The Oregon Literature Series

General Editor: George Venn
Managing Editor: Ulrich H. Hardt

Volume 1: Oregon Short Fiction

A project of the Oregon Council of Teachers of English

The Oregon Literature Series

The World Begins Here
An Anthology of Oregon Short Fiction

Glen A. Love

 Oregon State University Press
Corvallis, Oregon

Dedication

To all the Oregonians who helped to create it,
this book is dedicated.

Cover art: Detail from "Downhill" by Cie Goulet, monotype, 1991
Cover design: John Bennett
Text design: Jo Alexander
Permissions: Susanne Shotola
Art photographer: Susan Seubert

*The publication of this book is supported by a grant from the
National Endowment for the Arts in Washington, D.C., a federal agency*

The paper in this book meets the guidelines for permanence and durability of the
Committee on Production Guidelines for Book Longevity of the Council on Library
Resources and the minimum requirements of the American National Standard for
Permanence of Paper for Printed Library Materials Z39.48-1984.

Library of Congress Cataloging-in-Publication Data

The world begins here: An anthology of Oregon short fiction/edited by Glen A. Love
p. cm. -- (Oregon literature series ; v. 1)
Includes bibliographical references.
Summary: This first of a six-volume anthology of literature by Oregonians or
about Oregon contains old and new short stories and some Native American oral
tales.
ISBN 0-87071-369-8 (alk. paper, cloth). --ISBN 0-87071-370-1 (alk. paper, pbk.)
1. Short stories, American--Oregon. 2. Oregon--Fiction. [1. Short stories. 2. Oregon--
Fiction.] I. Love, Glen A., 1932-. II. Series.
PS571.O7W67 1993
813'.01089795--dc20   92-43642
                                                  CIP
                                                  AC

Acknowledgments

Without steady collaboration by many individuals, agencies, and institutions, the *Oregon Literature Series* would never have appeared in print. We wish to recognize here those who contributed support, time, and resources—more or less in the order in which their contributions were received—and knowing even now that the real evidence of our gratitude lies open before all of them now.

In 1986, the Executive Committee of the Oregon Council of Teachers of English (OCTE) began to discuss the idea of publishing a collection of Oregon literature. We wish to identify the members of that Executive Committee and thank them for their pioneering role: Lauri Crocker, Joe Fitzgibbon, Robert Hamm, Ulrich Hardt, Michelann Ortloff, and Ed Silling. Under then-OCTE President Ulrich Hardt, the Publications Committee was given the goal to further develop the idea of a state-based literary collection.

In 1988-89, the Executive Board of OCTE approved the pilot study by George Venn which became the *Oregon Literature Series.* We would like to recognize the members of that distinguished professional group of teachers by listing them here: Brian Borton, Sister Helena Brand, Suzanne Clark, Darlene Clarridge, Elaine Cockrell, Edna De Haven, Joe Fitzgibbon, Robert Boyt Foster, David Freitag, Debra Gaffney, Tim Gillespie, Irene Golden, Robert Hamm, Ulrich H. Hardt, Martha House, Ilene Kemper, Debbie LaCroix, Bill Mull, Thomas Nash, Debby Norman, Michelann Ortloff, Phyllis Reynolds, Eldene Ridinger, Mei-Ling Shiroishi, Andy Sommer, Daune Spritzer, Kim Stafford, Lana Stanley, Kathy Steward, Paul Suter, Nathaniel Teich, Linda Vanderford, George Venn, Michael Wendt, and Barbara Wolfe. Many members of that board gave many extra hours to reviewing the design, editorial guidelines, rationale, and budgets for that pilot project and other documents.

We would also like to acknowledge the following individuals from Oregon's literary and humanities community who reviewed the pilot proposal, made valuable suggestions, and gave their endorsement in 1988 to the idea of a collection of the best Oregon writing: Richard Lewis, Oregon Council for the Humanities; Brian Booth, Oregon Institute of Literary Arts; Peter Sears, Oregon Arts Commission; Jo Alexander, Oregon State University Press; Bruce Hamilton, Oregon Historical Society. OCTE President in 1988, Tim Gillespie, and Joe Fitzgibbon, OCTE President Elect, also reviewed the pilot proposal and made important contributions not only in these early stages but throughout the project.

When we presented the completed proposal for the *Oregon Literature Series* to the Editorial Board of Oregon State University Press in 1989, they broke with all precedent by signing a guaranteed publication contract and by agreeing to turn over editorial control of the content of the *Oregon Literature Series* to OCTE editors and appointees. We want to thank both press editors, Jeff Grass and 'Jo Alexander, and these members of that board who voted unanimously in favor of this project: Pat Brandt,

Larry Boersma, Richard Maxwell Brown, Bill Denison, Gordon Dodds, Mike Strelow, Dave Perry, Sandy Ridlington, and the late Marilyn Guin. Without their vote for collaboration and its implicit vote of confidence in us, we would have found it difficult to continue this project.

Our first financial support beyond OCTE was provided by a pilot grant from Eastern Oregon State College, School of Education. Specifically, we wish to thank Deans Jens Robinson, Gerald Young, and James Hottois for their willingness to grant a sabbatical and three years of part-time appointments to George Venn so that this project could be undertaken. At Portland State University, we want to thank Dean Robert Everhart, School of Education, for his steadfast support. He granted Ulrich Hardt a sabbatical to help launch the project, and he continued that support throughout the four years of the project. At Portland State University, we also want to acknowledge Interim Provost Robert Frank and Provost Michael Reardon for the faith they showed in the project by assigning graduate assistant Susanne Shotola to help us.

When we drafted our "Call for Editors" in 1989, we received helpful critiques from Kim Stafford, Edwin Bingham, Paul Suter, Sister Helena Brand, Edna DeHaven, Daune Spritzer, Lana Stanley, Michelann Ortloff, as well as other members of the OCTE Executive Board. When it was time to mail that "Call for Editors" to all Oregon libraries, newspapers, and other regional and national media, Lana Stanley assisted us. When it was time to select Volume Editors, these Publications Committee members assisted us: Robert Hamm, Marti House, Ilene Kemper, Debbie LaCroix, Mei-Ling Shiroishi, Michael Wendt, and Linda Vanderford. We'd like to thank them for the many hours they gave to evaluating the applications of 130 highly qualified individuals from Oregon and across the U.S. who applied for or were nominated for editorships.

When we needed to verify that these anthologies would, indeed, be both needed and used in the public schools, Portland State University School of Business Administration faculty member Bruce Stern gave us important assistance in designing a survey instrument, findings from which demonstrated a clear demand for the *Oregon Literature Series* in Oregon schools and homes. When we needed public relations expertise during editorial appointments, Pat Scott in the Portland State University Public Relations Office provided it.

When we needed legal advice, Leonard DuBoff and his firm of Cooney, Moscato, and Crew were more than helpful in contributing their contractual expertise.

As the project began to take a clear and definite shape in 1989, we received formal endorsements from these individuals whose confidence in the project made it possible to continue in spite of meager funding: Wes Doak, Oregon State Librarian, and Director, Center for the Book; Brian Booth, Director of Oregon Institute of Literary Arts; Kim Stafford, Director of the Northwest Writing Institute at Lewis and Clark College; Jennifer Hagloch, President of the Oregon Museums Association; Richard Lewis, Executive Director, Oregon Council for the Humanities; Joanne Cowling, President of the Eastern Oregon Library Association; Leslie Tuomi, Executive Director of the Oregon Arts Commission; Peter Sears, Oregon Arts Commission; Michael K. Gaston, President, Oregon Library Association; John Erickson, State Superintendent of Public

Instruction; Carolyn Meeker, Chair, Oregon Arts Commission; Carolyn Lott, Chair, National Council of Teachers of English (NCTE) Committee on Affiliates; Shirley Haley-James, President-Elect of NCTE; William Stafford, Oregon's past poet laureate; and Terry Melton, Director of the Western States Arts Foundation.

Essential financial support after 1989 came first from a generous allocation from the OCTE Executive Board. Later, we received modest one-time contributions from the Oregon Center for the Book and the Jackson Foundation. We would also like to state that this project was made possible—in part—by two minor grants from the Oregon Arts Commission.

Our sustaining patrons in the final three years (1990-93) of the project have been four; each of them contributed amounts in five figures so that the *Oregon Literature Series* could be completed in a timely and professional manner:

(1) the OCTE Executive Board, who sustained and underwrote us when regional foundations failed us;

(2) the Oregon Council for the Humanities, an affiliate of the National Endowment for the Humanities, which made and honored an exemplary three-year commitment ably administered by Robert Keeler;

(3) the National Endowment for the Arts, Literature Program, which assisted us at a time when we had been sent begging by all but one of the private foundations in Oregon;

(4) Portland State University, which granted multi-year support for graduate assistant Susanne Shotola to assist with the many details of the publication of the six volumes of the series;

(5) Oregon State University Press, where Jo Alexander and Jeff Grass contributed the vital tasks agreed to in 1989—designing, printing, and distributing these volumes. OSU Press set a national precedent by becoming the first university press in the United States to publish a multi-volume, comprehensive collection of a state's literature in the same state where the university press is located.

When we came to recommending graphics and cover designs for the *Oregon Literature Series* in 1992, we welcomed the generous and expert advice of three of Oregon's most knowledgeable art historians: Ron Crosier, Portland Public Schools; Gordon Gilkey, Curator, Portland Art Museum; and Nancy Lindburg, arts consultant and former staff member of the Oregon Arts Commission. Some of the works they recommended were selected by them from the slide inventory in Oregon's Percent for Art in Public Places Program. Other works were chosen from the Gordon and Vivian Gilkey Collection of Prints and Drawings at the Portland Art Museum, and from the Museum's collection of photographs. In addition to those three individuals, we were also fortunate to attract the services of John Bennett, book designer and publisher at Gardyloo Press in Corvallis, who collaborated on all features of the graphic design, and created covers for these volumes.

No literary project of this magnitude can be accomplished without skillful and reliable staff. The General and Managing Editors would like to express their profound appreciation to Susanne Shotola and Barbara Wiegele—both of Portland State

University—for their patient, professional, and timely attention to thousands of pages of details during the past four years: keeping accurate records, handling all permissions and finances, doing all the copying, typing, and mailing. We thanked them during the project and here we want to thank them again.

Unfortunately, this naming of our benefactors will be incomplete. We cannot list here all of those writers, families, and institutions who waived permissions fees; those innumerable librarians, archivists, storytellers, and historians who have safeguarded many of these pieces of writing for more than 100 years; those many who sent us notes of encouragement, those members of the public press who considered this project worthy of coverage. What we can say, however, is that every contribution moved us one page closer to the volume you now hold in your hands. Those others who failed us when we needed them most—they may eat—well?—cake?

Finally, George Venn would like to thank his wife Elizabeth who has tolerated great financial sacrifice for four years and who has begun to wonder about this tough, miserly Oregon muse her husband seems to have been serving at the expense of his art and her budget. Also, Ulrich Hardt would like to thank his wife, Eleanor, for her insights and interest in this project as Social Studies Specialist for Portland Public Schools, and for being more patient than could have been expected and tolerant of being alone many evenings and weekends while he was occupied with editorial responsibilities.

Ulrich Hardt, Managing Editor   *George Venn, General Editor*
Portland State University   *Grande Ronde Valley, Oregon*
Portland and Stuttgart
                    September 1992

Editor's Acknowledgments

I wish to thank the members of the Short Fiction Advisory Board of the Oregon Literature Series—Ron Abell, Kerry Ahearn, Bob Bumstead, Cecelia Hagen, Jim Heynen, and Ralph Teters—for their advice in choosing works for inclusion in this volume. The suggestions of my fellow-editors of the Series—Shannon Applegate, Stephen Dow Beckham, Gordon Dodds, Ulrich Hardt, Suzi Jones, Terence O'Donnell, Jarold Ramsey, Primus St. John, George Venn, and Ingrid Wendt, have also been most helpful. I am grateful as well for advice and assistance from Rebecca Lacy and Paul Pintarich of *The Oregonian*; from Rich Wandschneider of Fishtrap; from my University of Oregon colleagues Edwin R. Bingham, Fraser Cocks, Richard Heinzkill, Diane Hunsaker, Elizabeth McDowell, Earl Pomeroy, David Shetzline, Mike Stamm, and Quintard Taylor; and from fellow-Oregonians Brian Booth, Walt Curtis, Joe Franklin, Mildred Blair Hawkins, and Kim Stafford. Jo Alexander of the Oregon State University Press provided expert advice at all stages of the book's progress. Rhoda Love has been, in this project as in all our work together, a sound critic and helpful companion.

Glen A. Love, Editor

Contents

List of Art

General Introduction

The idea for the *Oregon Literature Series*, six anthologies of the best Oregon writing, was first proposed to the Oregon Council of Teachers of English (OCTE) in 1988. At that time, OCTE decided to depart from the conventional state literary anthology—a monolithic tome put together by a few academic volunteers and generally intended for libraries and adult readers. Instead, OCTE decided to create six shorter, genre-based anthologies: prose, poetry, autobiography, folk literature, letters and diaries, and short fiction. OCTE would publish a public "Call for Editors," and the most qualified individuals would be hired for their expertise and treated professionally—honoraria, expenses, research assistance, travel, etc. The anthologies would be intended as classroom/reference texts for students and teachers, and as introductory readers for the general public. Books would be designed to be easily held, carried, and read.

Numerous arguments were raised against this innovative proposal—most of them signaling Oregon's 150-year status as a literary colony. *No one had ever done this before. Oregon's literature was non-existent. There wasn't much writing of merit. Most scholars and critics have ignored Oregon literature—even in the best histories of Western literature. There's no literary history of Oregon. It will take years to find this work. In Oregon, literature has the least financial support of all the major arts. We had no publisher. It might rain.*

Nevertheless, in 1989, Ulrich Hardt and I were appointed by OCTE to complete the *Oregon Literature Series*. The work began when we signed a publication contract with Oregon State University Press, our first and most important professional collaborator. Next, from a pool of 130 applicants, OCTE chose these editors to discover Oregon's literary heritage: Shannon Applegate, Stephen Dow Beckham, Gordon B. Dodds, Primus St. John, Suzi Jones, Glen A. Love, Terence O'Donnell, Jarold Ramsey, and Ingrid Wendt. Appointed in August 1990, those individuals began the search for Oregon writing that eventually spread beyond every corner of the state—from ranch houses to university archives, from oral storytellers in longhouses to Chinese miners' writings in museums, from Desdemona Sands to Burns. Some editors traveled thousands of miles. Others corresponded with hundreds of authors. Most read thousands of pages. Poets, historians, folklorists, critics, scholars, teachers, and editors—they all benefited from and shared their research expertise. Even though honoraria were small, editors gave generously of their time. While the editors looked for Oregon writing, Ulrich Hardt and I sought out and received endorsements from many major cultural and arts organizations. Financial support was like rain in the time of drought, but we attracted a few wise, faithful, and generous patrons, as the Acknowledgments record.

Once the editors had discovered this vast, unstudied, and unknown body of writing, they assembled their manuscripts by using the following guidelines—guidelines that required them to choose writing—in its broadest sense—that might reveal the Oregon experience to both students and the public:

1. The volume must include a representative sample of the best Oregon writing from all periods, regions, occupations, genders, genres and sub-genres, ethnic, religious, political, and cultural backgrounds.
2. Oregon birth should not be used as a single criterion for inclusion. Oregon residence is important, but no arbitrary length of stay is required for a writer to be included.
3. Works about experience in Oregon are preferred, but editors are not limited to that criterion alone.
4. "Oregon" will be defined by its changing historical boundaries—Native American tribal territories, Spanish, Russian, British, U.S. Territory, statehood.
5. One or more translations and original from non-English languages should be included when appropriate to show that linguistic multiplicity has always been a part of Oregon.
6. Controversial subjects such as sexism and racism should not be avoided. Multiple versions of events, people, and places should be included when available.
7. Length of works must vary; limit the use of snippets when possible. Meet the need for diversity in reading, from complex to simple.
8. New, unknown, or unpublished work should be included.
9. Works will be edited for clarity but not necessarily for correctness. Editors may invent titles, delete text, and select text as appropriate and with appropriate notation.

Once assembled in draft, most of these manuscripts were two to three times longer than could be published by Oregon State University Press, so much fine writing had to be omitted, which all editors and our publisher regret. After being reduced to the requisite size, the manuscripts passed through two separate reviews: first, a different Advisory Board for each volume read and rated all selections; second, the Editorial Board composed of all fellow editors read, responded, and eventually voted to adopt the manuscript for publication. At all stages, both Ulrich Hardt and I worked closely with editors in many ways: readers, critics, fundraisers, administrators, arbitrators, secretaries, grant writers, researchers, coordinators, pollsters.

Now, we hope that these books will create for Oregon Literature a legitimate place in Oregon schools and communities, where the best texts that celebrate, invent, evaluate, and illuminate the Oregon condition have been invisible for too long. Here, for the first time, students will have books that actually include writing by Oregonians; teachers can find original, whole, local, and authentic texts from all regions, periods, and peoples in the state; librarians will be able to recommend the best reading to their patrons; the new reader and the general reader can find answers to the question that has haunted this project like a colonial ghost: "Who are Oregon's writers, anyway?"

Let it be known that an Oregon literary canon is forming—rich, diverse, compelling. Here, we give this sample of it to you. Let your love of reading and writing endure.

George Venn, General Editor
Grande Ronde Valley, Oregon
September 1992

Finding Oregon in Short Fiction

Think of the distinction between *space* and *place*. As geographer Yi-Fu Tuan describes the two, space is undifferentiated and open, devoid of value and support. Place is distinctive, bounded and known. Place is *defined* space, space that has been invested with value and identity and meaning through long human participation. For a geographic region such as Oregon, space becomes place when the people of that region have established a memorable relationship to it. One evidence and result of this relationship is art. Literature, poems, stories—these are the imaginative creations of human beings with a sense of themselves in an organized, meaningful territory, a place.

How long does it take to form the kind of imaginative transformation of space into place, out of which literature—stories—can grow? When the first European-American settlers arrived in the Oregon country in the mid-1800s, they found themselves in a region unfamiliar and strange to them, a geography of *space*. The native people whom the explorers and settlers encountered when they arrived had lived here for thousands of years. As H. L. Davis reminds us, the Wishram village which the first explorers encountered in the Columbia Gorge at the falls had existed much longer than any white settlement in North America. It was old when Europeans founded Saint Augustine or Jamestown or Santa Fe. And other indigenous peoples in the region we now call Oregon—such as the Chinook of the lower Columbia and Willamette Valley, the Tillamook, Alsea, and Coos along the Pacific coast, the Klamath and Modoc to the south, the Northern Paiute of the Great Basin, the Nez Perce and Cayuse of northeastern Oregon, and the Wasco and Warm Springs peoples of the north central region, at least forty distinct tribes in all—were similarly at home in their regions. They had an intimate and well-defined knowledge of the local features of land and weather and plants and animals. For them, Oregon was a place. And because it was a place, it inevitably had a rich literature— a flourishing oral tradition of storytelling, in this case—which gave the significance of myth to all aspects of their lives. Their existence was meaningful to them because their stories, their myths, made it clear why their homeland was what it was, and why things happened as they did.

These were, it needs to be emphasized, the original Oregonians, and the fact that they practiced a way of living which left the country, after millennia of their occupancy, ecologically healthy and beautiful ought to give us pause. Especially since Oregon has been diminished considerably in both the health and beauty of its land in the scant 160 years or so of white occupancy. The rich trove of oral literature of the original Oregonians was the linguistic record of that tradition. As Jarold Ramsey has shown us in *Coyote Was Going There: Indian Literature of the Oregon Country*, the natural features of the land, the cycles of the seasons, the migrations of salmon, of game, of the people themselves, were all deeply integrated into a oneness with this place. Although these people had no written language, and thus left no "prose" for us to read, we want to include some examples of native American stories in this anthology to suggest the power of that ancient tradition. Many more will be found in *Oregon Folk Literature*, a companion volume to this one.

The new European-American inhabitants had no such relationship to the land. If they had a mythology with respect to this place, it was, for the early explorers, as George Venn has pointed out, the mythology of the quest, of strangers in a strange land, a reciting of wonders. Later, for the first settlers, Oregon was a latter-day Eden, a place of hope and future promise, once the country and the Indians had been subdued. A new spirit of individualism and aggressive conquest accompanied these settlers, a spirit which opposed the communal oneness with the land that characterized the older native culture.

Still, because it is the nature of all human beings to create meaning and pattern from whatever environment they are placed in, the writers among the early permanent settlers of Oregon began the process of making sense of their new place. In some cases, as with Frederick H. Balch's *The Bridge of the Gods* and Joaquin Miller's *Unwritten History*, the recently arrived writers attempted to make some use of the Native American mythology which they found. But more often this heritage was dismissed or forgotten. Thus, in one way or another, the new writers took up the same task which had reached its culmination in the Native American stories of this prehistoric region. That process of storying the land continues today. And through our writers we have come some way toward creating a place—not merely a space—called Oregon.

Just how the space of Oregon becomes the place of Oregon for its new inhabitants is a matter of great interest. Historian Louis Hartz, in his book *The Founding of New Societies*, has posited a three-part process in the history of societies of colonial origin, like the United States, Canada, and Australia. The historical pattern of the colonists' presence, Hartz says, begins, in the first stage, with the colonial society as ill-defined and imitative, still subservient to the mother country. Space is not yet assimilated into place. This is followed by the second stage, one of a movement for separation and distinctiveness, accompanied by aggressive celebration of local values and scenes. This second stage may be a hundred years or more in arriving, but it encompasses the process by which the new people and the old land gradually come together. The third and final step for the new society is confident autonomy, accompanied by acceptance of international influences. The pattern might be seen to operate in the literature as well as the politics of new societies. And it might apply as well to a region like Oregon, which functioned, in its early days, much like a colony, a far-flung frontier, separated from its mother country by vast and forbidding distances. Oregon, too, had its imitative stage in its literature, as well as its aggressively regional stage, and, in recent times, its stage of entry into the international and multicultural arena.

This pattern, it should be added, ignores some features which are relevant to our interest in the Oregon tradition. For one, there is the presence of the indigenous people and their oral literature, both of which are largely displaced by the newcomers, but which later generations, like our own, will seek to reclaim. A second point of divergence from Hartz's model is the continuing process of immigration, of people who come from elsewhere, but who stay to become Oregonians and, more important, to become Oregon writers. In many cases, the process of rootedness takes place more quickly with these latecomers. One thinks of how such writers as William Stafford and Ursula LeGuin, who came to Oregon after World War II, seem to have found in Oregon a place that they were ready to respond to very quickly, perhaps because of their compatible backgrounds and values.

A final point of Oregon's divergence from the Hartz model might be in the new-found sense, even in our most sophisticated modern and contemporary writers, of the revaluing of region, of a new confidence in a place-conscious literature. The third step of Hartz's process must now make room for an ecological sense of the significance of place. No longer do writers feel that their region is merely something to outgrow, a step on their way to acceptance in the "cultural centers" of New York or Paris. Nowa-days, every place is recognized as equally real, and culture does not emanate from a few centers, but flows out from many regions like Oregon. As our consciousness of a threatened planet forces our attention back to the realities of our immediate environ-ment, we find ourselves resisting a life which amounts to only a vast network of interchangeable urban experiences. As Oregon writer William Kittredge has written recently, "There is no more running away to territory. This is it, for most of us. We have no choice but to live in community. If we're lucky we may discover a story that teaches us to abhor our old romance with conquest and possession." In an over-exploited earth, Oregon becomes more and more the place where we must put down new rootholds for our lives.

With these qualifications noted, then, we follow Hartz in arriving at the organiza-tion for this anthology. Tales from the Nez Perce, Nehalem Tillamook, Klickitat, and Northern Paiute people represent here the period of the original Oregonians. Euro-pean-American civilization, in its first, imitative stage, followed, but it was slow to develop. The early explorers, the fur traders, the mountain men, the pioneer diarists, the men and women who founded the new Oregon communities in the 1800s did not write fiction, for the most part. They had little leisure time for that. When Abigail Scott Duniway was trying to compose her 1859 novel, *Captain Gray's Company, or Crossing the Plains and Living in Oregon*, she lamented, in her introduction to the book, the lack of time which pioneer life afforded a writer, particularly "when a fron-tier farmer's wife undertakes to write a book, who has to be a lady, nurse, laundress, seamstress, cook and dairy woman by turns, and who attends to all of these duties unaided, save by the occasional assistance of an indulgent husband who has cares enough of his own." The early explorers and pioneers wrote, when they wrote at all, mostly what they saw and experienced. And so new, so strange, so unsettling was all of this that simply to record it seems to have engaged all their creative faculties.

When written literature in the form of stories and novels, poems and plays, did begin to appear in the Oregon country in the latter half of the nineteenth century, it was, as we might expect, for the most part a pallid version of the sort of writing being done in the nation's literary capital, the Northeast. This imitative stage of Hartz's progression is represented in the stories included here by Frances Fuller Victor, Joaquin Miller, Ella Higginson, and Alfred Powers. At this time, our ancestors still were not wholly at home in this place, and so early writers quite naturally paid less attention to the realities of life around them and transposed their materials into the conventions and practices of the dominant culture far to the east. Of the writers represented here, Frances Fuller Victor and Ella Higginson were among the first to begin to break out of this subservience to eastern models and styles. Then, too, Victor and Higginson suggested a feminine version of the western experience, one not of masculine adventure and heroism, but of nurturing family, home, and community. We can see in their work early attempts to use realistic local settings, attempts which were encouraged by regionally conscious new literary magazines of the Pacific coast like *The Pacific Monthly*. Still, the adherence of these first writers to the conventions of language and genre which they brought with them prevented them from achieving a wholly original interpretation of Oregon life.

The imitative stage hung on for a long time in Oregon, until the mid-1920s, by which time the vigor of the early writers had given way to writing which was genteel and vapid, in one respect, and crassly commercial, in another. Finally, under the influence of nationally prominent critics and writers like H. L. Mencken and Sinclair Lewis, the Northwest produced two brash but very talented young writers, H. L. Davis and James Stevens, who broke upon the local scene in 1927. They shocked the region's readers with an outrageously insulting little pamphlet, a satire attacking the feeble poetic twitterers and the literary Babbitts of the region. The pamphlet was entitled *Status Rerum* (The State of Things), and went on, in free-swinging and highly derogatory style, to call itself "A Manifesto Upon the Present Condition of Northwestern Literature Containing Several Near-Libelous Utterances Upon Persons in the Public Eye." Davis and Stevens named names and generally made things hot for the Northwest's literary establishment who, they claimed, had produced "a vast quantity of bilge, so vast indeed, that the few books which are entitled to respect are totally lost in the general and seemingly interminable avalanche of tripe." Harsh and embarrassing as it was, *Status Rerum* marked the end of the Emmeline Grangerford (of *Huckleberry Finn* fame) school of Northwest writing, and the clear advent of the stage of aggressive and self-conscious awareness in Louis Hartz's cultural progression. Reading the stories of the writers of the previous, imitative stage, we find ourselves listening to the diction and sentiments of another century. In the work of Davis and Stevens in the 1920s we hear for the first time the sound and the substance of an indigenous Northwest expression, as Karen Reyes has detailed in her historical study of Oregon writers between the two world wars.

With Davis and Stevens leading the way, along with a strong new regional literary magazine entitled *The Frontier*, edited by Harold G. Merriam of the University of Montana, the stage of confident regional awareness, the movement toward defined place, was well begun. Writers like Ernest Haycox and Albert Richard Wetjen joined with Davis and Stevens in the new, aggressive school of Oregon fiction, although the tendency of Haycox and Wetjen to write to a commercially successful formula may have weakened their work aesthetically. But Ernest Haycox, who began by writing formulaic cowboy westerns, later shifted toward more realistic regional stories and novels. He seems to have discovered that the myths of popular literature could not create an enduring sense of the Northwest as place. This aggressively regional stage of writing, in its attack upon the genteel tradition, was also aimed at what these writers perceived as the increasing over-refinement of Northwest literature. This feeling is particularly evident in *Status Rerum*. And it is worth noting that Walt Morey and Beverly Cleary, two of Oregon's most accomplished children's writers, reflect this same desire to put aside the genteel "niceness" of children's stories. Cleary, for example, born into an Oregon farming family in 1916, a generation after Davis and Stevens, pushes beyond the traditional, prim blandness of children's literature for an honest and humorous realism which is much in the spirit of the revolt against sterile gentility.

As Oregon literature began to find its own place, it became evident that the term "Oregon," itself, represents more of a political unity than a strictly regional and eco-logical one. The state of Oregon is composed of at least two—and as many as half a dozen—distinct geographic regions. H. L. Davis recognized this fact in his 1936 Pulitzer-Prize-winning novel, *Honey in the Horn*. There, he follows his main charac-ters through an Oregon odyssey which encompasses the lush valleys of the Willamette and the other great rivers to the south, the rain-lashed Pacific coastal strip, the steamboating towns along the Columbia, the wheatlands and dry-farming regions east of the Cascades, the high deserts, and the horse and cattle ranchlands of south-central Oregon. As Davis wrote in his essay "Oregon," "It used to be a saying in Oregon that people who lived there could change their whole order of life—climate, scenery, diet, complexions, emotions—even reproductive faculties—by merely moving a couple of hundred miles in any direction inside the state."

Recognizing the diverse mosaic of Oregon's regions, we have, in this volume, tried to select short fiction which represents that range of separate natural entities, from the white-topped surf of the Coast to the green-timbered western valleys and mountains, and to the gray sage country and rolling high deserts beyond the ranges. On the temporal and human scales, the fiction here presents and interprets life in Oregon from the time of the original inhabitants to the present, and from wild settings and pastoral outposts to the scattered small towns and cities to the state's only metropolis, Portland.

Can all of this diversity be made to hang together somehow? Should it? Perhaps these questions are best answered by the writers included under the final group of moderns and contemporaries. The last stage of Hartz's line of progression is said to suggest a mature acceptance of place in the world community. Necessarily this stage implies entering into a critical relationship with our sense of inhabited space. We might think of this as the stage of the examined myth. The arrival of Bernard Malamud in Corvallis in 1949 might serve as a kind of watershed moment for this latest stage of development. If Davis and Stevens had made it possible for Oregon writers to treat the region with honest self-awareness, their successors, like the Jewish outsider from New York, Malamud, or the fantasist Ursula Le Guin, announced that Oregon was open to the wider influences of the spirit. Percival Everett now gives us a sense of the black experience in Oregon, Elizabeth Woody writes of contemporary Oregon Native American life, and Juan Armando Epple portrays the Spanish-speaking exile from South America who now finds himself an Oregonian. And even home-grown products like Ken Kesey, William Kittredge, Molly Gloss, Craig Lesley, and Martha Gies have stretched out the borders of Oregon to include new territories of the imagination. Oregonians like these, not to mention our premier nature writer, Barry Lopez, whose assignments carry him, literally, to the ends of the earth, show us that our writers are now at home not only in their state, but in the world.

Learning to trust and use the region, rather than to apologize for it, is perhaps the most difficult of lessons for the writer of an emerging place. One of the functions of any region's literature is to convey a sense of that place's values to the larger world. Although, in its early stages, regional literature may appear to be a narrow or provincial view of life, it is actually a necessary and vital process, part of the inevitable competition between conflicting value systems by which cultures and civilizations are formed. National identities are only regional identities combined and written large. And it is important to the health of the national culture that individual regions offer alternative and corrective responses in the continuing debate over national character and expression. As Oregon writers and artists have turned space into place, they have helped to generate new values which have contributed to our evolving American identity.

Moreover, in the growing emphasis which we have come to place upon ecological thinking in modern life, it is increasingly important that regional identities come to the fore. Why? Because regional identities are most often formed not from within arbitrary political boundary lines—as may be the case with nations—but within natural and geographic borders, within ecosystems, which must be considered as wholes in order for us to deal with the growing numbers of environmental threats to our health and survival. As thirsty Southwesterners eye Oregon's rivers, and as the salmon spawned in these rivers are decimated on the high seas by drift-netters from across the Pacific, or are wiped out by hydroelectric dams which power our homes and industries, we increasingly come to realize how our region functions, or fails to function, as an ecological system, a whole. Richard Maxwell Brown has pointed out how Joel Garreau's book, *The Nine Nations of North America,* invited us to rethink the traditional political boundaries of North America along new regional lines, based upon emergent ecological and social forces which often cut across existing national boundaries. The environmental crisis has further encouraged such new awareness of regional identities, particularly in Oregon, with its reputation as an environmental leader among the states. Ecological consciousness seems to be an inevitable consequence of place consciousness. Having taken into our minds and hearts the beauty of Oregon, we recognize our responsibility not to defile it. Thus, though environmentalism is rarely a theme in the stories collected here, the environment is a strong and controlling presence in many of them.

"The world begins here," says the Nez Perce shaman. One of the most important contributions of a regional consciousness is the recognition that all art begins with some kind of particular experience. "All events and experiences are local, somewhere," says William Stafford, "and all human enhancements of events and experiences—which is to say, all the arts—are regional in the sense that they derive from immediate relation to felt life. It is this immediacy that distinguishes art. And paradoxically the more local the feeling in art, the more all people can share it; for that vivid encounter with the stuff of the world is our common ground." Surely there is value for all of us, as Oregonians, in realizing that our own places and peoples are the stuff from which literature is created, no less than Mark Twain's Hannibal or Robert Frost's New England or Willa Cather's Nebraska. Oregon is where we are. The world begins here.

Glen A. Love
University of Oregon

Works Cited

Balch, Frederick H. *The Bridge of the Gods: A Romance of Indian Oregon.* Chicago: A. C. McClurg, 1890.

Brown, Richard Maxwell. "The New Regionalism in America, 1970-1981." In *Regionalism and the Pacific Northwest,* ed. William G. Robbins, Robert J. Frank, and Richard E. Ross. Corvallis: Oregon State University Press, 1983, pp. 37-96.

Davis, H. L. *Honey in the Horn.* New York: Harper, 1935.

Davis, H. L. "Oregon" and "A Town in Eastern Oregon." In *H. L. Davis, Collected Essays and Short Stories.* Moscow, Idaho: University of Idaho Press, 1986, pp. 23-52.

Duniway, Abigail Scott. *Captain Gray's Company, or Crossing the Plains and Living in Oregon.* Portland: S. J. McCormick, 1859.

Hartz, Louis. *The Founding of New Societies.* New York: Harcourt, Brace, 1964.

Kittredge, William. *Owning It All.* St. Paul: Graywolf Press, 1987.

Love, Glen A. "Stemming the Avalanche of Tripe." In *H. L. Davis, Collected Essays and Short Stories.* Moscow, Idaho: University of Idaho Press, 1986, pp. 321-40.

——. "Oregon on the Literary Map: Regional Literacy and the Great Tradition." *Oregon English Journal,* 13:1 (Spring 1991), 3-8.

Miller, Joaquin. *Unwritten History: Life Among the Modocs,* ed. A. H. Rosenus. Eugene: Orion Press, 1972.

Ramsey, Jarold, ed. *Coyote Was Going There: Indian Literature of the Oregon Country.* Seattle and London: University of Washington Press, 1977.

Reyes, Karen S. "Finding a New Voice: The Oregon Writing Community Between the Two World Wars." Unpublished Master's Thesis. Portland State University, Department of History, 1986.

Stafford, William. "On Being Local." *Northwest Review,* 13:3 (1973), 92.

Stevens, James, and H. L. Davis. *Status Rerum: A Manifesto upon the Present Condition of Northwestern Literature Containing Several Near-Libelous Utterances upon Persons in the Public Eye.* The Dalles, Oregon: privately printed, 1927. Reprinted in *H. L. Davis, Collected Essays and Short Stories.* Moscow, Idaho: University of Idaho Press, 1986, pp. 357-66.

Tuan, Yi-Fu. *Space and Place: The Perspective of Experience.* Minneapolis: University of Minnesota Press, 1977.

Venn, George. "Continuity in Northwest Literature." In *Northwest Perspectives,* ed. Edwin R. Bingham and Glen A. Love. Seattle and London: University of Washington Press, 1979, pp. 98-118.

The World Begins Here

Native American Oral Tales

A Nez Perce Story

When the first settlers arrived in Oregon about 150 years ago, there were, anthropologists tell us, over forty Indian tribes in the region, speaking perhaps twenty-five different languages. Yet from what must have been the enormous number of Native American stories from the region only a few remain. As Jarold Ramsey laments in his collection of these texts, *Coyote Was Going There*, "whole tribes and their languages have vanished without leaving a trace of their mythological heritage behind." All the more reason to treasure those thousand or so remaining stories. They are our link to the mythic past of what is today our Oregon homeland. They are the taproot by which we may understand what it means to *belong* in this place. While there was no written language among Northwest Native Americans, hence no written stories as presented here, perhaps the following versions of their oral tales will suggest the importance of the storytelling tradition among the early Northwest inhabitants.

The story which follows, taken from *Coyote Was Going There*, is a powerful example of a universal archetype, the so-called Orpheus myth, which tells of an unsuccessful attempt to bring back a beloved person from the dead. "Coyote and the Shadow People" was originally recorded in 1929 by Archie Phinney, a Nez Perce who heard the story from his mother, Wayilatpu, who spoke no English. Phinney, who was educated at Columbia University and studied under the noted anthropologist Franz Boaz, was well qualified to span the two cultures, European-American and Indian, which are represented in the history of this story. That history is best told in Ramsey's chapter, "From Mythic to Fictive in a Nez Perce Orpheus Myth," from his book *Reading the Fire*, listed under Secondary Sources, below.

3

Coyote and the Shadow People

Coyote and his wife were dwelling there. His wife became ill. She died. Then Coyote became very, very lonely. He did nothing but weep for his wife.

There the death spirit came to him and said, "Coyote, do you pine for your wife?"—"Yes, friend, I long for her . . ." replied Coyote. "I could take you to the place where your wife has gone but, I tell you, you must do everything just exactly as I say; not once are you to disregard my commands and do something else."—"Yes," replied Coyote, "yes friend, and what could I do? I will do everything you say." There the ghost told him, "Yes. Now let us go." Coyote added, "Yes, let it be so that we are going."

They went. There he said to Coyote again, "You must do whatever I say. Do not disobey."—"Yes, yes, friend. I have been pining so deeply, and why should I not heed you?" Coyote could not see the spirit clearly. He appeared to be only a shadow. They started and went along over a plain. "Oh, there are many horses; it looks like a round-up," exclaimed the ghost. "Yes," replied Coyote, though he really saw none, "yes, there are many horses." They had arrived now near the place of the dead. The ghost knew that Coyote could see nothing but he said, "Oh look, such quantities of service berries! Let us pick some to eat. Now when you see me reach up you too will reach up and when I bend the limb down you too will pull your hands down."—"Yes," Coyote said to him, "so be it that thus I will do." The ghost reached up and bent the branch down and Coyote did the same. Although he could see no berries he imitated the ghost in putting his hand to and from his mouth in the manner of eating. Thus they picked and ate berries. Coyote watched him carefully and imitated every action. When the ghost would put his hand into his mouth Coyote did the same. "Such good service berries these are," commented the ghost. "Yes, friend, it is good that we have found them," agreed Coyote. "Now let us go." And they went on.

"We are about to arrive," the ghost told him. "There is a long, very, very long lodge. Your wife is there somewhere. Just wait and let me ask someone." In a little while the ghost returned and said to Coyote, "Yes, they have told me where your wife is. We are coming to a door through which we will enter. You will do in every way exactly what you see me do. I will take hold of the door flap, raise it up, and, bending low, will enter. Then you too will take hold of the door flap and do the same." They proceeded in this manner now to enter.

It happened that Coyote's wife was sitting right near the entrance. The ghost said to Coyote, "Sit here beside your wife." They both sat. The ghost added, "Your wife is now going to prepare food for us." Coyote could see nothing, except that he was sitting there on an open prairie where nothing was in sight; yet he could feel the presence of the shadow. "Now she has prepared our food. Let us eat." The ghost reached down and then brought his hand to his mouth. Coyote could see nothing but the prairie dust. They ate. Coyote imitated all the movements of his companion. When they had finished and the woman had apparently put the food away the ghost said to Coyote, "You stay here. I must go around to see some people."

He went out but he returned soon. "Here we have conditions different from those you have in the land of the living. When it gets dark here it has dawned in your land and when it dawns for us it is growing dark for you." And now it began to grow dark and Coyote seemed to hear people whispering, talking in faint tones, all around him. Then darkness set in. Oh, Coyote saw many fires in a long-house. He saw that he was in a very, very large lodge and there were many fires burning. He saw the various people. They seemed to have shadow-like forms but he was able to recognize different persons. He saw his wife sitting by his side.

He was overjoyed, and he joyfully greeted all his old friends who had died long ago. How happy he was! He would march down the aisles between the fires, going here and there, and talk with the people. He did this throughout the night. Now he could see the doorway through which his friend and he had entered. At last it began to dawn and his friend came to him and said, "Coyote, our night is falling and in a little while you will not see us. But you must stay right here. Do not go anywhere at all. Stay right here and then in the evening you will see all these people again."—"Yes, friend. Where could I possibly go? I will spend the day here."

The dawn came and Coyote found himself alone sitting there in the middle of a prairie. He spent the day there, just dying from the heat, parching from the heat, thirsting from the heat. Coyote stayed here several days. He would suffer through the day but always at night he would make merry in the great lodge.

One day his ghost friend came to him and said, "Tomorrow you will go home. You will take your wife with you."—"Yes, friend, but I like it here so much. I am having a good time and I should like to remain here."—"Yes," the ghost replied; "nevertheless you will go tomorrow, and you must guard against your inclination to do foolish things. Do not yield to any queer notions. I will advise you now what you are to do. There are five mountains. You will travel for five days. Your wife will be with you but you must never, never touch her.

Do not let any strange impulses possess you. You may talk to her but never touch her. Only after you have crossed and descended from the fifth mountain you may do whatever you like."—"Yes, friend," replied Coyote.

When dawn came again Coyote and his wife started. At first it seemed to him as if he were going alone yet he was dimly aware of his wife's presence as she walked along behind. They crossed one mountain and, now, Coyote could feel more definitely the presence of his wife; like a shadow she seemed. They went on and crossed the second mountain. They camped at night at the foot of each mountain. They had a little conical lodge which they would set up each time. Coyote's wife would sit on one side of the fire and he on the other. Her form appeared clearer and clearer.

The death spirit, who had sent them, now began to count the days and to figure the distance Coyote and his wife had covered. "I hope that he will do everything right and take his wife through to the world beyond," he kept saying to himself.

Here Coyote and his wife were spending their last night, their fourth camping, and on the morrow she would again assume fully the character of a living person. They were camping for the last time and Coyote could see her very clearly as if she were a real person who sat opposite him. He could see her face and body very clearly, but only looked and dared not touch her.

But suddenly a joyous impulse seized him; the joy of having his wife again overwhelmed him. He jumped to his feet and rushed over to embrace her. His wife cried out, "Stop! Stop! Coyote! Do not touch me. Stop!" Her warning had no effect. Coyote rushed over to his wife and just as he touched her body she vanished. She disappeared—returned to the shadow-land.

When the death spirit learned of Coyote's folly he became deeply angry. "You inveterate doer of this kind of thing! I told you not to do anything foolish. You, Coyote, were about to establish the practice of returning from death. Only a short time away the human race is coming, but you have spoiled everything and established for them death as it is."

Here Coyote wept and wept. He decided, "Tomorrow I shall return to see them again." He started back the following morning and as he went along he began to recognize the places where he and his spirit friend had passed before. He found the place where the ghost had seen the herd of horses, and now he began to do the same things they had done on their way to the shadowland. "Oh, look at the horses; it looks like a round-up." He went on until he came to the place where the ghost had found the service berries. "Oh, such choice service berries! Let us pick and eat some." He went through the motions of picking and eating berries.

He went on and finally came to the place where the long lodge had stood. He said to himself, "Now when I take hold of the door flap and raise it up you must do the same." Coyote remembered all the little things his friend had done. He saw the spot where he had sat before. He went there, sat down, and said, "Now, your wife has brought us food. Let us eat." He went through the motions of eating again. Darkness fell, and now Coyote listened for the voices, and he looked all around, he looked here and there, but nothing appeared. Coyote sat there in the middle of the prairie. He sat there all night but the lodge didn't appear again nor did the ghost ever return to him.

Suggested Further Reading

PRIMARY SOURCES

Phinney, Archie. *Nez Perce Texts.* Columbia University Contributions to Anthropology, vol. 25, 1934.

Ramsey, Jarold, ed. *Coyote Was Going There: Indian Literature of the Oregon Country.* Seattle and London: University of Washington Press, 1977.

Slickpoo, Allen P., Sr. *Nu Mee Poom Tit Wah Tit: Nez Perce Tales.* Lapwai: Nez Perce Tribes of Idaho, 1972.

SECONDARY SOURCES

Finne, Ron. "Tamanawis Illahee: Rituals and Acts in a Landscape." Film and video on the Indian heritage of the Northwest. 36526 Jasper Rd., Springfield, OR 97478.

Ramsey, Jarold. "From Mythic to Fictive in a Nez Perce Orpheus Myth." In his *Reading the Fire: Essays in the Traditional Indian Literatures of the Far West.* Lincoln, Nebraska: University of Nebraska Press, 1983.

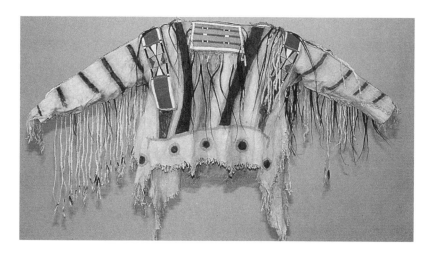

Two Nehalem Tillamook Tales

The Pacific Ocean was, for the Native Americans of the Oregon coast, the great and irrefutable evidence of nature's supreme power. Perhaps we can experience some of this same awe in such latter-day poets and writers of the Pacific Coast as Robinson Jeffers, Mary Barnard, Don Berry, and William Stafford. The evidence of the compelling authority of the ocean to Native American lives is present in the following two stories from the Nehalem Tillamook tribes. In the first story South Wind—who functions in the Tillamook mythology like Coyote in the stories of the interior tribes, as a trickster figure—has some success with Ocean, in marrying Ocean's daughter. But the full story of South Wind's escapades, found in *Nehalem Tillamook Tales*, records the more characteristic ups and downs of the Trickster and Transformer. In the second story, the uneasy alliance between the Tillamook people and Ocean is dramatized in the relationship between a man and that most human of Ocean's creatures, a seal.

Both stories are taken from the oral narratives of a remarkable Indian woman storyteller, Clara Pearson, as recorded by Elizabeth D. Jacobs in *Nehalem Tillamook Tales*, recently reprinted by Oregon State University Press.

South Wind

S outh Wind traveled in the winter. It was always stormy then. He had many different headbands. He would say, "I will put on my headband with which I run on trees. I will travel only on the limbs of trees." That was the time when the limbs broke off the trees. The limbs broke off and fell down when he walked on them. Sometimes he would say, "Now I will wear this headband with which I break off the tree tops." He had still another headband which he wore when he felled whole trees, just as if they had been chopped down. Very rarely he would start out saying, "This time I will wear the headband with which I pull trees up by the roots."

In his travels he always saw a beautiful girl on the ocean beach. She would be sitting by the waves at the edge of the beach. He was always attempting to catch her. But just as he almost touched her she would disappear. Ah, he thought about her. He wanted so much to catch her. He had seen her many times, but he did not know what kind of a girl she was. Finally Blue Jay told him, "Well, South Wind, do you still want to catch that girl?" "Yes, aunt," he replied, "would you tell me how to do it?" She told him, "When you see her, if you attempt to catch her do not blink your eyes. Just keep staring straight at her till you seize her with your hand. Then it will be all right. You will have caught her. Do you know who she is?" "No!" "She is that Ocean's daughter. Ocean is the chief of chiefs." South Wind had often destroyed things for Ocean to receive.

He found her the next time he went forth. He did as he had been advised, and he caught hold of her. He took her home, he took her south. He made her his wife. The girl did not like it. She said, "Oh, I have never had a home like this! My bed at home is soft. I did not sleep on a hard bed at home." South Wind had a wooden bed. After a while he asked her, "Do you want me to take you home to your father? Shall we go and stay with your father a while?" Yes, she wanted to go home. She was very pleased. He took her home. He saw many different things there. His father-in-law had everything! All sorts of living things were his pets. Those whales and many unattractive animals were his pets. They talked together. South Wind said, "Well, we will work together for the remainder of time. I will destroy things for you, so you can possess them. You must do your part. When I travel, you will be angry and drift things and drown things. In that way we will work together forever." Then he took his wife to his own home again. She took her belongings from her father's place since she was to remain with South Wind.

South Wind had one wife already when he was trying to catch that girl. She was continually getting angry and jealous. She would decide, "I will leave. I am not going to live with him any more. I am going away." She would start in the night and travel, travel as long as she could. She would think, "Well, I must be far away now." South Wind would arise in the morning and notice that his first wife was gone. He would look, there in the far corner of the room he would see her. There she would be, with her belongings scattered around, and her bed made there. She was never able to travel far enough to get out of South Wind's house. The whole world was South Wind's house!

That is ended.

The Man Who Was Husband to a Seal

The Tillamooks ate seals, but still they were afraid of them. They knew that those seals liked to get a girl or a man for a mate, they lusted for human beings.

A boat capsized. A female Seal caught that man. Everyone supposed that he was drowned. A long time went by. The man did not enjoy himself there with his Seal wives. He had a child at home and he wanted very much to go home. Somehow he managed to escape from his two Seal wives and returned. He had lost his good sense in the meantime. He did not want to enter the house at once, but sat around outdoors. He saw his little girl and asked her, "Where is your mother?" The child replied, "She is in the house." "Has your mother a husband?" "No, her husband, my father, was drowned long ago. They never found his body." Then he said, "You tell your mother to come out here. I want to talk to her. You whisper in her ear, 'I found my father outdoors.'"

The little girl went in the house, put her arm around her mother's neck, and whispered in her ear, "Mother! I found a person out there. He wants you to come out and talk to him. He said he is my father." The mother slapped her lightly, saying, "Oh! Be quiet! You must not talk that way." However, she went out. She saw him. It did indeed look very much as if he were her husband except that, all around the sides of his cheeks and chin and in places on his arms, patches of seal hair were growing. He told her, "I am not coming in the house immediately. You clean the house, carry fresh sand and put it all around the fire before I enter."

The woman went back inside, she got very busy, she picked up everything, cleaned house, packed sand, and spread it all around the fire. She was living in the home of her married brothers who did not know what she was doing that for. After a while she carried out a blanket, put it over her husband's head and brought him inside. He spoke to no one, he climbed in bed; he had a power. Then the woman told her sisters-in-law, "That person who climbed into my bed is my husband. He has come back. Seals had him but he got away and came home."

The man sang a few days, and people came from all around. He was changed, he did not act as he formerly had. He was afraid of water always, after that. But his brothers-in-law would ask him, "Do you want to come along? We will drift with our nets." Finally he went with them. They drifted. Soon that net was caught on a snag. They were unable to get it loose. All of those men, his brothers-in-law, dived to loosen that net, but were unable to do it. They all took turns, no one could do it. Then they said to him, "Say, brother! Why do you not try? You dive and see if you can loosen our net." He answered, "No! I cannot do that. I do not want to do it." They kept telling him to dive. Finally he looked in the water. "Oh, there are my wives," he said. "They look just the same. They are the ones who are holding that net. If I dive I will never come up again. They want me." He let them know, yet those men did not say, "Well, you do not need to dive then." Therefore he jumped overboard, and that net was loose immediately. But the man never came up again. He had indeed gone back to his Seal wives.

That is all.

Suggested Further Reading

PRIMARY SOURCES

Boas, Franz. *Chinook Texts.* U. S. Bureau of American Ethnology, Bulletin no. 20, 1894.

——. "Traditions of the Tillamook Indians." *Journal of American Folklore* ii (1898): 23-28, 133-51.

Jacobs, Elizabeth D. *Nehalem Tillamook Tales*, ed. Melville Jacobs. Eugene: University of Oregon Books, 1959. Reprint, with introduction by Jarold Ramsey, Corvallis: Oregon State University Press, 1990.

Jacobs, Melville. *Coos Myth Texts.* University of Washington Publications in Anthropology, vol. 8, no. 2, 1940.

SECONDARY SOURCES

Berry, Don. *Trask*. New York: Viking Press, 1960. Reprinted Sausalito, California: Comstock Editions, 1977.

Berry, Don. *To Build a Ship*. New York: Viking Press, 1963. Reprinted Sausalito, California: Comstock Editions, 1977.

A Story from Many Sources

The most widely known and recorded Native American legend of the Oregon country is called "The Bridge of the Gods." The story of a huge stone arch that once bridged the Columbia River where the present-day steel "Bridge of the Gods" stands appears in many Indian legends, and was retold by explorers and settlers from the early days.

Although the story of the Bridge of the Gods has certainly been changed considerably from the original tradition, it is included here because it is so well known, and because it became the inspiration for the first widely popular novel out of the Northwest, *The Bridge of the Gods*. This melodramatic adventure story, published in 1890 by Frederick H. Balch, overlaid the Indian myth with a deep layer of the religious evangelism found in many settlements in the early Northwest. Balch, who lived on the Washington side of the Columbia upriver from the Gorge, probably heard the legend first from the Klickitats, in whose culture the story seems to have had its origins. The version reprinted here is from Katharine Berry Judson's 1910 book, *Myths and Legends of the Pacific Northwest*.

The Bridge of the Gods

Long ago, when the world was new, Tyhee Sahale with his two sons came down Great River. They came near where The Dalles now are. The land was very beautiful and each son wanted it. Therefore they quarrelled. Then Sahale took his bow and shot two arrows. One he shot to the north; the other he shot to the west. Then Sahale said to his sons, "Go. Find the arrows. Where they lie, you shall have the land."

One son went north over the plain to the country of the Klickitats. He was the first grandfather of the Klickitats. The other son followed the arrow to the Willamette Valley. He was the first grandfather of the Multnomahs.

Then Sahale raised great mountains between the country of the Klickitats and the country of the Multnomahs. This he did that the tribes might not quarrel. White men call them the Cascade Mountains. But Great River was deep and broad. The river was a sign of peace between the tribes. Therefore Sahale made a great stone bridge over the river, that the tribes might be friends. This was called the Bridge of the Tomanowos.

The tribes grew, but they did evil things. They displeased Tyhee Sahale. Therefore the sun ceased to shine, and cold and snow appeared. The people were unhappy for they had no fire. Only Loo-wit had fire. Therefore the people sought to steal the fire of Loo-wit. Then Loo-wit fled and because the runners were stiff with cold, they could not catch her.

Then Loo-wit told Sahale of the need of the Indians. Loo-wit said the Indians were cold. So Sahale gave fire to the people. Thus Sahale built a fire on the bridge of the gods, and there the people secured fire. Sahale also promised to Loo-wit eternal youth and beauty. Thus Loo-wit became a beautiful maiden.

Then began the chiefs to love Loo-wit. Many chiefs loved her because she was so beautiful. Then came two more chiefs, Klickitat from the north and Wiyeast from the west. To neither would Loo-wit give an answer. Therefore the chiefs fought, and their people also fought. Thus did they anger Sahale. Therefore, because blood was shed and because Great River was no longer a sign of peace, Sahale broke down the Tomanowos Illahee. Great rocks fell into the river. They are there even to this day. When the water is quiet, buried forests can be seen even to this day. Thus Sahale destroyed the bridge of the gods. Thus the tribes were separated by Great River.

Then Sahale made of Loo-wit, Klickitat, and Wiyeast snow peaks. Always they were to be cold and covered with ice and snow. White men call them Mount St. Helens, Mount Adams, and Mount Hood.

Suggested Further Reading

PRIMARY SOURCES
Clark, Ella E. *Indian Legends of the Pacific Northwest.* Berkeley and Los Angeles: University of California Press, 1953.
Judson, Katharine Berry. *Myths and Legends of the Pacific Northwest.* Chicago: A.C. McClurg, 1910.

SECONDARY SOURCES
Balch, Frederick H. *The Bridge of the Gods: A Romance of Indian Oregon.* Chicago: A.C. McClurg, 1890.
Clark, Ella E. "The Bridge of the Gods in Fact and Fancy." *Oregon Historical Quarterly* 53 (March 1952), 29-36.
Jacobs, Melville. *The People Are Coming Soon.* Seattle: University of Washington Press, 1960.

A Northern Paiute Tale

This story was narrated by Doctor Sam Wata, a shaman of the Paiute region of Southeastern Oregon. Old Man Chocktoot, who appears in the tale, was a well-known chief of the Silver Lake Paiutes. The story tells not only of the origin of the earth but also of the coming of the whites to the Paiutes' country. As Jarold Ramsey has pointed out in *Coyote Was Going There*, the contrast in this story between the white people's love of silver for wealth and the native people's love of the silver beauty of shining streams of spring water is a telling one. So, too, is the ending which suggests the displacement of the Paiutes by a culture which is both more powerful and less aware of the earth than the native one.

The Beginning of the Earth

One time this was all water but just one little island. That is what we are living on now. Old Man Chocktoot was living on top of this mountain. He was living right on top of this mountain. In all directions the land was lower than this mountain. It was burning under the earth. Numuzo'ho was under there, and he kept on eating people.

The Star (pa'-tuzuba) was coming. When that Star came, it went up into the sky and stayed there. When that Star went up, he said, "That is too bad; I pity my people. We left them without anything to eat; they are going to starve." This Star gave us deer, and antelope, and elk, and all kinds of game.

They had Sun for a god. When the Sun came up, he told his people, "Don't worry, come to me; I'll help you. Don't worry; be happy all your life. You will come to me."

The Sun and the Stars came with the Water. They had the Water for a home. The Indian doctor saw them coming. He let his people know that they were coming. There were many of them. The little streams of spring water are the places from which silver money comes. It comes from the Sun shining on the water.

The first white man came to this land and saw that silver, but he lost himself and didn't get to it. Finally white people found this place, and they came this way looking for the silver. Those white men brought cattle, sheep, pigs, and horses. Before they came, there were no horses in this land.

The Sun told his people, "Deer belong to you. They are for you to eat." These white men don't know who put the deer and other animals in this land. I think it is all right for me to kill deer, but the white men say they will arrest me. Whenever I see cattle or sheep, I know they don't belong to me; I wouldn't kill them. I feel like going out and killing deer, but I am afraid. I am getting too old. Maybe white people don't know about the beginning of this earth.

Suggested Further Reading

PRIMARY SOURCES

Barker, M.A.R. *Klamath Texts.* University of California Publications in Linguistics, Vol. 30, 1963.

Kelly, Isabel. "Northern Paiute Tales." *Journal of American Folklore* 51 (October-December 1938) No. 202: 364-438.

Ramsey, Jarold, ed., *Coyote Was Going There: Indian Literature of the Oregon Country.* Seattle and London: University of Washington Press, 1977.

SECONDARY SOURCES

Beckham, Stephen Dow. *Requiem for a People: The Rogue Indians and the Frontiersman.* Norman: University of Oklahoma Press, 1971.

Stern, Theodore. *The Klamath Tribe.* Seattle: University of Washington Press, 1965.

Stories from the First Oregon Writers

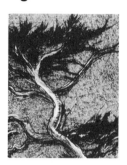

Frances Fuller Victor

Frances Fuller Victor (1826-1902) was born in Rome, New York. She and her sister, Metta, were child literary prodigies who married brothers. Frances and her husband moved to California and then to Oregon. There she wrote some of the earliest local color stories and poems of Oregon, and the histories of Oregon in H. H. Bancroft's series, and contributed other sections of his *History of the Pacific States.* Bancroft took the credit for much of her work, and for a time in her sixties she was so impoverished that she was compelled to sell toiletries door to door in Salem in order to earn a living. History has thankfully rescued her reputation, and she is now recognized as the writer who accomplished the most in early Oregon history and literature even while receiving the least reward and recognition. The story which follows was published in her collection, *The New Penelope,* in 1877, and shows Victor's attempt to combine realistic local settings—a summer colony near Seaside on the Oregon coast—with the conventional and formulaic love story of the time. The tale is also interesting in revealing early connections between Oregon and Hawaii.

On the Sands

Iwas summering at our Oregon Newport, known to us by the aboriginal name of Clatsop. Had a balloonist, uninstructed in the geography and topography of this portion of the Pacific coast, dropped down among us, his impression would have been that he had alighted in a military encampment, very happily chosen, as military encampments usually are.

Given, one long, low, whitewashed house enclosed by whitewashed pickets; a group of tents outside the enclosure and on the bank of a beautiful graveled-bottom, tree-shadowed stream, and you have the brief summing up of accommodations for summer visitors at Clatsop. The plentiful sprinkling of army buttons among the guests—for there are two forts within a three hours' ride of this beach—tend to confirm the impression of military possession. Besides, our host of the whitewashed hotel is a half-breed; and there is enough of the native element hanging about the place, picking berries and digging clams, to suggest an Indian family where a temporary station might be demanded. It would only be by peeping inside those tents where ladies and children are more numerous than bearded men, that one could be convinced of the gypsy nature of this encampment; though, to be sure, one need not press inside to find them, for the gay campers are sauntering about in all directions, ladies with their escorts, children with their nurses, parties returning from boating or fishing, or riding or bathing; everybody living out in the open air the whole day through on one pretense or another, and only repairing to the hotel at meal times, when the exquisite dishes prepared by French half-breeds suffer the most instant demolition—such hunger does open air inspire.

I had come here just invalid enough to be benefited by our primitive style of living; not too delicate to endure it, nor too robust to enjoy the utter vaga-bondism of it. There had been no necessity upon us to ape fashionable manners; no obligation to dress three times a day; no balls to weary ourselves with at night. Therefore this daily recurring picnic was just sufficient for our physical recreation, while our mental powers took absolute rest. For weeks I had arisen every morning to a breakfast of salmon-trout, French coffee (*au lait*), delicious bread, and fresh berries; and afterwards to wander about in the cool sea-fog, well wrapped up in a water-proof cloak. Sometimes we made a boating party up the lovely Neah-can-a-cum, pulling our boat along under the overhanging alders and maples, frightening the trout into their hiding-places under the banks, instead of hooking them as was our ostensible design. The limpid clearness of the water seemed to reflect the trees from the very bottom, and truly made a medium almost as transparent as air, through which the pebbles at the greatest depth appeared within reach of our hands. A morning idled away in this manner, and an afternoon spent in seeing the bathers—I never trust my easily curdled blood to the chill of the sea—and in walking along the sands with a friend, or dreaming quietly by myself as I watched the surf rolling in all the way from Tilamook Head to Cape Disappointment,—these were my daily labors and recreations. The arrival of a bundle of letters, or, still better, of a new visitor, made what variety there was in our life.

I had both of these excitements in one day. One of my correspondents had written: "I hope to see you soon, and to have the opportunity, long sought, of telling you some of the experiences of my early life. When I promised you this I had not anticipated the pleasure of talking over the recollections of my youth while listening with you to the monotone of the great Pacific, whose 'ever, forever' is more significant to me than to most lovers of its music. I never gaze upon its restless waves, nor hear the sound of their ripple upon the sands, or their thunder on the rocks without being reminded of one episode in my life peculiarly agitating to remember; but perhaps when I have told it to you, you may have power to exercise the restless spirit which rises in me at the recollection."

So here was promise of the intellectual aliment I had begun to crave after all these weeks of physical, without mental, action. I folded my letter with a feeling of self-congratulation, and turned to watch the movements of a newly arrived party for whom our half-breed host was spreading a tent, and placing in it rather an extra amount of furniture; for, be it known to the uninitiated, we had platform floors under our tents, real bedsteads, dressing-bureaus, rugs, and other comforts to match. That our new arrival exceeded us in elegant conveniences was, of course, duly noted by such idlers as we.

The party consisted of a lady, a little girl of ten, and a Kanaka servant. The lady's name, we learned, was Mrs. Sancy, and she was from the Sandwich Islands. More than that no one was informed. We discussed her looks, her manners, her dress, and her probable circumstances, as we sat around the campfire that evening, after the way of idle people. It occurred to me, as I glanced toward her tent door, illuminated by our blazing fire, and saw her regarding the weird scene with evident admiration of its picturesqueness, to ask her to come and sit with us and help us eat roast potatoes—roasted as they cook pigs in the Islands, by covering up in the ground with hot stones. The fact that the potatoes, and the butter which went with them, were purloined from our host's larder, gave a special flavor to the feast—accompanied as it was, too, by instrumental and vocal music, and enlivened by sallies of wit.

Mrs. Sancy seemed to enjoy the novelty of her surroundings, contributing her quota to the general fund of mirth and sparkling talk, and I congratulated myself on having acquired an interesting acquaintance, whose cheerfulness, notwithstanding the partial mourning of her dress, promised well for its continuance. Had she been sad or reserved, she certainly would not have been sought as she was by our pleasure-loving summer idlers, consequently my chances of becoming intimate with her would have been greatly abridged. As it was, she soon became, without question, one of the chief social attractions; easily falling into our vagabond ways, yet embellishing them with so much grace and elegance that they became doubly precious to us on account of the new charm imparted to them. All the things any of us could do, Mrs. Sancy could do better; and one thing she could do that none of the rest of us could, which was to swim out and float herself on a surf-board, like a native island woman; and seeing Mrs. Sancy do this became one of the daily sensations of Clatsop Beach.

I had known Mrs. Sancy about one week, and came to like her extremely, not only for her brilliant, social qualities, but on account of her native originality of thought, and somewhat peculiar culture. I say peculiar, because her thinking and reading seemed to be in the byways rather than the highways of ordinary culture. If she made a figure of speech, it was something noticeably original; if she quoted an author, it was one unfamiliar though forcible. And so she constantly supplied my mind with novelties which I craved, and became like a new education to me. One forenoon, a misty one, we were out on the beach alone, wrapped up in water-proofs, pacing up and down the sands, and watching the grey sullen sea, or admiring the way in which the masses of fog roll in among the tops of the giant firs on Tilamook Head, and were torn into fragments, and tangled among them.

"You never saw the like of this in the islands?" I said, meaning the foggy sea, and the dark, fir-clad mountains.

"I have seen *this* before;" she answered, waving her hand to indicate the scene as we then beheld it. "You look surprised, but I am familiar with every foot of this ground. I have lived years in this neighborhood—right over there, in fact, under the Head. This spot has, in truth, a strong fascination for me, and it was to see it once more that I made the voyage."

"You lived in this place, and liked it years ago! How strange! It is but a wilderness still, though a pleasant one, I admit."

She gave me a playfully superior smile: "We are apt to think ourselves the discoverers of every country where we chance to be set down; and so Adam thought he was the first man on the earth, though his sons went out and found cities where they learned the arts of civilization. So birth, and love, and death,

never cease to be miracles to us, notwithstanding the millions who have been born, and loved, and died, before our experience began."

"But how did it happen," I urged, unable to repress my curiosity, "that you lived here, in this place, *years ago?* That seems so strange to me."

"My parents brought me here when a little child. It is a common enough history. My mother was an enthusiast with brain, who joined her fortunes to those of an enthusiast without brain, and emigrated to this coast when it was an Indian country, in the vain hope of doing good to the savages. They only succeeded in doing harm to themselves, and indirectly, harm to the savages also. The spirit of the man became embittered, and the mean traits of his nature asserted themselves, and wreaked their malice, as is customary with mean natures, on the nearest or most inoffensive object. My poor mother! Maternity was marred for you by fear and pain and contempt; and whatever errors your child has fallen into, were an evil inheritance that only years of suffering and discipline could eradicate."

As Mrs. Sancy pronounced the last sentence, she seemed for the moment to have forgotten my presence, and stood, looking off over the calm grey sea, with absent unrecognizing gaze. After a brief silence she turned to me with a smile: "Pardon my mental desertion. It is not good to talk of our own lives. We all become Adams again, and imagine ourselves sole in the universe."

On this hint I changed the conversation, and we returned to the hotel to lunch, after which I saw no more of Mrs. Sancy for that day.

That afternoon, my correspondent Mr. Kittredge arrived; and as it was bright and sunny after the fog, we took a boat, and pulled along under the alders that shade the Neah-can-a-cum. It was there that I listened to this story:

"While I was still a young man, nearly fifteen years ago, I floated on this stream, as we are doing today. My companion was a young girl whom I shall call Teresa. She was very young, I remember now with sorrow, and very beautiful; though *beautiful* is not so much the word to describe her as *charming*—magnetic, graceful, intelligent. A lithe, rather tall figure, a high-bred, sensitive, fine face, and pleasing manners. She seemed older than she really was, on account of her commanding physique and distinguished manner.

"I will not go over the details of our acquaintance, which ripened rapidly into love;—so I thought. This was a new country then, even more emphatically than it is now; new with the charm of novelty—not new because it had ceased to progress, as is now the case. Scattered around here within a radius of a dozen miles were half-a-dozen other young men like myself, who had immigrated to the far west, in the spirit of romantic adventure; and once here, were forced to do whatever came to our hands to gain a subsistence. I lived on a farm which I improved, keeping house quite by myself, and spending my leisure hours in study. Of course, the other young men, similarly situated, often visited me, and we usually talked over authors, or such questions of the day as we were familiar with or interested in.

"But one evening love was the theme of our conversation, and incidentally, Teresa's name was mentioned among us. I don't know who first uttered it, but I observed at once that the faces of all three of my companions betrayed an interest too strong and too peculiar to be attributed to an ordinary acquaintanceship with the subject of our remarks. For myself, I felt my own face flushing hotly, as a horrible suspicion seized my consciousness, becoming on the instant, conviction too painful to endure.

"You being a woman, cannot imagine the situation. I believed myself to be Teresa's accepted lover; and so I knew intuitively, did all my three companions; their faces revealing their thoughts to me, as did mine to them. Whatever you women do in the presence of your rivals, I know not. Men rage. It is not often, either, that a man encounters more than one rival at a time. But three!—each of us poor rivals saw three rivals before him. Whatever of friendship had hitherto existed among us was forgotten in the extreme anguish of the moment, and we sat glaring at each other in silence, with heaving chests and burning brows.

"All but Charlie Darling—darling Charlie, we used to call him—his face was deathly white, and his eyes glowed like a panther's in the dark. Yet he was the first to recover himself. 'Boys,' said he, 'we ought not to have brought a lady's name into the discussion; but since Teresa's has been mentioned, we may as well have an understanding. I consider the young lady as engaged to me, and you will please remember that fact when you are talking of her.'

"He said it bravely, proudly, though his lip trembled a little, but he eyed us unflinchingly. No one replied for some moments. Then Tom Allen, a big clumsy, good-hearted, but conceited fellow, lifted his eyes slowly, and answered with a hysterical laugh: 'You may be her darling Charlie, but I'll be d—d if I am not to be her husband!'

"This was the match to the powder. Charlie, myself, and Harry King, each sprang simultaneously forward, as if we meant to choke poor Tom for his words. Again Charlie was the first to use reason:

"'Hold, boys,' cried he hoarsely, 'let us take a little time to reflect. Two of us have declared ourselves to be engaged to Teresa. Let us hear if she contemplates marrying King and Kittredge, also. What do you say, King?'

"'I say yes!' thundered King, bending his black brows, and bringing down his fist on the table by which he stood.

"'And *I* say, I contemplate marrying *her*,' was my answer to Charlie's challenge.

"Charlie flung himself into a chair, and covered his face with his hands. The action touched some spring in our ruder natures which responded in sympathy for our favorite, and had the effect to calm us, in manner at least. I motioned the others to sit down, and addressed myself to Charlie Darling. 'See here, Charlie?' I said, 'it seems that Teresa has been playing us false. A girl who could be engaged to four young men at once cannot be worth the regards of any of us. Let us investigate the matter, and if she is truly guilty of such falsehood, let us one and all quit her forever without a word of explanation. What do you say? do you agree to that?'

"'How are you going to investigate?' asked Tom Allen, roughly. 'Have we not each declared that she was committed to us individually, and what more can be said?'

"'It appears incredible to me that any girl, much less a girl like Teresa, could so compromise her self-respect as to encourage four suitors, each in such a manner that he expected to marry her. It is so strange that I cannot believe it, except each man swears to his statement. Can we all swear to it?'

"I laid my little pocket-bible on the table, and set the example of taking an oath to the effect that Teresa had encouraged me to believe that she meant to marry me. King and Allen followed with a similar oath. Charlie Darling was the last to take the oath; but as he did so, a gleam of gladness broke over his pale, handsome face; for he could word his oath differently from ours. 'I swear before these witnesses and Almighty God,' said Charlie, 'that Teresa Bryant is my *promised wife.*'

"'That takes the wind out of our sails,' remarked Allen.

"'Do you allow other men to kiss your promised wife?' asked King, with a sneer.

"Charlie sprang at King, and had his hand on his throat in an instant; but Allen and I interfered to part them. It was no difficult matter, for Darling, excited as he was, felt the force of my observations on the quarrel. I said: 'Shall a trifling girl make us enemies, when she has so behaved that no one of us can trust her. You, Darling, do not, cannot have confidence in her promise, after all you have this night learned. You had best accept my first suggestion, and join with the rest of us in renouncing her forever and at once.'

"'That *I* will not,' broke out King, vehemently. 'Her word is no better than her acts, and I have as much right to her as Charlie Darling, or either of you, and I'll not give up the right to a man of you.'

"'We'll have to fight a four-cornered duel,' remarked Tom Allen, beginning to see the ludicrous side of the affair. 'Shall we choose up, two on a side?'

"'I will withdraw my pretensions,' I reiterated, 'if the others will do so, or even if King and Allen will quit the field to Charlie, who feels himself bound by Teresa's promise to him.'

"'I have said I would not withdraw,' replied King, sullenly. And thus we contended, hot-browed and angry-voiced, for more than an hour. Then rough but practical Tom proposed a scheme, which was no less than to compel Teresa to decide between us. After long deliberation, an agreement was entered into, and I hope I shall not shock you too much when I tell you what it was."

Kittredge paused, and looked at me doubtingly. I glanced aside at the overhanging trees, the glints of sunshine on the bank, a brown bird among the leaves, at anything, rather than him, for he was living over again the excitement of that time, and his face was not pleasant to study. After a little waiting, I answered:

"I must know the remainder of the story, since I know so much; what did you agree upon?"

"A plan was laid by which Teresa should be confronted with her four lovers, and forced to explain her conduct. To carry out our design it was necessary to use artifice, and I was chosen as the one who should conduct the affair. I invited her to accompany me to a neighboring farm-house to meet the young folks of the settlement. There was nothing unusual in this, as in those primitive times great latitude was granted to young people in their social intercourse. To mount her horse and ride several miles to a neighbor's house with a single escort, not to return until far into the night, was the common privilege of any young lady, and therefore there was no difficulty about obtaining either her consent or that of her parents to my proposition.

"We set off just at sunset, riding along the beach some distance, admiring the gorgeous western sky, the peaceful sea, and watching the sand-pipers skating out on the wet sands after each receding wave. I had never seen Teresa more beautiful, more sparkling, or more fascinating in every way; and my heart grew 'very little' as the Indians say. It was impossible to accuse her even in my thoughts, while under that bewitching influence. She was so full of life and vivacity that she did not observe the forced demeanor I wore, or if she did, had too much tact to seem to do so. As for me, guarded both by my hidden suspicions and by my promise to my friends, I uttered no word of tenderness or admiration with my tongue, whatever my eyes may have betrayed.

"The road we were going led past my house. When we were almost abreast of it I informed Teresa that there were some of our friends waiting for us there, and invited her to alight. Without suspicion she did so. — Don't look at me that way, if you can help it. It was terribly mean of us fellows, as I see it now. It looked differently then; and we had none of us seen much of the world and were rude in our notions of propriety.

"When she came inside of the house and saw only three men in place of the girls of her acquaintance she expected to meet, she cast a rapid, surprised glance

all round, blushed, asked, 'where are the girls?'—all in the most natural manner. There was positively nothing in her deportment to betray a guilty
conscience. I recognized that, and so, I could see, did Darling. He made haste
to hand her a chair, which she declined, still looking about her with a puzzled,
questioning air. I was getting nervous already over my share in the business,
and so plunged at once into explanation.

"'Teresa,' I said, 'we four fellows have made a singular discovery recently, to
the effect that we each believed himself to be your accepted lover. We have
met together to hear your explanation. Is there a man in the house you are
engaged to?'

"She gave one quick, scrutinizing glance at our faces, and read in them that
we were in earnest. Indeed, the scene would have given scope to the genius of
a Hogarth. Alternate red and white chased each other in quick succession over
her brow, cheeks, neck. Her eyes scintillated, and her chest heaved.

"'Please answer us, Teresa,' said Darling, after a most painful silence of a
minute, which seemed an hour.

"She raised her flashing eyes to his, and her tones seemed to stab him as she
uttered, '*You?* you too?' Then gathering up her riding-skirt, she made haste to
leave us, but found the door guarded by Tom Allen. When she saw that she
was really a prisoner among us, alarm seized her, and woman-like, she began
to cry, but not passionately or humbly. Her spirit was still equal to the occasion, and she faced us with the tears running over her cheeks.

"'If there is a man among you with a spark of honor, open this door! Mr.
Kittredge, this is your house. Allow me to ask if I am to be retained a prisoner
in it, or what you expect to gain by my forcible detention?'

"Tom Allen whispered something unheard by any save her, and she struck
at him with her riding-whip. This caused both Darling and myself to interpose,
and I turned door-keeper while Allen retreated to the other side of the room
with rather a higher color than usual on his lumpish face. All this while—not a
long while, at all—King had remained in sullen silence, scowling at the pro-
ceedings. At this juncture, however, he spoke:

"'Boys,' said he, 'this joke has gone far enough, and if you will permit us to
take our leave, I will see Miss Bryant safe home.'

"Involuntarily she turned toward the only one who proffered help; but Darling and I were too angry at the ruse to allow him to succeed, and stood our
ground by the door. 'You see, Teresa, how it is,' continued King, glancing at
us defiantly: 'these fellows mean to keep you a prisoner in this house until they
make you do and say as they please.'

"'What is it you wish me to do and say?' asked Teresa, with forced composure.

"'We wish you to state,' said I, hoarsely, 'whether or not you are or have been engaged to either of us. We want you to say it because we are all candidates for your favor, and because there is a dispute among us as to whose claim is the strongest. It will put an end to our quarrel, and secure to you the instant return of your liberty, if you will declare the truth.'

"At that she sank down on a chair and covered her face with her hands. After a little time she gathered courage and looked up at Darling and me. I observed, even then, that she took no notice of the others. 'If I am promised to either of you, you know it. But this I say now: if I were a hundred times promised, I would break that promise after such insult as you have all offered me this evening. Let me go!'

"What Charlie Darling suffered all through the interview had been patent to each of us. When she delivered his sentence in tones so determined, a cry that was a groan escaped his colorless lips. To say that I did not writhe under her just scorn would be false. Tears, few, but hot and bitter, blinded my eyes. She took no further notice of any of us, but sat waiting for her release."

"You knew by this time," I said, "that you had been deceived."

"I felt by this time that I had been a fool—a poor, coarse fool; there had been treachery somewhere, and that all together we were a villainous lot. I was only hesitating about how to get out of the scrape decently, when Darling spoke in a voice that was hardly recognizable:

"'Teresa, we were engaged ; I told these others so before; but they would not believe me. On the contrary, each one claims to have received such encouragement from you as to entitle him to be considered your favored lover. Hard as it was for me to believe such falsehood possible to you, two of these claimants insisted upon their rights against mine, and they overruled my judgment and wishes to such a degree that I consented to this trial for you. It has resulted in nothing except shame to us and annoyance to you! I beg your pardon. More I will not say tonight.'

"Then she rose up and faced us all again with burning cheeks and flashing eyes. 'If any other man says I have given him a promise, or anything amounting to a promise, he lies. To Tom Allen I have always been friendly, and have romped with him at our little parties; but tonight he grossly insulted me, and I will never speak to him again. As to Harry King, I was friendly with him, too, until about a fortnight ago he presumed to kiss me rudely, in spite of resistance, since which time I have barely recognized him. If Mr. Kittredge says I have made him any promises, he is unworthy of the great respect I have always had for him;' and with that last word she broke down, and sobbed as if her heart would break. But it was only for a few minutes that she cried—she was herself again before we had recovered our composure.

"'What was it Tom Allen said to you?' asked Charlie, when her tears were dried.

"'He said he would have me, if the rest did cast me off. Thank you,' with a mocking courtesy to Allen. 'It is fortunate for you—and for you all, that I have no "big brother."'

"'I beg you will believe no "big brother" could add to my punishment,' Charlie answered; and I felt included in the confession. Then he offered to see her home without more delay, but she declined any escort whatever, only requesting us to remain where we were until she had been gone half an hour; and rode off into the moonlight and solitude unattended, with what feelings in her heart God knows. We all watched her until she was hidden from sight by the shadows of a grove of pines, and I still remember the shudder with which I saw her plunge recklessly into the gloom—manlike, careful about her beautiful body, and not regarding her tender girl heart."

"That must have been a pleasant half hour for you," I could not help remarking.

"Pleasant! yes; we were like a lot of devils chained. That night dissolved all friendships between any two of us, except between Darling and me; and that could never be quite the same again, for had I not shown him that I believed myself a favored rival? though I afterwards pretended to impute my belief to vanity."

"How did you account to yourself for the delusion? Had she not flirted, as it is called, with you?"

"She had certainly caused me to be deluded, innocently or otherwise, into a belief that she regarded me with peculiar favor; and I had been accustomed to take certain little liberties with her, which probably seemed of far greater importance to me than they did to her; for her passional nature was hardly yet awakened, and among our primitive society there was no great restraint upon any innocent familiarities."

"What became of her after that night?—did she marry Darling?"

The answer did not come at once. Thought and feeling were with the past; and I could not bring myself to intrude the present upon it, but busied myself with the leaves and vines and mosses that I had snatched from the banks in passing, while my friend was absorbed in his silent reminiscences.

"You have not heard the saddest part of the story yet," he said at last, slowly and reluctantly. "She kept her word with each of us; ignoring Allen and King entirely; and only vouchsafing a passing word to Charlie and me. Poor Charlie was broken-hearted. He had never been strong, and now he was weak, ill; in short, fell into a decline, and died in the following year."

"Did the story never get out?"

"Not the true story. That scoundrel King spread a rumor abroad which caused much mischief, and was most cruel after what we had done to outrage her feelings in the first instance; but that was his revenge for her slight—I never knew whether she regretted Darling or not. She was so sensitive and willfully proud that she would have died herself sooner than betray a regret for any one who had offended her. Her mother died, and her father took her away with him to the Sandwich Islands. It was said he was not kind to her, especially after her 'disgrace,' as he called it."

"She never forgave you? What do you know about her subsequent history?"

"Nothing of it. But she had her revenge for what went before. After she went to the Islands I wrote her a very full and perfect confession of my fault, and the extenuating circumstances, and offered her my love, with the assurance that it had always been hers. What do you think she wrote me in return? Only this: that once she had loved me; that she had but just made the discovery that she loved me, and not Charlie Darling, when we mutually insulted her as we did, and forced her to discard both of us; for which she was not now sorry."

"After all, she was not an angel," I said, laughing lightly, to his embarrassment.

"But to think of using a girl of sixteen like that!"

"You are in a self-accusing mood today. Let us talk of our neighbors. Bad as that practice is, I believe it is better than talking about ourselves:—Mrs. Sancy thinks so, I know."

"Who is Mrs. Sancy?"

"I will introduce you tomorrow."

Next to being principal in a romantic affaire de coeur is the excitement of being an interested third party. In consonance with this belief I laid awake most of the night imagining the possible and probable "conclusion of the whole matter." I never doubted that Mrs. Sancy was Teresa, nor that she was more fascinating at thirty-one than she had been at sixteen: but fifteen years work great changes in the intellectual and moral person, and much as I desired to play the part of Fate in bringing these two people together, I was very doubtful about the result. But I need not have troubled myself to assume the prerogative of Fate, which by choosing its own instruments saved me all responsibility in the matter.

As Mr. Kittredge messed with a party of military officers, and was off on an early excursion to unknown localities, I saw nothing of him the following morning. We were to ride on the beach after lunch, returning on the turn of the tide to see the bathers. Therefore no opportunity seemed likely to present itself before evening for the promised introduction.

The afternoon proved fine, and we were cantering gaily along in the fresh breeze and sunshine, when another party appeared, advancing from the opposite direction, whom I knew to be Mrs. Sancy, her little daughter Isabelle, and the Kanaka servant. The child and servant were galloping hard, and passed us with a rush. But the lady seemed in a quieter mood, riding easily and carelessly, with an air of pre-occupation. Suddenly she too gave her horse whip and rein, and as she dashed past I heard her exclaim, "The quicksands! the quicksands!"

Instinctively we drew rein, turned, and followed. We rode hard for a few minutes, without overtaking her; then slackened our speed on seeing her come up with the child, and arrest the race which had so alarmed her.

"There are no quicksands in this direction;" was the first remark of Kittredge when we could speak.

"What should make her think so?"

"There *were* quicksands there a number of years ago, and by her manner she must have known it then."

"And by the same token," I replied, "she cannot have been here since the change."

"Who is she?"

"My friend, Mrs. Sancy."

"Where is she from?"

"From the quicksands;" I replied evasively, as I saw the lady approaching us.

"I fear you have shared my fright," she said, as soon as she came within speaking distance. "When I used to be familiar with these sands there was a dangerous spot out there; but I perceive time has effaced it, as he does so many things;" smiling, and bowing to my escort.

"There are some things time never effaces, even from the sands," returned Kittredge, growing visibly pale.

"That is contrary to the poets," laughingly she rejoined; "but I believe the poets have been superseded by the scientists, who prove everything for you by a fossil."

I could not help watching her to learn how much or how little recognition there was in her face. The color came and went, I could perceive; but whether with doubt or certainty I could not determine. I felt I ought to introduce them, but shrunk from helping on the denouement in that way. In my embarrassment I said nothing. We were now approaching the vicinity of the bathing-houses, and seeing the visitors collecting for the bath, an excuse was furnished for quickening our paces. Mrs. Sancy bowed and left us. Mr. Kittredge seemed to have lost the power of speech.

Fifteen minutes after I was sitting on some drift-wood, watching the pranks of the gayest of the crowd as they "jumped the rollers," when Mrs. Sancy came out of a dressing-room, followed by her Kanaka with a surf-board. Her bathing-dress was very jaunty and becoming, and her skill as a swimmer drew to her a great deal of attention. To swim out and float in on the rollers seemed to be to her no more of a feat than it would be to a sea-gull, she did it so easily and gracefully. But today something went wrong with her. Either she was too warm from riding, or her circulation was disturbed by the meeting with Kittredge, or both; at all events the second time she swam out she failed to return. The board slipped away from her, and she sank out of sight.

While I gazed horror-stricken, scarce understanding what had taken place, a man rushed past me in his bathing clothes, running out to where the water was deep enough to float him, and striking out rapidly from there. I could not recognize him in that dress, but I knew it was Kittredge. Fate had sent him. The incoming tide kept her where she sank, and he soon brought her to the surface and through the surf to the beach. I spread my cloak on the sand, and, wrapping her in it, began rubbing and rolling her, with the assistance of other ladies, for resuscitation from drowning.

In three minutes more Kittredge was kneeling by my side with a brandy-flask, administering its contents drop by drop, and giving orders. "It is congestion," said he. "You must rub her chest, her back, her hands and feet; so, so. She will die in your hands if you are not quick. For God's sake, work fast!"

By his presence of mind she was saved as by a miracle. When she was removed to her lodgings, and able to converse, she asked me who it was that had rescued her.

"Mr. Kittredge," I said.

"The same I met on the beach?"

"The same."

She smiled in a faint, half-dreaming way, and turned away her face. She thought I did not know her secret.

I am not going to let my hero take advantage of the first emotion of gratitude after a service, to mention his wishes in, as many story-tellers do. I consider it a mean advantage; besides Mr. Kittredge did not do it. In fact, he absented himself for a week. When he returned, I introduced him formally to Mrs. Sancy, and we three walked together down to the beach, and seated ourselves on a white old cottonwood that had floated out of the Columbia River, and been cast by the high tides of winter above the shelving sands.

We were rather a silent party for a few minutes. In his abstraction, Mr. Kittredge reached down and traced a name in the sand with the point of my parasol stick—TERESA.

Then, seeing the letters staring at him, he looked up at her, and said, "I could not brush them out if I would. Time has failed to do that." Her gaze wandered away, out to sea, up towards the Capes, down toward the Head; and a delicate color grew upon her cheek. "It has scarcely changed in fifteen years," she said. "I did not count on finding all things the same."

With that I made a pretense of leaving them, to seek shells along the beach; for I knew that fate could no longer be averted. When I returned she was aware that I possessed the secret of both, and she smiled upon me a recognition of my right to be pleased with what I saw; what I beheld seeming the prelude to a happy marriage. That night I wrote in my diary, after some comments on my relations with Mr. Kittredge:

"It is best be off with the old love,
Before you are on with the new."

Suggested Further Reading

WORKS BY VICTOR

The River of the West. Hartford, CT: Columbian Book Co., 1870. Reprinted Missoula: Mountain Press, 1983.

The New Penelope and Other Stories and Poems. San Francisco: A. L. Bancroft, 1877.

History of Oregon, Hubert Howe Bancroft. San Francisco: The History Company, 1888. Reprinted New York: Arno Press, 1967.

The Early Indian Wars of Oregon. Salem: F. C. Baker, 1894.

WORKS ABOUT VICTOR

Mills, Hazel Emery. "The Emergence of Frances Fuller Victor—Historian." *Oregon Historical Quarterly* 62 (September 1961), 309-36.

———. "Travels of a Lady Correspondent." *Pacific Northwest Quarterly* 45 (October 1954), 105-15.

Morris, William A. "Historian of the Northwest." *Quarterly of the Oregon Historical Society* 3 (December 1902), 429-34.

Powers, Alfred. *History of Oregon Literature.* Portland: Metropolitan Press, 1935, pp. 305-16.

Joaquin Miller

Born Cincinnatus Hiner Miller in Indiana, Joaquin Miller (1837?-1913) adopted his new name from the Mexican bandit Joaquin Murietta, whom Miller had defended in an early writing. His family crossed the plains when he was an infant, and settled in the Willamette Valley near Coburg, just north of Eugene. As a young man he ran off to the California gold fields near Mt. Shasta, a portion of his life which he recorded in his unreliable but nevertheless fascinating autobiography, *Life Among the Modocs: Unwritten History*. Back in Oregon he worked as a surveyor, taught school, studied and practiced law, edited a newspaper, married Minnie Myrtle Dyer ("The Poetess of the Coquille") from Port Orford, and settled in Canyon City.

The marriage was a stormy one, however, and Miller left his family for San Francisco and London, where he made his reputation as "The Poet of the Sierras" or "The Byron of Oregon," dressing in outlandish western garb, and acting the part of a wild and woolly frontiersman. His florid poetry and prose and his flamboyant lifestyle brought him fame, as did his melodramas, *The Danites* and *Forty-nine*. His later years were spent on his estate in Oakland, California, "The Hights"—he was also eccentric in his spelling—where his memory is preserved in a public park named for him.

The selection which follows, from his autobiographical *Memorie and Rime*, is probably largely fictional, but is important as one of the first written accounts of the distinctions between Californians and Oregonians, differences which have now hardened into popular dogma.

An Old Oregonian in the Snow

I was once, when riding express, "snowed under" with a famous old pioneer in the great cañon that splits Camas Prairie in two and breaks the monotony of its vast levels.

A wild unpeopled and unknown land it was then, but it has since been made immortal by the unavailing battles of Chief Joseph for the graves of his fathers.

Joe Meek! The many books about him tell you he was a savage, buckskinned delegate to Congress from the unorganized territory of Oregon, who lived with the Indians. These statements are almost all untrue. His was a plain, pastoral nature, and he shunned strife and notoriety. He had none of Kit Carson's dash about him, none of Davy Crockett's daring, nor had he Fremont's culture and capacity for putting himself well before the world; yet he ranked all these men both in the priority and the peril of his enterprises.

Indeed, before the chiefest of them was really heard of he had called the people of the far Northwest together under the great pines by the sounding Oregon,* and made solemn protest against the pretensions of England to that region. These settlers sent this man over the plains alone, a journey of more than half a year, to beg the President that they might be made or remain a portion of the United States while most of the now famous mountaineers were yet at their mother's knee. I know no figure in our history that approaches his in grandeur except that of President Houston, of the Lone Star Republic. And yet you search in vain for his name among those who sat in our Capitol in those early days. Some say he arrived at Washington when Congress was not in session, and so did not present his credentials. Others say that he lost his papers on the way in one of his perilous passages of a stream. And then again I am told that he never had any credentials to present; that the territory had no official existence at that time, and as Congress had not then become as adept in coining States and Territories, the pioneers of the Oregon River gave him no authority to appear in Congress, but that his mission was entirely with the President.

But the spectacle of this man setting out in mid-winter to ride alone over an untracked distance of three thousand miles, the loyalty of this people, their peril from savages, as well as the cupidity of Great Britain, I count one of the finest on the page of pioneer history.

*Early name for the Columbia River.

I suspect that his mission was fruitful of little, for he was, as new people came pouring in, quietly relegated to the background, and never afterward came conspicuously forward, save as an occasional leader in the wars against the Indians. But the undertaking and the accomplishment of this terrible journey alone ought to keep his memory green forever. And, indeed, had fate placed him in any other spot than isolated Oregon, he surely now would not be so nearly forgotten.

When gold was discovered in Idaho—or Ida*h*ho, an Indian word meaning, in a broad sense, mountain of light—Joe Meek, now an old man, could not resist the temptation to leave his home in the woods of Oregon and again brave the plains.

But he was no longer in any great sense a conspicuous figure. He, so far from being a leader, was even laughed at by his own people, the Oregonians, the new, young people who had journeyed into the country after his work had been done—the old story of the ingratitude of republics. And if he was laughed at by the long-haired, lank and blanketed Oregonian, he was despised by the quick, trim, sharp and energetic Californian who had now overrun Oregon on his way to the new Eldorado.

I wonder if the world would believe the half that could be written of the coarseness, the lawlessness of these unorganized armies that surged up and down the Pacific coast in search of gold a quarter of a century ago? I know of nothing like these invasions in history since the days of the Goths and Vandals.

Two wild and strong streams of humanity, one from Oregon and the other from California, had flowed on inharmoniously, tumultuously, together on their way to the mines. On Camas Prairie winter swept suddenly over them, and there, down in the deep cañon that cleft the wide and wintry valley through the middle, this stream of life stopped, as a river that is frozen.

A hundred men, trying to escape the "blizzard," tumbled headlong into the cañon together, and took shelter there as best they could beside the great basalt that had tumbled from the high, steep cliffs of the cañon. They crept under the crags, anywhere to escape the bitter cold.

And how the Californian did despise the Oregonian! He named him the "webfoot" because his feet were moccasined and he came from the land of clouds and rain. The bitter enmity and the bad blood of Germany and France were here displayed in epitome and in the worst form. A wonder, indeed, if there would not be some sort of tragedy played here before the storm was over.

The Oregonians wore long hair at that date. A pair of leggings and a blanket, with his head thrust through a hole in the centre, made his chief raiment.

A tall, peaked hat, with a band about it something like the brigand of the stage, crowned his long, straight, and stringy hair. Sometimes he wore an old slouch hat; he was rarely without the blanket; he was never without the leggings.

The Californian wore the traditional red shirt in that day, with rarely an exception. He always wore a pistol, often two pistols, in the great leather belt, and a bowie-knife. He generally wore duck pantaloons, tucked inside of his great long-legged leather boots. If he was "on the shoot," or "come from the shoulder," a little investigation would in many cases disclose an extra pistol or two tucked down deep in these boots. And even whiskey bottles have been known to nestle there. He rarely wore a coat. The coat interfered with his locomotion, and he despised it. If he was cold he put on another shirt. And how he would howl at the long, lean, and silent Oregonian as he moved about in his moccasins and leggings, with his blanket tight about him and his hands quite hidden.

"Hello, webfoot," cried the Californian leader to old Joe Meek one day, "where's your hands? Come, show us your hands! Are you heeled?"

"Try me and see!"

The blanket flew back, two hands shot forward, and the garrulous and meddlesome Californian let the "webfoot" go, for he was "heeled."

We had but little wood here, and that was of the worst quality—willow—green and frozen. The little river gurgled and called plaintively for the first day or two as it struggled on the ground against its icy banks. But soon its lips were sealed, and the snow came down and covered the silent and dead waters as with a shroud.

The day after the little tilt between the Californian leader and quiet old Joe Meek, the Californians took occasion to walk up and down before his camp, and talk very loud and behave in a very insulting manner. The cañon was all on tiptoe. The men began to forget for a moment their miseries in the all-absorbing topic, the coming fight.

The blizzard only increased in terror. The mules and horses were freezing to death in their tracks on the snow plateau above.

It was terrible, pitiful. Death was imminent for both man and beast. The Californians outnumbered the Oregonians ten to one. They had secured the only real shelter from the storm, a sort of cavern under the over-hanging basaltic rocks, over which the snowy cyclone swept and left hanging huge masses of snow. The Californians were packed away like sardines, talking of the coming battle and firing the heart of their leader with hatred of the quiet old Oregonian, who, with his Indian sons, swung their half- frozen arms or walked up and down in the vain effort to keep warm.

Suddenly the Californian came up to one of the Indian boys and slapped him in his face. There was a shout from the cave. The old man only turned, threw back his blanket, tapped a pistol, pointed up to the plateau, and said:

"Them! Sunrise! Thar!"

The Californian was startled. He could not say a single word. He only nodded assent, and went back to his cave and his crowd. Never had duel been arranged so suddenly. He told his men, and they were wild, furious. A general battle was imminent.

Let us look at these silent, lean and despised Oregonians in their blankets. Comely they were not, nor graceful. They were not well read, nor had the eyes of the world been upon them as on the Californians. But be it remembered that away back before California was at all known these Oregonians had met under the pines, and most emphatically, as well as ungrammatically, proclaimed that they were a part of the United States, and not of England. They had declared war against aggressive tribes, had raised an army, maintained it in the field, and finally had coined their own money out of their own gold, paid off that army, and proclaimed peace, all on their own account. Their coin was pure gold—not a particle of alloy. The beaver on the one side of their crude coin showed the quiet industry of her pastoral people. The sheaf of wheat on the other side showed that plenty should reward the husbandman. People like that are not to be despised.

Against this record the Californian had little to exhibit. He had washed down hills and led rivers over the mountains; he had contributed much to the metallic currency of the world, but he had done little else.

The storm went down with the sun, and now how bitter cold! The moon hung high and clear right overhead. The stars stood out and sparkled in the frost-like fire. The keen, cold wind swept the plain above and threatened to fill the cañon with snow. Wolves, that had eaten only the dead horses up to this time, now began to devour the weak and dying ones. There were enough wolves gathering about us, howling, fighting, devouring our horses, to attack and eat us where we stood. But still the fight must go on. The deadly hatred must find some expression. Fortunate if it should end with this deadly duel just before us.

Clouds began to drive over the moon at midnight and stream away over toward Idaho to the east. The stars went out, as if the fierce wind had blown out the myriad lights of heaven. Then the snow began to fall again, thick and fast, massive, as the sombre Oregonians sat about their fire and talked of the coming duel. The group grew white as huddled flocks of sheep. Now and then a man would get up and shake himself, and the snow would slide off his shoulders in great avalanches. The fire began to perish under this incessant, unceasing dropping of snow. The snow simply possessed the world. The fire died out. It was dark, with a wild, a deadly darkness. They could not see each other's faces. When a man spoke it was as if some one called from deep down in a well. They groped about, feeling for each other. The Californians slept tranquilly and selfishly on in their cavern.

Snow above and snow below! The wolves howling from the hill. Snow that buried you, that lay on your shoulders like a burden, that loaded you down, that fastened upon you as if it had life and sense, and like a ghost that would never go away.

With the coming morning there came a sense of change. It was warm, warmer, sultry. The Chinook wind! But it was not light. There was only a dim, ghastly something in the air—the ghost of a dead day, and snow and snow and snow. Nothing but silence and snow!

I stop here as I write, and wonder if any one east of the Rocky Mountains knows what the "Chinook" wind is? One writes at a disadvantage here. But the world is learning. Ten years ago it would not have known what a "blizzard" or a "cyclone" meant. It knows now.

Well, this Chinook wind is a hot cyclone that leaps up from the Gulf of California, caroms from mountain-top to mountain-top toward the north, till it suddenly and savagely takes possession of the coldest and bleakest spot on the continent. It comes when the cold reaches a climax. This hot Chinook wind is born of the freezing blizzard. It is the one thing that makes this vast North-west habitable. Stick a pin here and remember. This Chinook wind is the most remarkable and phenomenal thing in nature.

The Oregonians threw back their blankets, stood erect, and breathed free for the first time in all these deadly days. Puddles of water began to form at their feet. Little rivulets began to seek the frozen river in the cañon. The snow began to slip and slump in avalanches down the steep sides of the mountains. The Indian boys tightened their moccasins, and with the first sign of breaking day hurried away over the hill, pistols in hand, to look after their horses. The old pioneer calmly waited for sunrise. He stood alone by the dead firebrands.

Suddenly there was a great, dull shock. Thud! An avalanche! The whole mountain side of snow had slid into the cañon and carried with it the overhanging masses above the cavern.

The swelling river, thus suddenly brought to a standstill, began to plunge and fret and foam at his very feet. The Indian boys returned, and began to move their effects out of the cañon. They dropped their loads at the sound of a second avalanche which seemed to close the cavern, and looked at each other in the gray dawn. They were glad; wild with delight. They chuckled at first; and then a yell—such a yell of pure satisfaction was never heard before.

Their father lifted his head, looked at them hard, and then plucking me after him, hurried down to the cavern's mouth.

The Californians were on their feet, falling over each other, dazed, confused, cursing, howling. The mouth of the cave was so closed by the snow that one had to stoop to enter.

They had thrown some pitch on the embers, and as it blazed up they stared at the apparition of the old man who stood there in their midst, in their power, and almost alone. A little white rabbit, driven in by the swelling water, came huddling at his feet. "What have you come in here for?" cried the leader, clutching a pistol.

"To save you."

"What!" And the pistol was raised to a level.

The old man did not heed or answer. He stooped and picked up the terrified little rabbit and held it kindly, as you would hold a kitten. The men looked at each other and then out at the booming flood, foaming at the door of the cavern, and dashing in the new dawn.

I turned and ran away and up toward our camp, for there was a cry of terror on every lip. The old man led them at a run, their guns in their hands, their blankets on their shoulders.

We reached the safe eminence where the Indian boys had made our new camp, and then old Colonel Joe Meek, turning to the Californian leader and pointing to the plateau beyond, said:

"Cap'n, it's sunrise."

"Colonel Joe Meek, I begs your parding. I'm licked!" cried the Californian, as he reached his hand in token of submission and peace.

Suggested Further Reading

WORKS BY MILLER

Life Among the Modocs: Unwritten History. London: Richard Bently and Son, 1873.
Reprinted, with an introduction by Alan Rosenus, Eugene, Oregon: Orion Press,
1972.

Forty-nine. San Francisco: California Publishing Co., 1882.

Memorie and Rime. New York: Funk and Wagnall's, 1884.

Joaquin Miller's Poems. 6 vols. San Francisco: Whitaker and Ray, 1909-10.

Selected Writings of Joaquin Miller. Ed. Alan Rosenus. Eugene, Oregon: Urion
Press, 1977.

WORKS ABOUT MILLER

Lawson, Benjamin S. *Joaquin Miller.* Western Writers Series number 43. Boise:
Boise State University, 1980.

Marberry, M. Marion. *Splendid Poseur: Joaquin Miller—American Poet.* New York:
Thomas Y. Crowell, 1953.

Ella Higginson

Born in Kansas, Ella Rhoads Higginson (1862-1940) crossed the plains to Oregon with her parents as an infant, and spent her early life in La Grande, in Portland, on a farm in the Willamette Valley, and in Oregon City.

After her marriage to Russell Higginson in Oregon City in the middle 1880s, the couple moved to Bellingham, where she lived until her death. Her poems and stories are set in both Oregon and Washington, though she felt that her childhood in Oregon influenced her work more than anything else. "Zarelda," set in Oregon City among working-class people, is a remarkable example of regional realism at the end of the nineteenth century, calling to mind the work of better-known rural New England writers like Sarah Orne Jewett and Mary Wilkins Freeman. Higginson's use of dialect and local patterns of life marks one of the earliest attempts by an Oregon writer to present the newly emerging culture in Oregon in its own terms.

Zarelda

"Reldy! Say, 'Reldy! *Za-rel-dy!*" The girl was walking rapidly, but she stopped at once and turned. She wore a cheap woolen dress of a dingy brown color. The sleeves were soiled at the wrists, but the narrow, inexpensive ruffle at the neck was white and fresh. Her thick brown hair was well brushed and clean. It was woven into a heavy, glistening braid which was looped up and tied with a rose-colored ribbon. Her shoes were worn out of shape and "run down" at the heels, and there were no gloves on the roughened hands clasped over the handle of her dinner-bucket.

"Oh, you?" she said, smiling.

"Yes, me," said the other girl, with a high color, as she joined Zarelda. They walked along briskly together. "I've been tryin' to ketch up with you for three blocks. Ain't you early?"

"No; late. Heard the whistle blow 'fore I left home. Didn't you hear it? Now own up, Em Brackett."

"No, I didn't—honest," said the other girl, laughing. "I set the clock back las' night an' forgot to turn it ahead ag'in this mornin'."

This young woman's dress and manner differed from her companion's. Her dress was cheap, but of flimsy, figured goods that under close inspection revealed many and large grease spots; the sleeves were fashionably puffed; and there were ruffles and frills and plaitings all over it. At the throat was a bit of satin ruffling that had once been pale blue. Half her hair had been cut off, making what she called her "bangs," and this was tightly frizzed over her head as far back as her ears. Her back hair—coarse and broken from many crimpings— was braided and looped up like Zarelda's, and tied with a soiled blue ribbon. She wore much cheap jewelry, especially amethysts in gaudy settings. She carried herself with an air and was popularly supposed by the young people of factory society to be very much of a belle and a coquette.

Zarelda turned and looked at her with sudden interest. "What in the name o' mercy did you turn the clock back for?" Em tossed her head, laughing and blushing.

"Never you mind what for, 'Reldy Winser. It ain't any 'o your funeral, I guess, if I did turn it back. I had occasion to—that's all. You wasn't at the dance up at Canemah las' night, was you?" she added suddenly.

"No, I wasn't. I didn't have anybody to go with. You didn't go, either, did you?"

"Unh-hunh; I did."

Em nodded her head, looking up the river to the great Falls, with dreamy, remembering eyes. "We had a splendid time, an' the walk home 'long the river was just fine."

"Well, I could of gone with you if I'd of knew you was goin'. Couldn't I? Maw was reel well las' night, too."

She waited for a reply, but receiving none, repeated rather wistfully—"Couldn't I?"

Em took her eyes with some reluctance away from the river and looked straight before her.

"Why, I guess," she said, slowly and with slight condescension. "At least, I wouldn't of cared if my comp'ny wouldn't; an' I guess"—with a beautiful burst of generosity—"he wouldn't of minded much."

"Oh," said Zarelda, "you had comp'ny, did you ?"

"W'y, of course. You didn't s'pose I went up there all alone of myself, did you?"

"You an' me ust to go alone places, without any fellow, I mean," said Zarelda. A little color came slowly into her face. She felt vaguely hurt by the other's tone. "I thought mebbe you went with some o' the other girls."

"I don't go around that way any more." Em lifted her chin an inch higher. "When I can't have an—escort"—she uttered the word with some hesitation, fearing Zarelda might laugh at it—"I'll stay home."

Then she added abruptly in a reminiscent tone—"Maw acted up awful over my goin' with him. Thought for a spell I wouldn't get to go. But at last I flared all up an' told her if I couldn't go I'd just up an' leave for good. That brought her around to the whipple-trees double quick, I can tell you. I guess she won't say much agen my goin' with him another time."

"Goin' with who?" said Zarelda. Em looked at her, smiling.

"For the land o' love! D'you mean to say you don't know? I thought you'd of guessed. W'y, that's what made maw so mad—she was just hoppin', I tell you. That's what made her act up so. Said all the neighbors 'u'd say I was tryin' to get him away from you."

In an instant the blood had flamed all over Zarelda's face and neck.

"Get who away from me, Em Brackett?"

"As if there was so many to get!" said Em, laughing.

"Who are you a-talkin' about?" said Zarelda, sternly. Her face was paling now. "What of I got to do with you an' your comp'ny an' your maw's actin'-ups, I'd like to know. Who *was* your comp'ny?"

"Jim Sheppard; he—"

"Jim Sheppard!" cried Zarelda, furiously. She turned a white face to her companion, but her eyes were blazing. "What do I care for Jim Sheppard? Aigh? What do I care who he takes to dances up at Canemah? Aigh? You tell your maw, Em Brackett, that she needn't to trouble to act up on my account. She can save her actin'-ups for somebody that needs 'em! You tell her that, will you?"

"Well, I will," said Em, unmoved. "I'm glad you don't mind, 'Reldy. I felt some uneasy myself, seein' 's how stiddy he'd been goin' with you."

"Well, that don't hender his goin' with somebody else, does it? I ain't very likely to keep him from pleasin' hisself, am I?"

"Don't go to workin' yourself up so, 'Reldy. If you don't care, there's no use in flarin' up so. My! Just look at this em'rald ring in at Shindy's. Ain't that a beaut'?"

"I ain't got time." Zarelda walked on with her head up. "Don't you see we're late a'ready? The machin'ry's all a-goin', long ago."

The two girls pushed through the swinging gate and ran up the half-dozen steps to the entrance of the big, brick woolen mills. A young man in a flannel shirt and brown overalls was passing through the outer hall. He was twirling a full, crimson rose in his hand.

As the girls hurried in, he paused and stood awkwardly waiting for them, with a red face.

"Good mornin'," he said, looking first at Em and then, somewhat shame-facedly, at Zarelda.

"Good mornin', Jim," said Zarelda, coolly. She was still pale, but she smiled as she pressed on into the weaving-room. The many-tongued roar of the machinery burst through the open door to greet her. Em lingered behind a moment; and when she passed Zarelda's loom there was a crimson rose in her girdle and two more in her cheeks.

Five hours of monotonous work followed. Zarelda stood patiently by her loom, unmindful of the toilers around her and the deafening noise; she did not lift her eyes from her work. She was the youngest weaver in the factory and one of the most careful and conscientious.

The marking-room was in the basement, and in its quietest corner was a large stove whereon the factory girls were permitted to warm their lunches. When the whistle sounded at noon they ceased work instantly, seized their lunch baskets, and sped pushing, laughing, jostling down the stairs to the basement. There was a small, rickety elevator at the rear of the factory, and some of the more reckless ones leaped upon it and let themselves down with the rope.

Zarelda was timid about the elevator; but that noon she sprang upon it and giving the rope a jerk went spinning down to the ground. As she entered the marking-room one of the overseers saw her. "What!" he exclaimed. "Did you come down that elevator, 'Reldy? I thought you had more sense 'n some o' the other girls. Why, it ain't safe! You're liable to get killed on it."

"I don't care," said Zarelda, with a short, contemptuous laugh. "I'd just as soon go over the falls in an Indian dug-out."

"You must want to shuffle off mighty bad," said the overseer. Then he added kindly, for he and all the other overseers liked her—"What's got into you, 'Reldy? Anything ail you?"

"No," said the girl; "nothin' ails me." But his kind tone had brought sudden, stinging tears to her eyes.

She went on silently to the stove and set her bucket upon it. It contained thick vegetable soup, which, with soda crackers, constituted her dinner. She sat down to watch it, stirring it occasionally with a tin spoon. Twenty other girls were crowding around the stove. Em was among them. Zarelda saw the big red rose lolling in her girdle. She turned her eyes resolutely away from it, only to find them going back again and again.

"Hey! Where'd you get your rose at, Em Brackett?" cried one of the girls.

"Jim Sheppard gave it to her," trebled another, before Em could reply. "I see him have it pinned onto his flannel shirt before the whistle blew."

"*Jim Sheppard!* Oh, my!"

There was a subdued titter behind Zarelda's back. She stirred the soup without lifting her eyes. "She went livid, though, an' then she went white!" one of the girls who read yellow novels declared afterward, tragically.

"Well," said Matt Wilson, sitting down on a bench and commencing to eat a great slice of bread thinly covered with butter, "who went to the dance up at Stringtown las' night?"

All the girls but two flung unclean hands above their heads. There was a merry outcry of "I did! I did!"

"Well, I didn't," said Matt. "My little lame sister coaxed me to wheel her down town, an' then it was too late."

"Why wasn't you there, Zarelda Winser?" cried Belle Church, opening her dinner bucket and examining the contents with the air of an epicurean.

For a second or two Zarelda wished honestly that she had a lame sister or an invalid mother. Then she said, quite calmly—"I didn't have anybody to go with. That's why." She turned and faced them all as she spoke.

With a fine delicacy which was certainly not acquired by education, every girl except Matt looked away from Zarelda's face. Matt, not having been to the dance, was not in the secret.

But Zarelda did not change countenance. She sat calmly eating her soup from the bucket with the tin spoon. She took it noisily from the point of the spoon; it was so thick that it was like eating a vegetable dinner.

"Didn't have anybody to go with?" repeated Matt, laughing loudly. "I call that good. A girl that's had steady comp'ny for a year! Comp'ny that's tagged her closer 'n her shadder! An' I did hear"—she shattered the shell of a hardboiled egg by hammering it on the bench, and began picking off the pieces—"that your maw was makin' you up a whole trunkful o' new underclo's all trimmed up with tattin' an' crochet an' serpentine braid with insertin' two inches wide on 'em, too. You didn't have anybody to go with, aigh? What's the matter with Jim Sheppard?"

Zarelda set her eyes on the red rose, as if that gave her courage.

"He took Em Brackett."

"Not much!" said Matt, turning sharply. "Honest? Well, then, he only took her because you couldn't go an' ast him to take her instid."

"Why, the idee!" exclaimed Em, coloring angrily and fluttering until the rose almost fell out of her girdle. "Zarelda Winser, you tell her that ain't so!"

"No, it ain't so," said Zarelda, composedly, finishing her soup and beginning on a soda cracker. "He didn't ask me at all. He asked Em hisself."

"My!" said Net Carter, who had not been giving attention to the conversation. "What larrapin' good lunches you do have, Em Brackett. Chicken sandwich, an' spiced cur'nts, an' cake! My!"

Em Brackett looked out of the cobwebbed window at a small dwelling between the factory and the river. "I wonder why Mis' Allen don't hide up that ugly porch o' her'n with vines," she said, frostily. In factory society "larrapin" was not considered a polite word and a snub invariably awaited the unfortunate young woman who used it. The line must be drawn.

When the whistle blew the girls started leisurely for the stairs. There would be fifteen minutes during which they might stand around the halls and talk to the young men. Zarelda fell back, permitting all to precede her. Em looked back once or twice to see where she was.

"Well, if that 'Reldy Winser ain't grit!" whispered Nell Curry to Min Aster. "Just as good as acknowledgin' he's threw off on her, an' her a-holdin' up her head that way. There ain't another girl in the factory c'u'd do that without flinchin', too."

When Zarelda reached the first hall she looked about her deliberately for Jim Sheppard. It had been his custom to meet her at the head of the stairs and going with her to one of the windows overlooking the Falls, to talk until the second whistle sent them to their looms. With a resolute air she joined Em Brackett, who was looking unusually pretty with a flush of excitement on her face and a defiant sparkle in her eyes.

In a moment Jim Sheppard came in. He hesitated when he saw the two girls together. A dull red went over his face. Then he crossed the hall and, deliberately

ignoring Zarelda, smiled into Em's boldly inviting eyes and said, distinctly—
"Em, don't you want to take a little walk? There's just time."

"Why, yes," said Em, with a flash of poorly concealed triumph. "'Reldy, if you're a-goin' on upstairs, would you just as lieve pack my bucket up?"

"I'd just as lieve." Zarelda took the bucket, and the young couple walked away airily.

This was the way the factory young men had of disclosing their preferences. It was considered quite proper for a young man and a young woman to "go together" for months, or even years, and for one to "throw off" on the other, when attracted by a fresher face, with no explanation or apology.

"Well," whispered Belle Church, "I guess there ain't one of us but's been threw off on some time or other, so we know how it feels. But this is worse. He's been goin' with her more'n a year—an then to stop off so sudden!"

"It's better to stop off sudden than slow," said Matt Wilson, with an air of grim wisdom. "It hurts worse, but it don't hurt so long. Well, if I ever! Just look at that!"

Out of sheer pity Frank Haddon had sidled out of a group of young men and made his way hesitatingly to Zarelda. "'Reldy," he said, "don't you want to want to take a walk, too?" The girl's eyes flamed at him. She knew that he was pitying her, and she was not of a nature to accept pity meekly. "No!" she flashed out, with scorn. "I don't want to—want to"—mimicking his tone—"take a walk, too. If I did, I guess I know the road."

She went upstairs, holding her head high.

When Zarelda went home that evening she found the family already at the supper table. The Winsers were not very particular about their home manners.

"We don't wait on each other here," Mrs. Winser explained, frequently, with pride, to her neighbors. "When a meal's done, on the table it goes in a jiffy, an' such of us as is here, eat. I just put the things back in the oven an' keep 'em hot for them that ain't on hand."

Zarelda was compelled to pass through the kitchen to reach the stairs.

"Well, 'Reldy," said her mother, "you're here at last, be you? Hurry up an' wash yourself. Your supper's in the oven, but I guess the fire's about out. It does beat all how quick it goes out. Paw, I do wish you'd hump yourself an' git some dry wood. It 'u'd try the soul of a saint to cook with that green stuff. Sap fairly *oozes* out of it!"

"I don't want any supper, maw," said Zarelda.

"You don't want any supper! What ails you? Aigh?"

"I don't feel hungry. I got a headache."

She passed the table without a glance and went upstairs. Her mother arose, pushing back her chair with decision and followed her. When she reached

Zarelda's room, the girl was on her knees before her trunk. She had taken out a small writing-desk and was fitting a tiny key in the lock. Her hat was still on her head, but pushed back.

She started when the door opened, and looked over her shoulder, flushing with embarrassment and annoyance. Then, without haste or nervousness, she replaced the desk and, closing the trunk, stood up calmly and faced her mother.

"Why don't you want any supper?" Mrs.Winser took in the trunk, the desk, and the blush at one glance. "Be you sick?"

"I got a headache." Zarelda took off her hat and commenced drawing the pins out of her hair. She untied the red ribbon and rolled it tightly around three fingers to smooth out the creases.

"Well, you wasn't puttin' your headache 'n your writin'-desk, was you?"

"No, I wasn't."

"Now, see here, 'Reldy," said Mrs. Winser, very kindly, coming closer and resting one large hand on the bureau; "there's somethin' ails you besides a headache, an' you ain't a-goin' to pull any wool over my eyes. You've hed lots an' lots o' headaches an' et your supper just the same. What ails you?"

"Nothin' ails me, maw."

"There does, too, somethin' ail you. I guess I know. Now, what is it? You might just as well spit it right out an' be done with it."

Zarelda was silent. She began brushing her hair with a dingy brush from which tufts of bristles had been worn in several places. Her mother watched her patiently for a few moments, then she said—"Well, 'Reldy, be you goin' to tell me what ails you?"

Still there was no reply.

"You ain't turned off in the fact'ry, be you?"

Zarelda shook her head.

"Well, then," said Mrs. Winser slowly, as if reluctantly admitting a thought that she had been repelling, "it's somethin' about Jim Sheppard."

The girl paled and brushed her hair over her face to screen it from her mother's searching gaze.

"Have you fell out with him?"

"No, I ain't fell out with him. Hadn't you best eat your supper before it gets cold, maw?"

"No, I hadn't best. I ain't a-goin' to budge a blessed step out o' this here room tell I know what ails you. Not if I have to stay here tell daylight." After a brief reflection she added—"Now, don't you tell me he's been cuttin' up any! I always said he was a fine young man, an' I say so still."

"He ain't been cuttin' up any," said Zarelda. "At least, not as I know of."

She laid down the brush and pushing her hair all back with both hands, fronted her mother suddenly, pale but resolute.

"If you want to know so bad," she said, "I'll tell you. He's threw off on me."

Mrs. Winser sunk helplessly into a chair. "Threw off on you!" she gasped.

"Yes, threw off on me." Zarelda kept her dry, burning eyes on her mother's face. "D'you feel any better for makin' me tell it?"

Certainly her revenge for the persecution was all that heart could desire. Her mother sat limp and motionless, save for the slow, mechanical sliding back and forth of one thumb on the arm of her chair.

After a while Zarelda resumed the hair-brushing, calmly. Then her mother revived.

"Who—who in the name of all that's merciful has he took up with now?" she asked, weakly.

"Em Brackett."

"What!" Mrs. Winser almost screamed. "That onery hussy! 'Reldy Winser, be you a-tellin' me the truth?"

"Yes, maw. He took her to the dance up at Canemah las' night, an' she told me about it this mornin'!"

"The deceitful jade. Smiled sweet as honey at me when she went by. You'd of thought sugar wouldn't melt in her mouth. I answered her 's short as lard pie-crust—I'm glad of it now. Has he took her any place else?"

"He took her walkin' at noontime. Stepped right up when she was standin' alongside o' me an' never looked at me, an' ast her right out loud so's all of 'em could hear, too."

"Well, he'd ought to be ashamed of hisself! After bein' your stiddy comp'ny for more'n a year—well onto two years—an' a-lettin' all of us think he was serious!"

"He never said he was, maw."

"He never said he was, aigh? 'Reldy Winser, you ain't got enough spunk to keep a chicken alive, let alone a woman! 'He never said he was,' aigh? Well, ain't he been a-comin' here three nights a week nigh onto two year, an' a-takin' you every place, an' never a-lookin' at any other girl? An' didn't he give you an amyfist ring las' Christmas, an' a reel garnet pin on your birthday? An' didn't he come here one evenin', a-laffin' an' a-actin' up foolish in a great way an' holler out—'Hello, maw Winser?' Now, don't you go a tellin' me he never meant anything serious."

"Well, he never said so," said the girl, stubbornly.

"I don't care if he *never* said so. He acted so. Why, for pity's sake! You've got a greasespot on your dress. I never see you with a grease-spot before—you're so tidy. How'd you get it on?"

"Oh, I don't know."

"Benzine'll take it out. Well—I'm a-goin' to give him a piece o' my mind!"

Zarelda lifted her body suddenly. She looked tall. Her eyes flamed out their proud fire.

"Now, see here, maw," she said, "you don't say a word to him—not a word. This ain't your affair; it's mine. It's the fashion in fact'ry society for a girl an' a fellow to go together, an' give each other things, without bein' real engaged; an' she has to take her chances o' some other girl gettin' him away from her. If he wants to throw off on her, all he's got to do 's to take some other girl to a dance or out walkin'. An' then, if he's give her a ring or anything, it's etiquette for her to send it back to him, an' he'll most likely give it to the other girl. I don't think it's right, an' I don't say but what it's hard—" her voice trembled and broke, but she conquered her emotion stubbornly and went on—"but it's the way in fact'ry society. There ain't a girl in the fact'ry but what's had to stand it some time or other, an' I guess I can. You don't want me to be a laffin'-stawk, do you?"

"No, I don't." Her mother looked at her in a kind of admiring despair. "But I never hear tell of such fashions an' such doin's in all my born days. It's shameful. Your paw an' me 'd set our minds on your a-marryin' him an' gettin' a home o' your own. It's been a burden off o' our minds for a year past."

"Oh, maw!"

"Just to feel that you'd be fixed so's you could take care o' your little sisters in case we dropped off. An' there I've went an' made up all them underclo's!" She leaned her head upon her hand and sat looking at the floor with a forlornly reminiscent expression. "An' put tattin' on three sets, an' crochet lace on three, an' serpentine edgin' on three. An' inserting on all of 'em! That ain't the worst of it. I've *worked his initial in button-hole stitch* on every blessed thing!"

"Oh, maw, you never did that, did you?"

"Yes, I did. An' what's more, I showed 'em all to old Miss Bradley, too."

"You might just as well of showed 'em to the whole town!" said poor Zarelda, bitterly.

"They looked so nice I had to show 'em to somebody."

"Sister," piped a little voice at the foot of the stairs, "Mis' Riley's boy's come to find out how soon you're a-comin' over to set up with the sick baby."

"Oh, I'd clear forgot." Zarelda braided her hair rapidly. "Tell him I'll be over 'n a few minutes."

"Now, see here, 'Reldy," said her mother, getting up and laying her hand affectionately on the girl's arm, "you ain't a-goin' to budge a single step over there to-night. You just get to bed an' put an arnicky plaster on your forehead—"

Zarelda laughed in a kind of miserable mirth.

"Oh, you can laff, but it'll help lots. I'll go over an' set up with that baby myself."

"No, you won't, maw." She slipped the last pin in her hair and set her hat firmly on the glistening braids. "I said I'd set up with the baby an' I will. I ain't goin' to shirk just because I'm in trouble."

She went out into the cool autumn twilight. Her mother followed her and stood looking after her with sympathetic eyes. At last she turned and went slowly into the poor and gloomy house; as she closed the door she put all her bitterness and disappointment into one heavy sigh.

The roar of the Falls came loudly to Zarelda as she walked along rapidly. The dog-fennel was still in blossom, and its greenish snow was drifted high on both sides of her path. Still higher were billows of everlasting flowers, undulating in the soft wind. The fallen leaves rustled mournfully as she walked through them. Some cows were feeding on the commons near by; she heard their deep breathing on the grass before they tore and crushed it with their strong teeth; she smelled their warm, fragrant breaths.

She came to a narrow bridge under the cottonwoods where she saw the Willamette, silver and beautiful, moving slowly and noiselessly between its emerald walls. The slender, yellow sickle of the new moon quivered upon its bosom.

Zarelda stood still. The noble beauty of the night—all its tenderness, all its beating passion—shook her to the soul. Her life stretched out before her, hard and narrow as the little path running through the dog-fennel—a life of toil and duty, of clamor and unrest, of hurried breakfasts, cold lunches and half-warm suppers, of longing for knowledge that would never be hers—the hard and bitter treadmill of the factory life.

A sob came up into her dry throat, but it did not reach her lips.

"I won't!" she said, setting her teeth together hard. "I hate people who whine after what they can't have, instead o' makin' the best o' what they've got."

She lifted her head and went on. Her face was beautiful; something sweeter than moonlight shone upon it. She walked proudly and the dry leaves whirled behind her.

Suggested Further Reading

WORKS BY HIGGINSON

From the Land of the Snow Pearls. New York: Macmillan, 1897.

A Forest Orchid. New York: Macmillan, 1897.

When the Birds Go North Again. New York: Macmillan, 1898.

Mariella; of Out-West. New York: Macmillan, 1904.

The Voice of April-Land. New York: Macmillan, 1906.

Alaska, the Great Country. New York: Macmillan, 1908.

WORKS ABOUT HIGGINSON

"Ella Higginson." In *History of Oregon Literature*, Alfred Powers. Portland: Metropolitan Press, 1935, pp. 415-440.

Alfred Powers

Known best as the author of the important reference work, *History of Oregon Literature* (1935), Alfred Powers (1887-1983) grew up on cattle ranches in the Southwest and came to Oregon as a young man, receiving his bachelor's degree from the University of Oregon in 1910. He served as a private in World War I, and returned to work in Oregon higher education, where he held various faculty and administrative positions during his career, including professor of creative writing. He also served as editor of the *Oregon Historical Quarterly* and edited many books for Binfords and Mort, the Portland publisher of regional literature. Besides being a scholar and editor, Alfred Powers wrote many books of regional interest. "Marooned in Crater Lake," the story included here, is representative of his ability to create suspenseful adventure in local settings for the young reader.

Marooned in Crater Lake

In October, 1910, before George Washington's profile had displaced the picture of Benjamin Franklin on the one-cent stamps, Jim Turner bought a book of this denomination at Medford, Oregon, securing only twenty-four of the green rectangles for twenty-five cents. But the protective book was well worth a penny when carrying stamps in a warm pocket. He tore out five of them as postage for five scenic postcards which he mailed, three for his aunt and two for Mrs. Harry Smith. Mailing postcards was one of his duties as the only boy member of the two-car tourist party which included his uncle and aunt and Mr. and Mrs. Smith. He put the book with its nineteen remaining stamps in a hip pocket of his khaki trousers and promptly forgot all about it until two days later, at the edge of the blue waters of Crater Lake, when he had occasion to use it under circumstances that made those nineteen one-cent stamps of greater value to him than nineteen dollars or even nineteen hundred dollars.

When the man on mule back who accidentally discovered Crater Lake cast the first white man's gaze down the precipitous and far-descending walls of that deep basin, it was his belief that the unruffled blue water, a thousand feet below, would forever remain inviolate to human touch—it would never slake thirst, or wash dirt from hand or face, or be navigated.

Yet Jim Turner, on that October day in 1910, had done all that the discoverer, seeing no possibility of man's descent down those sheer precipices, thought never would be done. Lying prone, with no cup but the lake itself, he had taken a drink of the cold, satisfying water. He had dipped up in his hat some of it with which to loosen the jelly that clung to his fingers from the sandwiches of his lunch. Finally, that morning at eleven o'clock, he had come in a rowboat to the tiny beach upon which he still stood, dismayed by a universal solitude, menaced by approaching night—deserted, alone!

At six o'clock that October evening he still remained there, the only soul anywhere about the edges of the lake, the unattainable rim itself virtually left unpeopled. The winds that rocked the firs far up on that rim, descended to him with abated strength. But the cold crept down, piercing and numbing, so that he had to pace his cramped beach for warmth.

Gathering dusk had already changed the indigo water to black and was blurring the silhouette of Wizard Island out in the lake. The stars brightened and increased. He imagined they were visible to him earlier than to others, as he looked up from the darkening depths of that vast hole in which he stood. Those stars promised that the first snows, due at this season of the year, mercifully would not come that night.

Weather and chance could do with him as they pleased. He could not help himself. He could not attract the help of others. He was marooned in Crater Lake!

All around, in a grim circle, rose the almost perpendicular walls, from eight hundred to two thousand feet high. In front of him extended the silent and now forsaken waters of the lake, two thousand feet deep. It was impossible to scale the one. It was equally impossible to swim the other.

As he paced up and down on the narrow strip of beach, with darkness closing in around him, Jim had opportunity to review the events that had made him a captive in that majestic prison.

With his uncle and aunt and the Smiths, he had reached Crater Lake on the last day of the season. The Lodge was already closed to guests, and a single caretaker of the property had been left to prepare everything against the approach of winter. Late in the season as it was, a half-dozen automobile parties had come up to look at the lake, for the bad weather, though expected at any time, had not yet set in. The man in charge offered to give this late-season group boat service on the lake until four o'clock in the afternoon. But he explained that this was the last time he would go down the trail and that, before returning to the Lodge, he would haul out the boats for winter.

But it was not this circumstance alone that had brought about Jim's plight.

On the long motor trip, he had been in the habit of riding sometimes in his uncle's car and sometimes in that of the Smiths. After the trip to Crater Lake the two cars expected to separate. His aunt and uncle intended to go back to Portland by way of Medford and the Pacific Highway, while the Smiths meant to tour the country a week longer, returning to Portland by way of Klamath Falls and Eastern Oregon. Jim was free to go with either, but had not yet made up his mind.

He was still postponing his decision when, at the edge of the lake, Mr. and Mrs. Smith took passage in one crowded motor-boat, his uncle and aunt in another, while he selected a rowboat with two cordial strangers, inclined, like himself, to fish for the famous trout of Crater Lake.

He was having some luck with the fish and was by no means ready to go, when his aunt and uncle hailed him from a motor-boat that drew up to take him aboard.

"Are you going with us or the Smiths?" they asked. "We are starting right away and expect to get to Medford tonight. The Smiths won't be leaving for a couple of hours. We have already told them our plans. They said to be at their car at four o'clock, if you are going with them. If you are not on hand at that time, they will know you have gone with us."

Jim was reluctant to give up his fishing, and this reluctance prompted his decision.

"I'll go with the Smiths," he said. "Take these three fish for your supper at Medford. Good-by. I'll see you next week in Portland." "Good-by," returned his aunt and uncle. "Be sure to be at the Smiths' car not later than four o'clock. We won't see them again."

At a small recession in the universal wall, on a tiny shelf or beach, where the water was deep and where the fishing seemed even more promising than from the boat, Jim asked to be put ashore. He told the men in the rowboat that he would catch one of the launches as it came by and that they did not need to wait for him or bother to call for him later.

Glad of the chance for two hours more of fishing, he expected to catch the motor-boat in which the Smiths were touring the lake. But this boat failed, after a long interval, to appear. He remembered now that it had come this way when it started out. He saw it, far on the other side of the lake, going in the direction of the landing and the foot of the trail. He shouted, but they did not hear him. He waved his hands and his handkerchief, but they did not see him. The boat disappeared from sight!

He expected that another boat of some sort would be along, but as he scanned the surface of the lake he saw none. None put out from behind Wizard Island. He looked at his watch. It was a quarter of four. He remembered what the caretaker of the Lodge had said—at four he would begin hauling out the boats for winter. Even now he was probably covering them with tarpaulin. No more oars would dip in the blue waters before the next summer. The deep silence would be unbroken by the *chug-chug* of a motor. Navigation had ceased upon the lake, which was being left to its long winter solitude.

He was stranded!

He began to shout at the top of his voice, but he was more than two miles from the boat landing, and the near-by walls caught and returned his calls in echoes. He kept shouting until he was hoarse and his throat was sore. It did no good. Nobody heard him, nor was it possible for him to be heard.

The chance was no better that anybody would see him. The wall back of him went straight up for a hundred feet. From that point it slanted backward toward the rim. He had noticed this topography when he had approached it by boat in the morning. If the whole face of the wall had been perpendicular, there would have been more hope of attracting the attention of a possible observer from above. But the sloping upper part and the sheer drop at the bottom put him in a concealed position. He could no more be seen than some one leaning close against the side of a house could be seen by a person sitting on the ridge of the roof. He was completely out of the line of sight.

Nobody knew that he was shut up in that great caldron. His aunt and uncle thought he was with the Smiths. The Smiths thought he was with his aunt and uncle. It would be a week before they would see each other in Portland and find out that he was missing.

The caretaker of the Lodge would not be coming back down to the lake. He had made his final visit. He would be working back at the Lodge. There was no way to attract his attention.

Could he survive until his uncle found out what had happened, or was he doomed to a grave in the lake he had so long looked forward to seeing? He had two jelly sandwiches and two raw fish. He would not starve, but if winter set in, scantily clad as he was, he could not live through the cold of seven autumn nights. His imagination took a tragic direction. Maybe his aunt and uncle would never find him. The next summer, boats would pass by the little beach where he stood. The deep snows in the meantime would have come and gone. The people in the boats would be startled by what they saw there. The world would know that a boy had been left to perish in that great abyss of the Cascades, giving fresh fears to the Indians, who refuse to look upon its enchanted waters.

He recalled the Indian legends of the lake and of its sinister toll of savage life. He had read them idly in a folder. They now assumed an oppressive meaning. For an hour or more he was entirely miserable.

Then his thoughts began to take a more practical turn. If he could get over to Wizard Island diagonally in front of him, he might signal successfully from its top. But three quarters of a mile or so of deep water intervened between him and it. He couldn't swim it clothed; he doubted whether he could swim it at all. If he stripped and succeeded in getting across, there was no telling how long he would have to remain, exposed to the October chill of mountain nights, before attracting help. He would surely freeze.

Around the edge of the lake from where he stood, it was more than two miles to the boat landing and the beginning of the trail. There would be a few short stretches of beach along which he could walk, or shallow water which he could wade; but, for the most part, there would be deep water bordered by perpendicular walls offering no supporting hold for a cold and exhausted swimmer. Again, he would have to leave his clothes behind. The frigid October night that kept him walking his little beach for warmth, reminded him that such a course would be suicide.

It would be better, he decided, to wait till his uncle began a search, rather than try to gain Wizard Island or the trail, with almost certain failure ahead in either attempt.

His mind worked round to the idea of a signal. He took an inventory of his possessions in the dark. He had two raw fish, as has been said, and two jelly sandwiches, wrapped thickly in newspaper. He had his watch, his jack-knife, one hundred feet of heavy three-ply trolling line, with fifteen feet of leader, fifty feet of smaller fishing line, with a short leader, and an alder pole that he had cut while coming down the trail that morning. For the purpose of getting a signal up to the rim, there seemed no value in all this. He included his clothes in the inventory. Although he had done so several times before, he felt again for matches, but found none. All he found in his pockets, in addition to his handkerchief, knife, purse, and watch, was what he remembered was a little book of one-cent stamps, which seemed worthless enough at that place and time. In his impatience at finding this stamp-book instead of matches, he had an impulse to send it sailing out into the lake. But he put it back in his pocket.

Upon reflection, he was less disappointed about the matches. He had nothing to burn except a small pine board which he had found upon his little beach, the newspaper in which his sandwiches were wrapped, the stamps, and possibly his green alder fishing rod, if it were whittled into fine enough shavings. Such scant fuel would not produce a flame that would be discernible over the thousand-foot precipice that shut him in, nor produce a volume of smoke that would rise to such a height before dissolving into the air. With a match, however, and this meager supply of wood, he might have been able to cook one of his fish.

He realized he couldn't give a signal, for he had nothing to give it with— nothing that could remotely be worked into a signaling device of any kind. He would simply have to wait a week until his uncle began a search, and trust that meanwhile the Cascade storms would hold off.

His teeth chattered with the cold. The prospect of spending seven such nights as this was dismal enough.

His mind tired out with thoughts that got him nowhere, and his legs weary from pacing his small refuge, he sat down with his back against the wall, put his coat over his head, and attempted to get some sleep. He dozed fitfully. Frequently he would have to get up to exercise his cramped and chilled legs and to thaw out his congealed blood.

In the morning he ate one of his two jelly sandwiches. He would eat the second one the next day; after that, the raw fish.

He had no more idea of how he was going to get out of Crater Lake than he had had the night before. But he was more reconciled to his plight, and his mind, freed from panic, was clearer.

While rummaging in his pockets, he idly took out the book of one-cent stamps and turned through the green rectangles of the pictured Ben Franklin. He wet his finger and tested the gummed lower surfaces. This time he had no impulse to throw them into the lake. He wouldn't have traded the little stamp-book for ten thousand matches. He put it carefully back into his pocket as though it were a great treasure.

He had hit upon a possible way of giving a signal. He meant to work out his plan with great care, taking all the time necessary. The man undoubtedly was still at the Lodge. He could scarcely have finished his work so soon. If this man's attention could be attracted, Jim felt there was a good chance that he would be rescued. But the only way was to get a signal above that thousand-foot wall that hemmed him in. It wasn't likely that the caretaker of the Lodge, who was an old-timer in the region, would give any particular scrutiny to Crater

Lake scenery. He might not find it convenient to walk down to the edge of the rim to look out over the magic blue waters of the lake. At best, he would be a passive observer. An occasional and indifferent glance across the lake, as he straightened up from his labors, was as much as could be expected from him. To catch and hold the man's eyes during one of their casual and roving inspections of the landscape—that was what Jim meant to do.

Gradually, he was figuring it all out. He was certain he could do it if the wind would blow—blow only hard enough to ruffle the smooth water shut in by those protecting walls. The afternoon before, he had seen it shake the firs on the rim, like prune-trees under the hands of the harvesters, and had felt it descend a thousand feet to where he stood, not wholly becalmed. A breeze, a breeze—that, above all else, he wanted. That necessity alone was now absent from his inventory, which he took once more, this time with definite purpose.

Laying aside his remaining sandwich for the next morning's consumption, he smoothed out the newspaper that had wrapped it and its fellows. In one place a jelly stain had soaked through, moistening and weakening the fabric beyond all use, but this was in such a position that an unharmed area of paper two feet square could be secured. He placed the paper on a dry rock. He picked up the pine board, whittled off some shavings to test its soundness, and placed it beside the paper. To the collection on the rock he added his hundred feet of trolling line, his smaller fishing line of fifty feet, and the leader from both lines. On top of all he placed the little book of stamps as the crowning jewel of his possessions. If any one had been there to see, he would have wondered what purpose this miscellany was meant to serve.

The first thing Jim did was to untwist the three strands of his trolling line, securing three hundred feet of cord instead of one hundred. In the same way, he got one hundred feet from his fifty feet of small line. The untwisting of the kinky and cork-screwing strands completed, he surveyed the resulting four hundred feet of stout cord, but regarded it as only a good beginning toward his complete needs.

He pulled off his high-topped boots, removed his long woolen socks, put his boots back on bare feet, and began unraveling the socks. These yielded two big balls of thread. But as he tested the strength of the yarn he was not satisfied. Reversing the process of the fishing lines, he twisted the two strands tightly together until the two balls of yarn formed a double cord. This had cut the length in half, which wasn't enough for his purpose. He drafted still another garment—he took off his sweater and reduced it likewise to twine, which he doubled and twisted as in the case of the yarn from the socks. At last he had, all told, slightly more than two thousand feet of string. This cordage manufacture, however, had consumed the whole day. Darkness came and forbade further labor.

Once more, sleep was difficult, in spite of the fact that it was greatly in arrears. He suffered from the cold more than he had the night before, for he was now deprived of his socks and sweater. The hours seemed interminably long, but he obtained a few brief periods of repose.

In the morning, while it was still dark, he ate his last sandwich; and, as soon as it was light enough, he took his knife and whittled from the pine board three straight thin strips. Two of these splits were about twenty-three inches long. The third was about fifteen inches long. The two longer ones he crossed in the form of an "X," but with the intersection three or four inches from the center toward the upper ends. The third and shorter he placed horizontally across the other two, its center at their intersection. He lashed the joint with cord. Around the outside, in grooves previously cut in the six ends of the three sticks, he stretched the leader of his trolling line, so that he had a strong and rigid six-sided framework.

With his knife, he cut from the newspaper a covering of the same shape as the framework, but with an inch margin all round.

On a smooth, dry place on his little beach he laid down the paper and, over this, the framework of sticks and catgut. He then took out of his pocket the book of stamps. With his knife he slit each of the nineteen stamps into four pieces, making in all seventy-six gummed seals, quite narrow, but long enough in each case to have much adhesive tenacity. With these stickers he fastened down the border of paper, which he folded over the catgut rim.

Crossing and adjusting three strings with great care and exactness, he fashioned a "bridle," and arranged a short pendant loop at the lower end.

To the crossed strings, or bridle, he tied one end of his two thousand feet of twine. He tore his handkerchief into strips, which he pieced into a string and which he tied in the center of the pendant loop. Then from his shirt, he slashed off a section of additional cloth and tied it to the lower end of the handkerchief string.

The signal was ready to carry upward its message of an imprisoned boy. Jim had built a kite!

A breeze to fly it was the next need. He held it up in front of him, but the pressure against it was hardly noticeable. Something of the calm of morning still prevailed. He looked across and up at his barometers on the rim—the trees—and saw by their comparative quiet that the wind had not yet come in from the mountain-tops. He would be patient until the afternoon.

At two o'clock, from a perch as high up as he could gain, he held the precious kite above his head. If it ever dropped into the water, all his labor would be lost. He held the kite up and threw it from him, but it dropped down, not to the water, for he gave it but little line, and, besides, he held the tail in his hand. It seemed a lifeless thing.

Many times he tried. Always it dropped. It seemed without buoyancy. It was heavy and spiritless, without the grace and lightness of flight. His heart sank. It would not fly!

He adjusted and readjusted the bridle. He subtracted from and added to the tail. Still it fell like a shot bird. For an hour he tried.

In the meantime, the wind increased. The firs on the rim no longer stood still, but bowed and courtesied. Out from shore the surface of the water had lost some of its glassy smoothness. The reflection of the wall in front of him trembled slightly. The sweat that came out on his face from his anxiety and his labors was evaporated quickly.

He kept trying, and at last began to have periodical promises of success. Finally, a breath of wind bellied the kite and tautened the paper against the sticks back of it. He threw it out several feet. A timely breeze that he felt against his cheek caught it. It shot out straight, and even rose a little. He dropped the tail and gradually let out line. The kite darted from side to side, and once it made a quick dart downward like an airplane on a tail-dive—it was a dangerous moment. But it rallied like an airplane, though the tail dripped a few drops of water as it rose. Steadied by that tail, it climbed diagonally up- ward above the blue of the lake slowly toward the blue of the sky. It began to pull so strongly that Jim had a new alarm. But he let out string—two hundred feet, five hundred, a thousand, and at last two thousand.

It hung in the air at a great altitude, its tail, the crudities of which were softened by the distance, waving beneath it. It soared high enough above the sunken waters of the lake and far enough away from the encircling cliffs so that it could surely be seen from the Lodge, if there was anybody at the Lodge to see.

He took what remained of the newspaper, tore it into round pieces the size of saucers, punched a hole in the center of each, and strung them on the kite- string in his hand. From time to time he would let one of these loose and watch it scud up the string to the kite. He hoped these might help to guide the caretaker of the Lodge to the base of the string and to himself.

But it began to be dusk, and still no sign that anybody had seen the kite. After all, had the man fastened up the doors, prepared the building against the winter storms, and left? Had no stray and late-season tourist paused for a mo- ment on the edge of the crater? He was beginning to debate whether to pull the kite in or risk leaving it up all night. He might have trouble or find it altogether impossible to get it to fly again in the morning, if he drew it in. But if he left it out, there might be snow or rain, the wind might grow too strong or die down, the all-night pull might weaken the string, and any of these con- tingencies would be hazardous to the kite.

At last, he heard the exhaust of a motorboat in the direction where the trail led up from the lake to the Lodge. The staccato beats at first sounded a great distance away, but soon the *chug-chug* grew closer and friendly calls were added to the sounds of navigation.

"Where are you?" he heard. "Where are you?" repeated frequently and loudly.

"Here," answered Jim. "Here—over here!"

The boat came up to the little beach, and Jim, still holding the kite-string, greeted the caretaker of the Lodge.

"It's a good thing you flew that kite," Jim's rescuer told him. "I never dreamed anybody was down here. I thought it was a bird at first. But I looked over there several times from where I was working at the Lodge and thought it wasn't quite natural for a bird to do like that—to stay high up in the air above the lake in about the same place, not moving much and sort of hanging there like it was held up by a string from the sky. A smaller bird kept right underneath it. So I came down to the edge of the rim and got a closer look. You can imagine how surprised I was when I saw it was a kite and that the second bird was the kite's tail. I couldn't figure it out. The only way I could explain it was that maybe somebody had left it flying without my noticing it before. I took a squint through the field-glasses that I brought along and saw pieces of paper mounting up to it, and remembered how we used to do that when I was a boy. So I reckoned somebody was down here at the bottom end of the kite-string, who was signaling and who needed help pretty bad. It made me kind of shiver when I realized it was probably some one everybody had forgotten and left at some part of the lake where he couldn't get back to the trail. So I beat it down here faster than I ever did before. Jim did you say your name is? Well, turn loose the string and let 'er go. It'll probably land over on the other side of the lake somewhere. It saved your life and no mistake, for you might never have got out of here. Jump into the boat, Jim, and we'll go. There's a warm fire in the fireplace at the Lodge and something to eat. You must be about frozen— here, put on my coat—and I expect you could eat a whole ham.

"It sure was lucky," he went on, as he started the motor-boat, "it sure was lucky you flew that kite. But how did you make it, Jim? Where did you get your stickem? When I was a boy we used to make paste out of flour and water. Did you have a tube of glue or paste in your pocket, maybe?"

"No, I used postage-stamps," said Jim; "one-cent stamps," he added, as though two-cent stamps and the multiple image of George Washington might not have had the same result at all. "You see," he explained, "Ben Franklin's picture on the stamps suggested the idea of a kite to me."

Suggested Further Reading

WORKS BY POWERS

Marooned in Crater Lake: Stories of the Skyline Trail, the Umpqua Trail, and the Old Oregon Trail. Portland: Metropolitan Press, 1930.

History of Oregon Literature. Portland: Metropolitan Press, 1935.

Prisoners of the Redwoods. New York: Coward-McCann, 1948.

True Adventures on Westward Trails. Boston: Little, Brown, 1954.

Early Modern Fiction
Aggressively Oregonian

H. L. Davis

H. L. (Harold Lenoir) Davis (1894-1960) won the
Pulitzer Prize for fiction for his 1935 novel, *Honey in
the Horn*, the only Oregon fiction writer to receive that
award. H. L. Mencken, America's foremost literary
critic at the time, called it the best first novel ever
published in America. Some years earlier, in 1919,
Davis's poetry won the nationally prestigious Levinson
Prize. His short stories and essays, told in a laconic,
frontier-wise narrative voice, have also been widely
admired. Davis thus has a strong claim to the title of the
best Oregon writer, even though his authorship—with
James Stevens—of a blistering attack upon the Oregon
literary scene (see the Introduction to this volume)
made him *persona non grata* with the state's artistic
establishment. He left the Northwest in 1932, although
he continued to write about it. He knew Oregon well,
having spent his early years in the towns and settlements
along the Umpqua River, and later in Antelope and in
The Dalles, where he graduated from high school in
1912 and worked at a variety of jobs before becoming a
writer.

Old Man Isbell's Wife

The cow-town started as an overnight station on the old Military Road through Eastern Oregon into Idaho. The freighters wanted a place to unhitch and get the taste of sagebrush out of their mouths. They were willing to pay for it, and one was built for them by the people who like, better than anything else, money that has been worked hard for—not to work hard for it themselves, but to take it from men who do.

The cow-town itself was a kind of accident. When they built it, they had no idea beyond fixing up a place where the freighters could buy what they wanted. They fixed it up with houses—houses to eat in, houses to get drunk in, houses to sleep in, or stay awake in, houses to stable horses in; and, as an afterthought, houses for themselves to live in while they took the freighters' and cattlemen's money. And money came—not fast, but so steadily that it got monotonous. There were no surprises, no starvation years, no fabulous winnings or profits; simply, one year with another, enough to live on and something over. They got out of the habit of thinking the place was an overnight station to make money in. They began, instead, to look at it as a place to live in. That, in Eastern Oregon, meant a change of status, a step up. The risk of the place being abandoned was over; there, straddling the long road between Fort Dalles on the Columbia and Fort Boise on the Snake River, was a town.

The new status had no effect upon its appearance. Ugly and little it had begun, and ugly and little it stayed. The buildings were ramshackle and old, with the paint peeled off; and, including the stack of junk behind the blacksmith shop, the whole thing covered an area of ten blocks. Two acres of town, in the middle of a cattle range of ten thousand square miles. Yet in those ten blocks a man could live his entire lifetime, lacking nothing, and perhaps not even missing anything. Food, warmth, liquor, work, and women; love, avarice, fear, envy, anger, and, of a special kind, belonging to no other kind of life, joy.

Over the ten thousand miles of range, whole cycles of humanity—flint Indians, horse Indians, California Spaniards, emigrants, cattlemen—had passed, and each had marked it without altering its shape or color. The cow-town itself was one mark, and not the biggest, either; but that was a comparison which none of the townspeople ever made. They were too much used to it, and they had other things to think about. What interested them was their ten blocks of town, and the people who lived in it.

All country people keep track of each other's business as a usual thing, because they haven't anything else to think about. But the cow-town people did it, not in idleness, but from actual and fundamental passion. They preferred it to anything else in the world. It was not in the least that they were fond of one another though, of course, some of them were. That had nothing to do with their preference. It was merely that what their town did was life clear, interesting, recognizable; and nothing else was. They stuck to what was familiar. It must be remembered that these people were not chance-takers. They were more like the peddlers who follow an army, not fighting themselves, but living on the men who do. The freighters and cattlemen, and the men from the range, were a different race; the range itself was a strange element; and they were too small to have much curiosity about either. The women were the smallest. It was they who backed the movement to ship Old Man Isbell out of town.

II

Old Man Isbell lived in the cow-town because there was no other place he could live. He had ridden the range, at one job or another, for more than fifty years, and the town would have been strange and foreign to him, even if it had made him welcome. It did not. For one thing, he was not a townsman, but a member of the race which they preyed on. For another, he was eighty-five years old, slack-witted, vacant-minded, doddering, dirty, and a bore. It took an hour to get the commonest question through his head, and another hour for him to think up an answer to it. He never tied his shoes, and he had to shuffle his feet as he walked to keep them from falling off. Nor did he ever button his trousers, which fact was cited by the women as indicating complete moral decay. He ought to be sent away, they said, to some institution where such cases were decently taken care of.

The clerk in the general store agreed with them, and perhaps he, at least, had a right to. It was his job, every day, to sell Old Man Isbell a bill of groceries, and the old man could never remember what it was he wanted. Sometimes it took hours, and while he was there ladies couldn't come in the store, on account of his unbuttoned trousers and his pipe.

His pipe was another just ground for complaint. It was as black as tar and as soggy as a toadstool, with a smell like carrion and a rattle like a horse being choked to death. To get it lit took him hours, because his hand shook so he couldn't hold a match against the bowl. It was his palsy, no doubt, that was to blame for his unbuttoned trousers, his dangling shoestrings, and the gobs of food smeared on his clothes and through his whiskers. But that was not conclusive evidence that he was feeble-minded. Even a sane man would have trouble tying a bow-knot or hitting a buttonhole if his hands insisted on jumping two inches off the target at every heart-beat. The ladies added it to their evidence, but it should not have been allowed to count. Old Man Isbell's chief abnormality was of longer standing. He was simply, and before anything else, a natural-born bore.

The dullness of his speech was a gift of God. He had lived his eighty-five years through the most splendidly colored history that one man could ever have lived through in the world—the Civil War, the Indian campaigns in the West, the mining days, the cattle-kings, the long-line freighters, the road-agents, the stockmen's wars—the changing, with a swiftness and decision unknown to history before, of a country and its people; yes, and of a nation. Not as a spectator, either. He lived in the middle of every bit of it, and had a hand in every phase. But, for all the interest it gave to his conversation, he could just as well have spent his life at home working buttonholes.

"I remember Lincoln," he would say. "I drove him on an electioneerin' trip, back in Illinoy. Him and Stephen A. Douglas. I drove their carriage."

One would sit up and think, "Well! The old gabe does know something good, after all!" Expecting, of course, that he was about to tell some incident of the Lincoln-Douglas debates—something, maybe, that everybody else had missed. But that was all. So far as he knew, there hadn't been any incidents. They electioneered. He drove their carriage. They rode in it. That was all that had impressed him.

Or he would remember when there had been no Military Road, and no cow-town, nor even any cattle; only, instead, great herds of deer pasturing in grass belly-deep to a horse. A herd of over a hundred big mule-deer trotting close enough for a man to hang a rope on, right where the town was. But when you tried to work him for something beside the bare fact that they had been there you struck bottom. They had been there. Hundreds of them. He had seen them, that close. That ended that story. I asked him, once, if he remembered anything about Boone Helm, an early-day outlaw and all around mean egg. He considered, sucked his pipe through a critical spell of croup, and finally said, "They used to be a road-agent by that name. He cut a feller's ears off."

It was not a prelude, but a statement of what he remembered. Some old men remember more than what actually happened; some remember things that never happened at all. Old Man Isbell remembered the exact thing, and, that being done, he stopped. He ought to have been writing military dispatches. Or had he? It never came into his head to tone up or temper down the exact and religious truth, and amplifying what he had seen simply wasn't in him.

To events that went on in the town he never appeared to pay the smallest attention. Indeed, he paid none to the people there, either, and, though they laid that to the condition of his wits, it irritated them. Yet it was no more than an old range-man's indifference to things which he considers immaterial. He was sharp enough when anything was going on that interested him—cattle-branding in the corrals below town, or the state of the water on the range. South of town was a long slope, with a big spring almost at the top, ringed with green grass except when the spring went dry. Then the grass turned brown. The old man never failed to notice that. He would stop people in the street and point it out.

They laughed at him for it, behind his back. What did it matter to him whether the cattle had a dry year or not? He had an Indian War pension to live on, and he would get it whether the cattle throve or died to the last hoof. But, of course, he remembered what cattle looked like when they died of thirst, and swelled and popped open in the unmerciful heat, their burnt tongues lolling in the dust. It excited him to think of it, and he made a nuisance of himself about it. Sometimes he would stop strangers to tell it to them, which gave the town a bad name. Beside, his critics added, he smelled bad. Not being able to wait on himself, and never having been particular about washing or laundry, he did smell bad. The place for him, they agreed, was in some nice home where he could be waited on decently. He needed looking after.

In that they were right. He did need looking after. The trouble was that their plan involved sending him away from the sagebrush country, and that would have been the same thing as knocking him in the head with an ax. He was an old sagebrusher. To take him out of sight of his country—the yellow-flowered, silver-green sage, the black-foliaged greasewood, blossoming full of strong honey; the strong-scented, purple-berried junipers, and the wild cherry shrub, with its sticky, bitterish-honied flowers and dark sour fruit; the pale red-edged ridges, and the rock-breaks, blazing scarlet and orange and dead-black—to lose them would have killed him. By these things, an old sagebrusher lives. Out of reach of them, silly as it sounds to say so, he will die. I've seen them do it.

Old Man Isbell, incapable and slack-witted, helpless with age, and, so far as anybody could tell, without any suspicion of what the townspeople were thinking about him or that they were making designs against his life, did the one thing that could save him. He had nobody to take care of him. It was to see him taken care of that they wanted to send him away; and, surely without knowing it, he stumbled on the way to head them off. He got married.

The wedding threw the town into a perfect panic of delighted horror. This was one of the things that made life a fine thing to live. Other people, other communities, had diversions which the cow-town did without; this made up for them. The justice of the peace, having performed the ceremony, put out for home on a gallop to tell his wife the news. Hearing it, she came out with her hair down, and canvassed the houses on both sides of the street, knocking at every door, and yelling, without waiting for anybody to open—"Old Man Isbell's got married! You'll never guess who to!"

III

The bride alone would have made a rich story. She was about twenty-eight years old—Old Man Isbell being, as I've mentioned, eighty-five—and the rest of her was even more incongruous than her youth. She weighed close to three hundred pounds, being almost as broad as she was tall, and she had to shave her face regularly to keep down a coarse black beard, which showed in the wrinkles of fat where a razor could not reach.

As Old Man Isbell was the town nuisance, she was the town joke. Even in that scantily-womaned place, where only the dullest girls lived after they were big enough to look out for themselves, she had never had a suitor. The men were not too particular, but nobody dared pay court to her, for fear of getting laughed at. She was so fat that to walk downtown for Old Man Isbell's order of groceries took her almost an hour. It made one tired to watch her. Even the Indian squaws, riding through town, their matronly bellies overhanging the horns of their saddles, drew rein to admire Old Man Isbell's bride for an adiposity which laid theirs completely in the shade. They were fat, all right, but good heavens! They cackled and clucked to each other, pointing.

Housewives ran to peep through the curtains at the twenty-eight-year-old girl who had been hard up enough to marry an old, dirty, feeble-minded man of eighty-five. Store loafers perked up and passed remarks on her and on the match. But in spite of them all, in spite of the tittering, and the cruelty and the embarrassment, and her own exertion, she carried home the groceries every day. She cooked and cleaned house, too; and kept it clean; and one of the first things she bought after her marriage was a clothesline. It was full every day, and the clothes on it were clean. So were Old Man Isbell's. He sat on his front porch, wobbling matches over his black gaggling pipe, without a thing in the world to bother his mind except his pipe and the spring on the slope south of town. His trousers were fully buttoned, his shoes tied, and his beard and clothing washed, brushed and straightened, without a speck upon them to show what he had eaten last, or when.

Town joke or not, the fat woman was taking care of him. She was being a housewife, attending to the duties of her station exactly as the other married women in town attended to theirs, and that was something they had not expected. There wasn't any fun for them in that. They wanted her to remain a joke; and they couldn't joke about her housework without belittling their own.

They took it out on her by letting her alone. There was no woman in town for Old Man Isbell's wife to talk to, except my mother, who, being the schoolteacher's wife, didn't quite belong to the townspeople, and would probably have repudiated their conventions if she had. Across the back-fence she got all of the fat woman's story—not all of it, either, but all its heroine was willing to volunteer.

The fat woman had come to the country with her father, who took up a homestead on Tub Springs Ridge. But he got himself in jail for vealing somebody else's calf, and she moved into town to live till he served out his time. For a while she lived by selling off the farm machinery he had left. But it didn't take very long to live that up—"not that I eat so much," she hastened to add, "I really don't eat as much as . . . as ordinary folks do . . ."—and when that was gone she was broke. That was what induced her to listen, she said, to Old Man Isbell, when he first began to talk about getting married. She was desperate. It seemed the only resort, and yet it was so unheard of that she hesitated.

Finally, she borrowed a lift from a stage-driver, and went to the county jail to ask advice from her father. He knew the old man. It would be all right, he said, for her to marry him. But not unless she realized what kind of job she was taking on, and was game to live up to it. She mustn't bull into it and then try to back out. The old man would have to be tended exactly like a small infant— the work would be just as hard, and just as necessary—and, in addition, he was uglier, meaner, and dirtier. If she wanted to undertake the contract, all right; but she must either stick to it or let it entirely alone. When Old Man Isbell died, she would get what money he had saved up, and his Indian War pension. Enough to keep her, probably, for life. But it was up to her to see that she earned it.

"He made me promise I would," she told my mother, "and the Lord knows I have. It's just exactly like pa said, too. He's just like a little baby. To see him set and stare at that spring for hours on end, you wouldn't believe how contrary and mean he can be around the house. All the time. He'll take a notion he wants something, and then forget the name of it and get mad because I don't guess it right. I have to pick up things and offer 'em to him, one at a time, till I manage to hit the one he's set his mind on. And him gettin' madder every time I pick up the wrong thing. Just like a baby. And his clothes—they're the same, too." She sighed into her series of stubbly chins. "It keeps me goin' every minute," she said. "It's mighty hard work."

"You do keep him clean, though," my mother said. "He was so dirty and forlorn. Everybody's talking about how clean you keep him now."

"They talk about how I married him to get his pension," the fat woman said. "How I'm just hangin' around waitin' for him to die. I know!"

"That's only some of them," my mother said. "They don't know anything about it. You work right along, and don't pay any attention to them."

"None of the ladies ever come to call on me," said the fat woman.

"I shouldn't think you'd want them to," my mother suggested. "You must be so busy, you wouldn't have time to bother with visitors. They probably think you'd sooner not be disturbed at your work."

"I do want 'em to, anyway," said the fat woman. "And they call on all the other married ladies, whether they're overworked or not. They call on Mis' Melendy, across the way, and she's got teethin' twins."

"Well, I wouldn't care whether they came to see me or not," said my mother.

"I do, though," the fat woman insisted. "I've got a house, and a husband, just the same as they have. I do my housework just the same, too. I'd like to show 'em all the work I do, and what a care it is to keep things clean, and how clean I keep 'em. If they'd come, they'd see."

My mother assented. There was no earthly chance that any of them would come, and she knew it. But the fat woman didn't know it, and it was the one thing in the world that she had her head set on. Everything else that women take pride in and nourish conceit upon she had given up; and for that very renouncement she stuck all the more fiercely to the idea of being visited by the neighbor ladies, of being received as an established housewife, like the rest of them. There might not be any sense in the notion, but she wanted it. No matter how they came, or why, she wanted them. Even if they came prying for things to discredit her with, to trot around and gabble about, she wanted them anyway. When other women got married the neighbor ladies came to call. Now she was married, and they didn't.

The worst of it was, there was no way of breaking it to her that they weren't going to. My mother made several tries at letting her down easy, but got nowhere. She wanted it too much to give it up. Some days she would come to the fence elated and hopeful, because one of the ladies had nodded to her; sometimes she would be depressed and glum.

"I know what's keeping 'em away," she told my mother. "It's him!"

She yanked a fat arm in the direction of her husband, sitting in the sun with his mouth hanging open.

"Oh, no!" my mother protested. "Why—"

"Yes, it is!" the fat woman insisted. "And I don't blame 'em, either! Who wants to come visitin', when you've got to climb around an object like that to get into the parlor? I don't blame 'em for stayin' away. I would, my own self."

"But you've got to take care of him," my mother reminded her.

"Yes. I've got to. I promised pa I wouldn't back out on that, and I won't. But, as long as I've got him around, I won't have any visitors to entertain. I might as well quit expectin' any."

She sighed, and my mother tried to console her, knowing how deep her idiotic yearning was, and how impossible it was to gratify it. She had tried to persuade the neighbor ladies to call. There was no use wasting any more time on them. Yet, to come out bluntly with the fact that they had all refused would be silly and cruel. My mother was incapable of that. Concealing it, she did her best with promises and predictions, taking care to be vague, while Old Man Isbell dozed, or poked matches at his choking black pipe without any thought of human vanity or hope or disappointment, or anything but the Winter stand of grass on the range. Nobody could believe, from his looks, that he could have asked the fat woman to marry him. It was much more likely that she had hazed the notion into him. Some day, I thought, we might find out, when he could forget the range long enough.

But we never did. He died before the Winter grass got ripe enough for the cattle to sample.

IV

It was on a morning in October that my mother was awakened, about day-light, by yelling and crying from the Isbells' house. She got up and looked across, and saw, through their window, a lamp still burning, though it was already light enough to see. As she looked, the lamp went out—not from a draft, but because it had run dry. That meant that something was up which was keeping them too busy to tend to it. My mother dressed, and hurried over.

Old Man Isbell was dying. The fat woman had been up watching him all night. She sat beside the bed, while he plunged and pitched his thin hairy arms and yelled. Across her knees lay an old, heavy Sharp's plainsman's rifle.

"Watch 'em, watch 'em!" yelled Old Man Isbell. "They cut sagebrush, and push it along in front of 'em to fool you while they sneak up! If you see a bush move, shoot hell out of it! Shoot, damn it!"

The fat woman lugged the immense rifle to her shoulder and snapped the hammer. "Bang!" she yelled.

"That's you!" approved the old man, lying down again. "That's the checker! You nailed him that time, the houndish dastard! You got to watch 'em, I tell ye."

"He thinks he's standin' off Indians," the fat woman explained. "He's young again, and he thinks he's layin' out on the range with the hostiles sneakin' in on him. I've had to—All right, I'm watchin' close," she told him. "Bang!"

My mother got her something to eat, and built a fire, so that when the neighbor ladies came to help they could have a warm room to sit in. Their resolution to stay away held good only in life. When anybody was dying, social embargoes collapsed. Beside, a death was something they couldn't afford to miss. They came; all the women whom the fat woman had set her heart on being friends with; and nobody thought to remark that, instead of being responsible for their staying away, it was Old Man Isbell who had the credit of bringing them there, after all.

But the fat woman was past bothering about whether they came or stayed away. Even their remarks about the cleanness of her house went over her unnoticed. She had livelier concerns to think about. The old man was driving stage. He was going down the Clarno Grade, and a brake-rod had broken. The stage was running wild, down a twenty percent grade full of hairpin switchbacks. He was flogging his horses to keep them out from under the wheels. He yelled

and swore and pitched and floundered in the bedclothes, screaming to his wife that she must climb back and try to drag the hind wheels by poking a bar between the spokes.

"And hurry, damn it!" he yelled. "Drag 'er, before that off pointer goes down!"

The neighbor women gaped and stared. This was something they had never heard of. They didn't even understand what kind of emergency the old man was yelling about. But the fat woman paid no attention to them, and did not hesitate. She climbed along the edge of the bed, reached a broom from the corner, and, poking the handle down as if into a wheel, she set back hard. Her mouth was compressed and firm, and she breathed hard with excitement. She appeared to be taking the game almost as seriously as the old man did, crying back to him that she was holding the wheel, as if it meant the saving of both their lives, though hers was in no danger, and his was burning out like a haystack flaming in a gale.

The women brought food and put it into her mouth as if she was something dangerous. They weren't used to games like this, except in children and dying men. Being neither, the fat woman had no business playing it; and they poked buttered bread into her mouth sharply, frowning as if to show her that they saw through her nonsense, and considered it uncalled for. Neither their buttered bread nor their disapproval made any impression on her. The old man was yelling that she must hold the wheel, and she, with her chins trembling with fatigue and sleeplessness, cried back that she had it where it couldn't get away.

In the afternoon he had another one going. He was in a range-camp at night, and there was a herd of wild mustangs all around his fire, trying to stampede his pack-horses. The fat woman pretended to throw rocks to scare them off.

"There's the stud!" he mumbled. "Where in hell is that gun of mine? Oh, God, if it wasn't for bringin' down them damned Siwashes, wouldn't I salivate that stud? Don't shoot! Don't you know them Injuns'll be all over us if they hear a shot? Hit him with a rock! Watch that bunch over yon! Look how their eyes shine, damn their souls! Throw! Do you want to lose all our horses, and be left out in Injun country afoot?"

All day, and till after dark, the neighbor women watching her, she threw when he ordered; and when, at dark, he switched to heading a stampede of cattle, she charged with him to turn them, swinging an imaginary rope with her fat arm, yelling and ki-yi-ing as he directed, and jouncing the bed till the whole house rocked.

About midnight he had burned his brain down to the last nub, and there the fat woman was no longer needed. He lifted himself clear of the bed, and said, "Well, hello, you damned old worthless tick-bit razor-back, you! How the hell did you get out to this country?" He sounded pleased and friendly. It had never occurred to the townspeople that he had ever had any friends. Even as it was, the fact was lost on some of them, for while he spoke he looked straight at one of the visiting women, as if he were addressing her. Somebody tittered, and she left indignantly, banging the door. Everybody jumped, and looked after her. When they looked back, Old Man Isbell was lying on his pillow, dead.

The fat woman did not want to leave him. She was dull and almost out of her head with weariness, but, when they took hold of her, gently, to put her to bed where she could rest, she fought them off.

"He might come to again," she insisted. "You can't tell, he might flash up again. And he might think of something he'd need me for. You leave me be!"

They explained to her that it wasn't possible, and that, even if it was, she must have some sleep. She mustn't kill herself to humor a man out of his mind.

"I want to!" she said. "I want to do that! All them things he's done, and been in, and seen—he never let on a word to me about 'em, and I want to hear 'em! I never knew what an adventured and high-spirited man he was. I like to do what I've been doin'!"

She fought them until they quit trying and left her. When they came back, she had gone to sleep by herself, beside her dead husband; a fat woman, twenty-eight years old, beside the corpse of a man eighty-five.

V

She came to call on my mother after the funeral. Her mourning habit had come from a mail-order house, and, though there were yards of it, enough, I judged, to make three full-size wagon-sheets, it needed to be let out in one or two places, and she wanted advice.

"How to fix it so I can wear it, right away," she explained. "I could send it back, but I don't want to wait that long. I want to show 'em that my husband was as much loss to me as theirs would be to them. He was, too. He was a sight better man than any of theirs."

She rubbed the tears out of her eyes with the back of her wrist. My mother consoled her, and mentioned that now, at least, everybody knew what care she had taken of him.

"I don't care whether they know it or not," said the fat woman. "None of 'em come to see me, and they can all stay away for good, as far as I'm concerned. The way they acted the one time they did come settled 'em with me."

"But they helped out during your bad time," my mother said. "They meant kindly."

"Yes. Helped out. And then they come smirkin' and whisperin' around how I ought to be glad my husband was out of the way. How I must have hated takin' care of him, and what a mercy it was to be rid of him. I told 'em a few things. They'll stay away from me a spell, I can promise you that!"

She sat straight in her chair, and dropped the mourning dress on the floor.

"I was glad to take care of him," she said. "Yes, sir! I was proud of my husband. The things he'd done, and the risks he'd been through, when the men in this town was rollin' drunks and wrappin' up condensed milk. . . ."

She drew a breath, and, forgetting that my mother had been there, began to tell about the time when he had been surrounded by the Indians, creeping in on him with sagebrush tied to their heads. He fought them back and outgamed the whole caboodle of them; and her voice rose and trembled, shrilling the scenes she had enacted with Old Man Isbell when his numb old brain was burning down through the pile of his memories, spurting a flame out of each one before they all blackened and went to nothing.

She shrilled the great scenes out defiantly, as if it were her place to defend them, as if they belonged to her, and were better, even at second hand, than anything that any of the townspeople had ever experienced. None of their common realities had ever touched her. Beauty had not; love had not, nor even friends. In place of them, she had got an eighty-five-year-old dotard and the ridicule of the townspeople. Watching over the old man when he died was the one time when she had come anywhere within reach of heroism and peril and splendor; and that one time, being worthy of it, she passed them all. And that one time was enough, because she knew it.

"The hostiles aprowlin' around," she cried, her voice blazing. "The houndish dastards! . . ."

Selections for Further Reading

WORKS BY DAVIS

Status Rerum: A Manifesto upon the Present Condition of Northwestern Literature Containing Several Near-Libelous Utterances upon Persons in the Public Eye. With James Stevens. The Dalles, Oregon: Privately Printed, 1927. Reprinted in *H. L. Davis, Collected Essays and Short Stories.* Moscow, Idaho: University of Idaho Press, 1986.

Honey in the Horn (winner of Pulitzer prize). New York: Harper and Brothers, 1935.

The Selected Poems of H. L. Davis. Ed. Orvis C. Burmeister. Boise, Idaho: Ahsahta Press, 1978.

Winds of Morning. New York: William Morrow, 1952.

Team Bells Woke Me, and Other Stories. New York: William Morrow, 1953.

Kettle of Fire. New York: William Morrow, 1959.

WORKS ABOUT DAVIS

Bain, Robert. *H. L. Davis.* Boise State University Western Writers Series, Number 11. Boise, Idaho: Boise State University, 1974.

Bryant, Paul. *H. L. Davis.* Boston: Twayne Publishers, 1978.

James Stevens

James Stevens (1892-1971), along with his friend and one-time literary collaborator H.L. Davis, brought the realism of people at work into Oregon literature. Because of Stevens, we know something of life in the old logging camps and mines and mills of the region. Self-supporting since he was fifteen, Stevens worked at such jobs as logger, millworker, and teamster before becoming a recognized, published writer at age 32, in 1924. He authored several books about the legendary logger-giant of the woods, Paul Bunyan, books which brought Stevens his first fame. But it is the fiction based upon his own experiences as logger, mill hand, and teamster which has become his most notable contribution to Oregon letters. The story which follows is typical of Stevens' ability to catch something of the heroic and epic qualities present in many of the demanding physical jobs of a post-frontier Oregon.

The Old Warhorse

The big Menominee & Tacoma mill—sawing average, two hundred thousand feet, board measure, per ten hours—was roaring close to the end of a payday shift. It was a rainy February day and the lights had gone on at four o'clock. There was a white blaze of them over the markers at the head of the long green-chain, and over every sawing machine. Saw steel glittered from trimmer, edger, resaw, and slasher, as the sharp teeth of circulars and bands bit and ripped through boards, cants, and slabs. The screaming songs of the saws and the rumble of live rolls filled the big millhouse with a tumult of sound.

At the headrig the sixty-foot bandsaw was a silver flash of ripping steel. A brute of a stick seven feet through and eighty long was on the carriage. The two doggers and the setter had to climb the log's side to catch the signals from the head sawyer's cage.

In that cage, with the log deck on his left, the carriage and its gigantic burden squarely in front of him, and the wide silver ribbon of the big band flashing on his right, stood old Johnny McCann. He had stood his ten hours a day in this cage for twenty-five years. He had stood in others like it back in Saginaw for fifteen more.

Head sawyer. Boss of the millhouse floor. A great lumbering operation centering around the skill of his eye and hand. A mighty life. Ay, it was a tremendous job, this one of sawing up the big timber. You felt like a general or a king when you got a great beauty of a log like this one off the deck and lined up for the bandsaw. Your eyes sized up the hundreds of year rings in its end. An old-timer. A tall tree before Columbus hit this new world. Ripe for lumber now.

The sapwood is deep. Slab her heavy and hard. Square her down to the sweet fine-grained clear. Keep the figures of your orders in your head, Johnny, old horse! Get the taper of the log! Signal the carriage crew with your left hand—why the hell is the lad so slow, that setter, that boy of yours, young Johnny McCann? Ease over this lever in your right hand, now—she moves— the old headsaw sings—boom! down the live rolls goes the first slab! Back with the carriage, the big beauty of a log showing a face of clear sapwood. On again—down the rolls—back—ahead—now a jiggle of the left-hand lever to lift the mighty steel gooseneck hook of the turner—slab her on!

Forty years of it in a head sawyer's cage, still old Johnny McCann could thrill like a youth at the cutting of an ancient giant from the forest. The years rolled away from him then. So did his troubles. He even forgot the hot lead in his feet and the shooting pains in his legs. He forgot his worry about the superintendent bending over the sheets on the log-scaler's desk. He was a head sawyer in all the glory of fighting a great bulk of sawlog into lumber. He felt the levers in his hands, he saw the steel hook of the turner jerking the log down on its slabbed face, and the carriage plunging ahead; and he heard the screaming thunder of his bandsaw as it ripped through bark and grain; he felt, saw, and heard no more. He was a hero, a king—and then the quitting whistle boomed through the mill.

The roar of machinery and the screams of the saws died away in a drone. Old Johnny McCann leaned on his levers and gazed miserably at the great log on the carriage. He had lost it. The night shift head sawyer would have it now. The sawyers and helpers were streaming for the door, all black shapes in the glaring light. The broad-beamed young setter swung away from the carriage, calling over his shoulder:

"Won't be home for supper, dad. Eatin' downtown."

II

Old Johnny didn't hear. His gaze was on the superintendent, who was slowly approaching from the scaler's desk. Old Johnny felt his legs giving way under him. He gripped the levers hard. His mind seemed to be turning numb from the burning ache in his feet; they shot pain clear to his eyes. That's the way she goes, lads. Forty years of it, forty years of standing dead still and at a strain in a head sawyer's cage, then the old legs and feet give out, the old hands get a little shaky and slow, and the super comes up, flushes, hems and haws, and finally blurts out the sad, sad news. The time has come. Life's got you down at last. You're old, you're old. No use to buck it. But it's—well, hell, let 'er go. . . .

Old Johnny McCann walked alone from the company office to his home above the tideflats. On other payday nights the blue check in his pocket had made a glow that spread all over him, but now it was cold. He hobbled along, the wind blowing rain over his bowed head. Back of him the great domes of waste burners and the small lighted squares of millhouse windows shone through smoke and darkness. Old Johnny McCann was feeling like an exile, a man driven from his native city. Forty years as the king of a millhouse floor, and now . . . the superintendent's words kept pounding in his ears. . . .

"Sorry, Johnny. Sorrier'n hell. But you know yourself—we got to hold the cut up to two hundred thousand—you've dropped to one-ninety-five, then ninety—eighty-five—losing two hundred dollars a shift, the company is. . . . Hrrumph! . . . It's all right—all right! You've made us thousands extra in your twenty-five years. You've got a pension coming. You're going to be treated right. Take it easy rest of your days—that's better, huh? Hrrumph. . . . The lad? Sorrier'n hell about the lad, too, Johnny. Looked like he'd step into your shoes till a while back. Can't stand for head sawyers hitting the redeye now, Johnny. Times have changed since the old Saginaw days. . . . Well, maybe you *have* got it coming. Well—I'll give you another month—one more payday, Johnny—just one more. A chance to go out sawing on your highest average— I'll give you that. . . . Forget it. Us oldtimers got to stick together, Johnny. . . ."

The words kept hammering through old Johnny's head. A chance. Not a chance to keep himself from the waste pile—the shooting pains in his legs, the hot lead in his feet told him that. But for young Johnny, the broad-beamed lad who thought he could lick anything in life with a grin, a joke, or at the worst with a swing of his big white fist—ah, the hell of it, thought Johnny McCann. Blowing his check all night over the bar of the Owl. Laughing and joking all he could think of, with that soft streak in him. Would it turn hard at the chance for a real fight? Would he be willing to stand and battle by the old man's side? Old Johnny had his doubts. He only knew that he himself would make one mighty effort to go out in a grand smash of sawing. . . . Well, a bit of supper, a spell of rest, then to look up the lad. . . . Old Johnny McCann hobbled on, his head bowed against the winter rain.

III

Shag Hogan, day edgerman in the M. & T. mill was picking a cigar from a box on the Owl bar. He was making his selection carelessly, without even examining the box, for he was gazing sideways at young Johnny McCann. The broad-beamed young setter had just ordered another round of drinks for the M. & T. gang. A contemptuous grin was on the edgerman's swarthy face. Old Johnny McCann saw that first, as he stepped through the swinging doors of the Owl. He knew what it meant; he knew what thoughts were in the edgerman's head. Something like:

"Keep it up, my fine buck. Drink the redeye down. But watch friend Shag take a cigar. Drink yourself out of your last chance at the headsaw, son; hop to 'er, lad, for that makes Shag Hogan boss of the big rig when your old man saws himself off his feet."

Sure, those were his thoughts, though he spoke aloud so friendly and fine:

"Certainly I'm a friend of yours, Johnny. I just ain't drinkin' tonight, that's all. Don't mind my takin' a cigar now, hey Johnny?"

"Cert'nly not, Shag. Good ol' Shag, bes' edgerman on the tideflats! Take dozen s'gars on me, good ol' Shag Hogan."

Old Johnny felt his hands unclench, turn nerveless and cold. What was the use? That was the nature of the lad—puling drunk one minute, the next slobbering over the man who was all set to knock him out. No use—so old Johnny turned to go. As he did so he noticed that J. Michael Murphy, proprietor of the Owl, was conversing grandly with a nabob. As he talked he pointed at a faded and streaked steel engraving that was framed above the bar mirror.

"That picksher yer inquirin' about—yeah, it's been in my fambly for a hundred years," J. Michael was saying. "A fine, rare picksher it is. Come from the old country. Can't ye smell battle in it, though? And look at the harse. Ye never saw a braver harse in a picksher. Yeah, a fambly heirloom."

Old Johnny's gaze followed the pointing finger, and he grinned. The steel engraving was familiar to him. J. Michael had bought it from a pedler and hung it in his saloon back in the old Saginaw days. J. Michael had risen in the world out here on the Sound; he was a political influence and conversed with nabobs. Family heirlooms! Old Johnny felt an impulse to tell the nabob the facts about the engraving, but it was smothered by a sudden swell of emotion in his heart. In an instant the engraving had come to life with meaning for him.

It pictured the repulse of a cavalry charge in one of Napoleon's battles. The thing was vivid with an illusion of movement in a mass of panic-stricken horses. The background showed the enemy cavalry looming in pursuit. The battlefield was strewn with wounded and dying horses and men. But it was a hamstrung old warhorse in the center of the scene which had caught old Johnny's eye.

He was an old warhorse by the saber scars on his flanks, which the artist had taken pains to distinguish from his new wounds. His hind legs were sprawled impotently under him. Yet the heart of the old warhorse still throbbed with the fire of battle. That was beautifully shown. His lean, scarred, bleeding body was braced up on his sound front legs. His mane waved like a torn banner from his proud, arched neck. His teeth were bared at the onrushing enemy.

"Ah!" whispered old Johnny to himself, with huge astonishment. "To have known that picksher for so long and to have never really *seen* it afore! Why— why, it's me!"

Old Johnny McCann half-closed his eyes. The shine of the mirror turned into a bright mist. He saw himself as Roaring Johnny, a bully young sawyer in the white pine country far away. He mingled with the gang of his youth again. Tramped along with it to the big, red mill, the frost steaming off the sidewalk boards. He saw the cool, clear blue of a morning sky, he stepped high as the keen, frosty air tickled his ribs, he lifted his chest and was Roaring Johnny when he "helloed" his friends. Far out and away a snowy peak rose against the blue. Then a dark-green ridge of virgin timber, then stump-speckled, cut-over hills rolled down, with a light-green blanket of second-growth on the older lands near town. Steam wafted up in the sunlight from the booms in the mill-pond, the quiet water shining between the logs. The big, red mill, the black smokestacks, the white drifts of sawdust smoke, the whiter clouds of steam that puffed out from the exhausts. And the smells. The keen breeze bore down fresh and balmy smells from the green woods. It blew into his face the rousing pungent smells of green lumber and green sawdust. . . . Ah, it was a life to live over again! . . .

The life of the timberlands. His no more. Only to remember. But was it now? Old Johnny opened his eyes and stared hard at the warhorse in the engraving. By thunder, there he was! There was his story! He, too, had a grand life behind him! And, by the holy old mackinaw, he was going down fighting in just that style! And right here and now he'd show the lad, Shag Hogan, and all the rest of the gang, who was still the head sawyer of the M. & T. mill! Yea, bullies! Sawdust and shavings are going to fly! Come on, old warhorse, look up at your old tilicum in the picture there, square your shoulders, shake the hobbles out of your legs, and horn in! . . .

IV

"Only takin' cigars to-night, huh? Better put some redeye under your belt, Shag Hogan, and get some life into your carcass! For you've got a month of hell ahead of you, old-timer!"

There was a hush of amazement among the M. & T. men at the bar. Only one or two of the old-timers among them had ever heard their head sawyer's Saginaw bully roar. And old Johnny appeared about six inches taller and ten years younger to-night, as he jammed in between young Johnny and Shag Hogan. Old Johnny saw the wide stares of the sawdust savages and he shot a grim glance up at the old warhorse. More and more he was knowing how the brave old devil was feeling. It was kind of glorious, actually. The last grand stab in a mighty game.

"What are you buggin' your eyes about, Shag? Ain't you heard? Hell, I thought everybody in the mill knew I was due for the waste pile in another month. But you don't know, huh, Shag—you don't know you was brought here to take the headsaw when I passed out? Damn' innercent, ain't yuh?"

"Why, Mr. McCann, what you talkin' of?"

"Don't 'Mr. McCann' me, old-timer! I ain't no super. You know what I'm talkin' of—my last month on the headsaw. And I'm here to tell you it's goin' to be one grand smash! I'm tellin' you and the whole M. & T. outfit I'm out to bust all records for my finish! Two hundred thousand feet a shift won't be nothin' this next month! I'll send the cants down the rolls to the edger so fast you'll wish you'd never heard of a sawmill, Shag Hogan! You'll be skin and bone, time this month is out!"

The edgerman's pride was stabbed, and he roared.

"Th' hell I will! You never saw the day you could cover me up, you stove-up old Siwash! Nev—"

The last word was choked in the middle as he saw the flash of a big, white fist swinging at his mouth. Young Johnny had turned from puling to fighting. He bellowed and swung—but a gnarled old hand knocked the blow down and clamped his wrist.

"Just a minute, lad. I ain't ready to start on *you* yet." Old Johnny turned on the edgerman again. "I'm warnin' you fair, Shag. You'll have to cinch your leather apron up tight, spit on your hands and keep your carcass full of life if you handle the cants I'll roll down this month. Rest up good to-morrer, for Monday you ketch hell and halleluiah!"

Old Johnny smacked a double-eagle on the bar.

"Set 'em up, bartender! Three rounds for the house on Roarin' Johnny McCann! Promenade to the bar! Drink to a month of sawin' such as has never been seen this side of Saginaw! Drink 'er down with an old warhorse of the timberlands!"

Shag Hogan drank with the others. He felt kind of sick, like he needed something. He could swear that the old sawyer was drunk. But old Johnny was steady on his feet, though his straight body swayed like a pine in a big wind. Maybe it *would* be hell and halleluiah. It was almost that right now, wrestling the big cants and tugging on the heavy edger levers. The toughest edging job he'd ever seen. He wouldn't stay on it an hour if it wasn't for the chance at headsawing which the super had promised him soon. A few shifts of extra heavy cutting might do him up. He was no fool. There was more to this than just a grandstand play on the part of old Johnny McCann. The old stiff had more on his mind than that. The kid—that was it, by the holy old mackinaw! He wondered now. If the old head sawyer was playing a game for the kid—

"Outside with you, lad. I've something to say to you alone."

Young Johnny obediently pushed his big frame from the bar and unsteadily followed the old man out through the swinging doors. Shag Hogan scowled after them. He was suspicious. He had good reasons to be.

V

There was a space of clear glass at the top of the glazed front window of the Owl Saloon. Standing on the avenue curb, one might look up and through the oblong of clear glass and see the steel engraving above the bar mirror.

The old sawyer kept his gaze fixed on the battle scene as he stood and talked to the big lad at his side. About them were the trolleys, the horses and buggies in the wide avenue, the black shadows of store buildings behind dim street lights, the bright spots along the sidewalks, marking the saloons, and the saw-mill men stringing by, hilarious over a payday night. But neither man was conscious of the life of the avenue as old Johnny had his say. One looked at a picture that had come to life for him; the other grew sober under words spoken in a voice that carried him back to the years when he was a small boy flushed with the pride of his dad being the head sawyer in the biggest mill on the tideflats. Looking past the corner of the Owl Saloon, young Johnny McCann could see the red domes of the burners, the lights of millhouse windows. He began to feel something of what that meant to the old man. Maybe life was something more than blowing your paycheck, hogging down the redeye, sporting with the girls, raising hell, cocky and proud.

It had hurt when the old man talked to him about being an old warhorse on his last legs; then throwing it into him about having a soft streak, saying it looked like he'd need another setter to go out in the grand smash of sawing he'd planned. It was the hurt of a scolded boy, and something else from boyhood welled up in young Johnny now. That feeling of his dad being a hero— it had stirred again at this talk of ending up like an old warhorse. That was it, right enough. The old man had sawed his way from the white pine sticks of Bangor and Saginaw to the big firs of Puget Sound. Battled the big sticks from a sawyer's cage for forty years. Young Johnny wanted to throw his arm around the stooped shoulders. But you could only bristle and bluster when words were coming at you like the licks of an ax.

"Your cocky hell-raisin' has left you jug-headed on the setworks, and that's what's knocked down my cut more'n any failin' of mine! The super knows. He didn't bring Hogan here on my account! You ain't got a chance to step into my shoes now, son!"

"To hell with it!"

"Yeah. All right. Hold your dander down. I ain't out for no lecksher. I'm thinkin' of myself, my finish. How I make it is up to you. You *are* the best setter on the tideflats when you want to be; you're the only one, son, who can help me bust all sawin' records this last month and go out like an old warhorse." Old Johnny's voice quavered a little there, then it sounded steady and hard. "If you're goin' to lay down, say so, and I'll find a setter who'll see me through, anyway. I want to know now."

"Who the hell you think you're talkin' to, some ten-year-old? Certainly I won't lay down!"

"That's all I wanted to know." Old Johnny felt his knees shaking with relief, but he wouldn't soften. "Then come on home."

VI

A head sawyer needs legs like two tough timbers. He stands on one spot and in a strain all through his shift. When the last cant is dropped from a sawlog and the carriage is shot back and ground to a stop in front of the log deck, the sawyer steps on a plunger with his left foot and the dogs that hold the first of the log deck turn are released. The sawyer's left foot then shoves a foot throttle down, steam pounds into a cylinder below the mill floor, and huge steel arms leap up and shove the new sawlog against the carriage headblocks. The sawyer then has both feet to stand on until the log is ripped into cants. His right foot hardly moves in its place until the noon and night whistles blow. Forty years of it, and any head sawyer needs new legs for his job.

Old Johnny McCann was needing new legs on the eleventh day of his battle. The first ten had made sawmill history on the tideflats. Everything had been right. There had been a noble run of the logs from the woods, all sticks between four and six feet in diameter. The only orders on the boards were for small timbers. So old Johnny only had to grade the clears out of each sawlog after slabbing off a face, and then knock off four- to ten-inch cants for the edger.

It was beautiful sawing. And young Johnny had been with him all the way. Whenever old Johnny had felt that he couldn't last another minute, that he'd have to give in to the pains that throbbed to his bones, to the "weak trembles" of his knees and the burning numbness in his feet that made him feel like his shoe soles were hot lead—then old Johnny only had to look up and out of the cage, across the sawlog on the carriage, and see the broad-beamed young setter at his dial, showing new life in every move of him, and then the leg pains were fought down again.

It was marvelous what a change had shown in the lad that first Monday. Even the super had noticed it, remarking that it was too bad old Johnny hadn't got his hand in before Shag Hogan was put on the edger and promised the headsaw. Old Johnny had managed a twisted grin, though a ten-hour shift was done and his legs were about killing him. And he had said under his breath, "Don't be too sure who's to take my headsaw, Mr. Super. 'Tis only the first day of battle." A mighty day it had been. The cut had jumped to two hundred and twenty thousand feet, a record for the mill. And Shag Hogan was like a dishrag. He was more suspicious of old Johnny than ever. He had more reasons to be.

For the record was broken by two thousand feet the next day, and through the week it had climbed on, until two hundred and thirty thousand feet were marked up by the scaler for Saturday. It had been a good thing for old Johnny that shift was a Saturday. Young Johnny had to go for a livery rig to take him home. But it was all right; the lad stayed away from the saloons that night; and he stuck home all day Sunday. He still bristled and blustered at every word that was said to him, bragged about the big drunk he would have when this month was over, and the like of that. Old Johnny wished him in hell and declared he'd fire him off the carriage in a second, once another decent setter showed up in the mill. One would have thought the two were sworn enemies. But what a week of sawing it had been!

Monday was a blue day. The cut dropped to two-fifteen. Still high over the average, but not enough. Shag Hogan had been freshened by a Sunday's rest, also, and he left his edger with something of a swagger Monday night. Tuesday morning old Johnny's eyes were bleak and his face was drawn with desperate determination as he hobbled into his cage. That day he cut two-thirty-five, with the edger table choked every minute of the shift. Wednesday and Thursday the old sawyer held the cut up to the high mark, and last night Shag Hogan, his long body as limp as an empty sack, his face sweat-streaked, his hair a wet tangle over his eyes, argued furiously with the superintendent. The super shrugged his shoulders and turned away, meaning that if the wrathy edgerman didn't like it he could quit. Old Johnny had to be carted home again, but there was a thrilling hope in his heart that more than made up for his wrecked legs.

It was hot lead in his feet, running snakes of fire in his muscles and the palsy in his knees this afternoon of the eleventh day. There was a cold spot in his heart from the feeling that this day was his last one—the old warhorse was licked—enemy was looming closer and closer above him, like a black cloud. Still it was never-say-die with old Johnny. He was sawing away at a mightier lick than ever. At midafternoon the scaler's figures showed that one hundred and ninety thousand feet of logs had already gone through the big headrig. If he could shove them on as fast he'd hang up two-forty for the ten hours, maybe more. The edger table was choked with cants; the lineup men were stacking them; and Shag Hogan was hog-wild. Maybe it'll be his Black Friday, thought old Johnny. The thought was made like a prayer, for he could feel his own finish drawing near.

VII

He might last the day, but never the week, never tomorrow. Flesh and blood couldn't stand it. He could fight pain, fight it like an old warhorse, but when the old right leg began to sink under him as he tripped a log from the deck, he knew that the enemy was drawing close, ready to beat him down. Looking over at young Johnny, who was all wildfire for the grand smash of sawing his old man was making, showing it in the shine of his eyes, the flush of his face, his swagger and bluster forgotten now—that would make old Johnny fight pain, but it couldn't keep the strained old knees from buckling. . . . Was he going now? Not on your life ! Be an old warhorse, Johnny McCann, to the last snort! . . . Rear up and show your teeth to the last damn' gasp!

He forced his mind back to the sawing. It slowed just so much whenever he let himself feel pain or think. His right hand quickened on the lever that stuck up from the floor by his right foot, and the carriage shot behind the flashing teeth of the bandsaw so much the faster. Quicker again, and the carriage hardly seemed to stop before it was plunging forward, then slowing at the instant the log's end touched the ripping teeth, then crowding through, and another cant boomed down the rolls. Back and forward, back and forward, signal the setter—he's just the setter now, and not the big lad—now that much quicker with the left-hand lever—the giant gooseneck hook of the turner leaps up, stabs down into the sawlog, twists it like a cat twisting a ball of yarn, lifts, drops from sight as the steel arms set the log against the headlocks. . . .

Saw on! Saw on! Keep a-sawing to break another record to-day, Johnny McCann! Aye, old warhorse, you're Roaring Johnny again! . . .

The whistle shrilled for the millwrights. Black smoke rolled up from the edger with a stink of burning leather. Shag Hogan had stuck a cant in his circulars and slipped his drive belt. Take just one glance at him, old Johnny! See him jumping and waving his fists like a maniac. Saw hard now, old-timer! Pile the cants ten feet high on the edger table! Beautiful logs on the deck! Roll 'em along! . . .

The super was bawling into his ears, so as to be heard above the singing roar of the big band. What say—ease up?

"Ease up, hell! You want your big cut, don't you, hey? I'm sawin' logs!"

Forget the burning aches and pains! Quick on the levers, now, like you had the youth of the lad there behind the setter's dial ! Hearken to the old saw's song! Better than a bugle call, hey, Johnny McCann? See the cants drop and boom down the rolls not a dozen feet apart! Ain't that some heavy artillery, old Johnny? Pile 'em ten feet high on the edger table! Pile 'em up, you lineup men! Got to put 'em somewhere—the old warhorse of the timberlands is busting another record to-day—two-forty—two-forty—two-forty—you're going to make that figure, Johnny McCann! . . .

What's that down behind the edger table? Sneak just one look and see what's going on. Hell, it's Shag Hogan, shaking one fist at the pile of cants and his other in the super's face ! And the super's bawling back at him—good glory, Johnny McCann, it looks like—yea, lad, there he goes! Off comes his leather apron, he jumps on it, heads for his locker, grabs his hat and coat, and out he goes, still shaking his fists, through the millhouse door! The super's taking the edger. . . .

Hey, old warhorse, you've licked 'em! Old-timer, the last battle is yours! It's yours. . . .

Ah, Johnny lad, it's all right now . . . all right . . . and the old warhorse needs a bit of help . . . he's sinking down . . . can't you see, Johnny lad . . . it was all put on . . . where's your big young arm?

The big, young arm was around old Johnny a second after he had fallen between his sawyer's levers. From out of the grip of it a weak, old voice whispered:

"Take the headsaw, lad. She's yours."

Suggested Further Reading

WORKS BY STEVENS

Paul Bunyan. New York: Alfred A. Knopf, 1925

Status Rerum: A Manifesto upon the Present Condition of Northwestern Literature Containing Several Near-Libelous Utterances upon Persons in the Public Eye. With H.L. Davis. The Dalles, Oregon: Privately Printed, 1927. Reprinted in *H.L. Davis: Collected Essays and Short Stories.* Moscow, Idaho: University of Idaho Press, 1986.

Homer in the Sagebrush. New York: Alfred A. Knopf, 1928.

Big Jim Turner. Garden City, New York: Doubleday 1948. Reprint: Albuquerque: University of New Mexico Press Zia Book, 1975.

WORKS ABOUT STEVENS

Claire, Warren L. "Introduction." *Big Jim Turner.* Albuquerque: University of New Mexico Press, 1975.

Love, Glen A. "Stemming the Avalanche of Tripe." in *H.L. Davis: Collected Essays and Short Stories.* Moscow, Idaho: University of Idaho Press, 1986, pp. 321-40.

Ernest Haycox

Ernest Haycox (1899-1950) is perhaps best known as a master of the formula Western, along with such other famous practitioners as Zane Grey and Louis L'Amour. But he also helped to enlarge and deepen the formula Western, especially in his later work, and to give us a more realistic version of Western history, as may be seen in the following story.

Haycox was born near Portland, and by the age of 20 had served a tour of military duty on the Mexican border and in France during World War I. After his discharge from the Army in 1919, he attended Reed College and then transferred to the University of Oregon, where he majored in journalism and learned how to write popular western fiction for big-selling magazines. Later, he developed a more dramatic style, centered upon character, which led to such successes as "Stage to Lordsburg" in 1937. This story became a John Ford film, *Stagecoach* (1939), in which John Wayne made his debut as a star. Many of Haycox's other stories have been made into films. Professor Richard Etulain has shown how Haycox turned increasingly to Oregon history in his last novels, and how, especially in *The Earthbreakers*, he reached toward a unique Oregon regionalism which approached that of H. L. Davis.

Cry Deep, Cry Still

At four o'clock that morning when John Mercy rose to search out and yoke the oxen, it was a mud-black world. The scudding clouds of a southwest storm were breaking in violence against the hills and releasing a fat rain which searched through the cabin walls and became a humid sweat upon everything. Today would be only a sullen, end-of-the-world twilight, as yesterday had been, and for as many days back as Mrs. Mercy cared to remember.

Mercy returned for breakfast, the heat of the room dyeing his wind-stung cheeks to blood crimson. He said brief grace and looked about the table, to his wife Martha, to Caroline in her flannel nightgown, to young Tom still drugged with sleep. "The devil's crying at the eaves but he can't get in." The hard work of a first fall in Oregon, the laying up of the cabin and the breaking of land, had taken twenty pounds from him, but he was cheerful, his eyes as blue as old velvet. "I'll let Tom milk and fetch water. It will save me an hour. It's a slow sixty miles each way, the Yamhill and the Tualatin to ford. They'll be high."

"You can't ford the Willamette or the Columbia," Mrs. Mercy said. "What'll you do?"

"At the Willamette's mouth I'll find some Indians to canoe me to the fort."

"And leave wagon and beasts for them to steal."

"I don't contemplate it," he said. "Eight days ought to see me back here."

"How can those pawky little canoes carry you, two millstones and a barrel of flour? You'll sink. What would we do, left three alone out here two thousand miles from home?"

"Don't contemplate that either," he said. He rose and made slow work buttoning on his overcoat while he watched his wife. "You'll be all right?"

"Worry for yourself."

"It might be nine days instead of eight," John Mercy said.

"If you see anybody along the way that we came over the plains with—though that would be like finding a penny in the ocean—tell them hello and say we're doing well."

"So we are," he said agreeably.

"Just say it," she retorted.

He went about the table to kiss the top of his daughter's head. He said, "Magpie for sharp," and he nodded at his son. "Do the chores without being asked and cause your mother no worry. You're the man here." He took up the sack of food and moved to the door, but there he swung to give his wife a grave moment's look.

She was aware of it and suddenly fell briskly to her chores about the fireplace, ignoring him. She said, "Well, you'd better get started," and then noticed the mud he had brought into the house with his shoes. "Dirt, dirt, I'll die of it." He looked at her but said nothing, and went into the darkness.

Wind rushed past him with its fat, stinging rain. He threw the food into the wagon and walked abreast the oxen to prod them into motion. "Hup, Dandy, Babe! Hup!" The beasts stirred the covered wagon forward, into the meadow and across it toward a valley lying blind in the night.

Fort Vancouver, toward which he was bound for millstones and flour, was sixty miles northward through a country inhabited by scarcely more than a hundred white people; this was December and the year of 1842 came to its gusty ending in rain and wind. He bent his head and trudged forward over the spongy soil. . . .

After he was well gone, Martha Mercy opened the door to look after him, sighting nothing now. She listened to the dashing roar of the wind in the fir tops high over the cabin; the sound of it drew her mouth into a displeased line and she closed the door and walked to the fireplace, a young woman with a clear brown face rarely lighted by a smile, with restless hands and a preoccupied manner. "Tom," she said, "the cow can hook off that top rail of the gate. You take a piece of rope and tie it."

The wind's rustling was endless, and she noted the glitter of water seeping through the log spaces. She turned to frown at the room: the beds and table and chairs cramping it, the boxes piled over boxes, the extra bedding and furniture stored above the rafter crosspieces, the crowded shelves, the clothing hanging from pegs everywhere; she saw the mud near the door and it was a match exploding her discontent. She seized the broom and went vigorously around the room, under the beds and under the children's feet at the table. Caroline said, "I want to dress now."

"Light the lantern, Tom. Put on the heavy coat."

She pulled the big kettle, with its simmering water, from the crane and scalded the milk bucket. Bundled against the weather, young Tom went out into the darkness, and as soon as he had gone Caroline changed from nightgown to clothes.

Martha Mercy got the comb, and stood back of the chair for half an hour's patient combing of the girl's hair, forming its exact part, braiding it and tying the braids. Momentarily, she was pleased. Caroline was pretty.

"Now, then, if you're sharp as a magpie, as your father says, do the dishes," Martha said.

She went to the shed and carried in the full pans of another day's milk, took off the cream and dumped the skim into a bucket for the pigs; she scalded the pans and filled them with the fresh milk young Tom brought in. Young Tom went slowly out to feed the pigs, a first light then creeping like dirty water into the morning. She thought: *He's tired for some reason,* and began to worry about him; he never had Caroline's bubbling health.

She put on her big cloak and tied a scarf around her head. From the shed she got an armload of pitchwood and stove sticks and carried them to the outdoor fireplace. She laid the pitch wood, brought a bucket of coals from the cabin and got the fire going, the variable currents of wind throwing smoke into her face. When the fire was strong she hoisted a great iron scalding pot and lodged it on the rock ledge above the flame and took a bucket behind the cabin.

A barrel stood here on stilts, a tub beneath it. Fire ashes filled the barrel, the rain washed through the ashes, and lye water trickled into the tub; she made three trips from tub to kettle with the lye water, then got an egg from the house and dropped it in the lye water for a test. The egg floated, its end barely above surface. Out of the cabin she brought the grease saved from butchered deer, from two bears Mercy had shot, from bacon drippings. This went into the kettle with the lye water.

She fed the fire and stepped into the cabin, the lower half of her dress and her shoes sodden. The dishes were done, and Caroline stood dreaming at the fire.

"You take your book and go through your letters," said Mrs. Mercy.

"I'd rather make soap."

"You'll get to make it someday," said Mrs. Mercy, "and wish you didn't need to." She put on Mercy's extra pair of boots, her feet entirely lost within them, and returned to the kettle to find that the inslanting rain had dampened the fire. She brought more pitch kindling and chunks of dry fir bark from the shed. Tom watched her. She said, "Tom, take the milk clabber to the chickens. Count and see if they're all there—and get the eggs."

She fed the fire with wood standing ricked by the shelter, the sharp smoke making her cry. The morning moved on, such as it was. The plowed field beyond the foot of the hill—where the winter wheat lay—was black as coal from its month-long soaking; sullen clouds skimmed the earth and lodged in the timber so heavily that a fine fog sparked all about her. Young Tom returned

from the chicken shed and ducked into the shelter of the cabin's doorway. "Six eggs, chickens all right." His face was solemn, his shoulders drawn up.

Trying to imitate his father, she thought, but she looked closely at him, not quite sure; this was the way he sometimes appeared just before coming down with cold. She said, "Take the ax and go strip me some cedar bark, about this long." She spread her arms to indicate the length. "A lot of it."

"You'll kill the trees."

"We've got trees to kill," she said.

At noon the soap was half thick in the kettle, young Tom had stacked a pile of cedar bark in the back shed, and both of them were soaked. She made a meal of cold scraps and fried eggs and sassafras tea, immediately going back to the tedious chore at the fire. By four o'clock the soap was a clear, clean jelly the color of isinglass; she heard it splatter as it bubbled, and judged it right, and drew it from the fire, ladling the soap into the wooden tub. She stored the tub in the shed and returned to clean out the kettle while a premature night whirled down about the cabin.

"Time for milking, Tom."

After supper a greater wind and rain rushed against the cabin and stormed through the trees with the sound of a river cataract. She put Tom to his arithmetic and took the lantern out to look at the chickens huddled in their small house; still restless, she went to the corral to make sure Tom had tied the top rail well enough. To get anything in this country was very hard; to lose anything was a tragedy.

She went on to the store shed, playing the lantern's light along the shelves, over the salt crocks, the potatoes, cabbages and apples and pumpkins given them by their nearest neighbors, the Teals, four miles away. She brooded over the scantiness of the bacon and the half-empty salt-pork tub; it was six months before the garden came on or a hog could be killed, a close thing with four mouths to feed. When she stepped into the cabin she saw young Tom shiver, and she knew that he was going to be sick.

"You go to bed."

She stood at the fire after both of them had settled for the night and gave Mercy a moment's thought, he camped somewhere in a dripping grove fifteen miles away; but he would be inside the wagon cover and he would be warm. She drew the fire together, laid her hand on young Tom's cheek, feeling no fever there yet, and snuffed out the lights. "Turn your back," she said to him and got ready for bed.

The firelight performed its golden, leaping dance on the walls. They were both young, but work was making them old too fast, all because Indiana had got too small for Mercy's notions and he wanted a mile of land in Oregon and his own grist mill. The endless rain was hard to bear, for it took her back to her home where the snow now was a shining crust on the ground and the cold wonderful air shook down the brown oak leaves, banking them in windows against the rail-fence lines. She saw the little town with its houses spaced in their blocks, and the church bell's sound was strong in her ears. Past Pennoyer's, Gregg's and Jackson's she walked, rattling her knuckles against the fence pickets, over the packed snow to Burglon's store, whose shelves were so common then and seemed so rich now. Bob Burglon, learning the business from his father, waited on her; she stirred on the bed and closed him from her mind with effort.

Above the storm she heard a sound beginning, like the tearing of cloth. It grew suddenly to a snapping and whining, and she sat upright in terror and felt the cabin tremble—actually jump—as the tree struck close by with its roar and its dying shower of falling branches.

Caroline whimpered and young Tom woke and began to cough. She listened to her heart's pounding; wind yelled through blackness, and the blackness was heavier than lead. This was the hour when, no matter how she tried to stop it, she thought of Ellen Mercy, born dead, lying inside the rail fence beyond the meadow. The blackness and the wet cold earth brought the thought to her.

Early on the fourth day she rose to make broth from a piece of salt meat simmered with potatoes and onions. On young Tom's waking she fed him against his will, but stopped when she saw he could hold no more down. Fever had cracked his lips, and his arms showed a first thinness, and though he was sleepy he could only catnap. She got Caroline's breakfast, took care of the milk and fed the chickens. Using two water buckets at a time, she made four trips to the creek, a hundred yards distant, to fill the water barrel in the shed; on her return from the final trip she found Caroline in the cabin's doorway, her eyes round as dollars.

"There's a dog. He went around back of the barn."

Mrs. Mercy dumped the water into the barrel. "There's no dog. There's nobody but the trapper yonder and he's got no dog. The Teals are across the river. It couldn't be their dog." Young Tom was at the moment sleeping and she hated to disturb him, but his face was so bright a red that she touched it with her hands. "There's no dog," she said.

"I saw him, right in the yard. He went back of the barn."

Mrs. Mercy looked at her daughter, shaken by a dreadful coldness. She pulled her into the cabin and closed the door and got the rifle from its pegs; she found a cap for the rifle's nipple. "Stay here till I come back and don't open the door." She let herself into the yard and stopped to look through the gray light, toward the meadow, toward the hills. She circled the house, half afraid to turn the corners, going on to the cowshed.

There was nothing to be seen between cabin and shed, and beyond the shed the trees cast a thick shadow. She swung to come straight upon the open door, to see inside the cowshed before she got too close to it; the cow stood forlornly there, disliking the rain. She drew a long breath of relief and walked toward the far side of the shed; before she got quite to its corner she caught sight of motion in the darkness of the trees, and a long, sunken-flanked wolf came silently into the clearing, saw her and stopped.

He was evilly thin, of a dirty, rusty gray, and his eyes were a strange green staring at her with an unhuman steadiness; he had a mind and he was thinking whether he should be afraid or whether he should jump at her—that she knew in the paralyzing moment of her stillness. She never thought of the gun in her hand, never realized she had it. She said, "You dirty thing—get!"

The sound of her voice startled the wolf. He made an easy turn of insolence and went shadowlike into the timber. Then she remembered she had a gun, but he was gone.

She ran to the shed, seized a piece of rope and fixed it to the cow's halter, leading the cow to the cabin door and tying it there. When she opened the door, Caroline stood waiting.

"Where's the dog—why's the cow here?"

"If it was a dog, he might hurt the cow. I didn't see the dog."

She rested the gun beside the door. "Don't touch that." She went to the fire and rested her head against her hands to let the waves of weakness go through her. Maybe he wouldn't come this near to the house, but maybe he was hungry enough to dare; she had to leave the door open to watch the cow. She turned, hearing Tom threshing on the bed. He was awake but he looked at her in a strange way and she knew the fever, still strong, made him lightheaded.

It was more than a cold and he was in danger. She laid her hand softly on his chest, and he rolled his head, looking up to her with fear in his eyes.

"Am I going to die?"

"It's just a little thing. It's a cold. You've had colds before."

She held him up for a drink of water, pulled the quilt over him and briskly turned to her work. She made Caroline a bite to eat, she scalded the churn, and brought the milk from the shed; seated at the doorway, the churn between her legs and her eyes on the yard, she worked the dasher up and down.

Down the meadow, a voice hailed the cabin, shocking her, and in a moment Mrs. Teal, skirts dripping from a four-mile walk through wet meadow grasses, appeared at the door; with her was the oldest Teal boy, a basket in each arm.

Mrs. Teal said, "I missed your visit Sunday and got to wonderin'."

"Mercy's away to Fort Vancouver." A great relief from loneliness came upon Mrs. Mercy, so great that for an instant she was happy. But she could not reveal to this woman her weakness; she showed Mrs. Teal a steady face, and rose to accept the baskets with proper thanks.

"Just some garden things," said Mrs. Teal. "They'll rot in our storehouse, we've got so much. It'll be the same with you when your garden's started. First year's always a hard thing—nothing to do with." Mrs. Teal saw young Tom on the bed and walked over and bent and looked at him. Her voice was quiet: "What's ailin' him?"

"A cold," said Mrs. Mercy.

"If we just had some mustard for a plaster," said Mrs. Teal. "There's never anything. I'll be happy when there's a store." She looked again at young Tom, silently and long; she was worried, Martha Mercy realized. The Teal boy stood beyond the doorway, waiting.

Mrs. Mercy looked at young Tom and Caroline and spoke to Mrs. Teal: "Maybe your son could take the gun and go look on the other side of the cowshed. There's a dog around." She added quietly: "A gray dog, Caroline thinks."

"Oh, dear," murmured Mrs. Teal. "They do bother in winter when they get hungry. Joe—" But Joe, reaching for the rifle, had already gone. "Have you got any turpentine? On a rag soaked with water, it would draw."

"No."

Mrs. Teal looked at her narrowly and lowered her voice: "You got another baby started?" When Martha Mercy shook her head, the other woman murmured, "Well, then, it's weariness. You been up most of the night, I guess. That's a terrible big tree that fell. Mercy better clear more away. I'll leave Joe here to sleep in the shed tonight. And to fetch me if you have need."

"It's a trouble for him."

"Great stars!" said Mrs. Teal. "What's people for? And there's no need to stand off. Not out here. People have got to have each other. Even if they don't like each other, they got to get along. Well, it's soon dark and I'll go." She gave a last look to young Tom and went into the yard, calling to her son. Joe Teal appeared from the timber a moment, listened to his mother's words, and went back into the timber, as lean and easy and insolent as the wolf itself.

Caroline Mercy sat down before the churn, lifting and lowering the dasher in steady rhythm. Covertly from time to time Mrs. Mercy threw a glance toward young Tom. The fever was growing, the breaking point hadn't been reached. She kneaded the butter and took it to the storehouse, poured buttermilk into a jug and brought young Tom a glass of it; when she lifted him upright to drink she felt the fiery heat of his body. He drank the full glass and fell back on the bed, fretful and weak. She brought up the quilts around him.

Darkness came down with a rising wind and rain. She made supper for Caroline and for Joe Teal, who, coming out of the darkness, ate as though in a haste to be back at his hunting. "I'll sleep in the cowshed," he said, and took a blanket from her and led the cow away. She ate nothing, having no appetite. She washed the dishes, combed and put up Caroline's hair and sent her to bed.

"The light's in my eyes," said Tom.

She snuffed the candles and drew a chair beside young Tom's bed, holding his hot hand. "Now, then," she said, "you'll be better in the morning. This fever's about burned out the corruption, and then it'll go and you'll eat like a pig." His breathing was fast and heavy, the labor of it exhausting him; his heart alarmed her with the violence of its pulsing against his skin.

A terrible helplessness came upon her and out of it came bitter thoughts and a moment of hatred for John Mercy. He was an ambitious man who couldn't abide the thought of being small in Indiana—believing that a mile of land, a mill and someday a store out here would make them happy and leave the children well off. But what good was that to young Tom now, half dead with fever? It wasn't a healthy country, no freezing weather to kill the putrid things in the earth and air each year, only this wetness which sickened people and kept them damp winter long.

In sleep, young Tom cried. She sat in the slowly chilling room, listening to the fever have its way, holding his hand and silently praying her will into him. She feared to let his hand go and she feared to move. Mercy, about now, would be starting back over a country without roads or bridges; she had no tenderness in her thinking of him, only a feeling that if young Tom should die, her mind would die.

Pain struck her in the back of the neck, and she seized the edges of the chair to avoid falling. She had slept a few moments and her hand had fallen away from young Tom's hand. She searched for it, and panic came upon her at the quietness that was upon him. She bent, placing her head near his face; his breath rustled against it, but the sound of hard struggle was gone; and when she touched his face the heat, too, had gone.

He was motionless; he was in the sleep of exhaustion and the fever was broken. She pulled the covers around him and, removing only her shoes, she got into bed beside Caroline and lay awake, too tired to be relieved. . . .

On the seventh day the rain stopped; and the water-beaded trees around the house were all asparkle. A wolf hide hung in the cowshed, shot by Joe Teal, who had gone home. Young Tom sat propped around with pillows, his eye sockets deep and a waxiness on his face, too weary to complain at being in bed; but he was hungry and he was better.

She carried ten pails of freshet-yellowed water from the Cobway and set on the washtub. "You're not so sick you can't do some studying," she told him. "It's time wasted that's sinful, and I'll not have you ignorant like that trapper. Caroline, get that arithmetic book for him." She hoisted the boiling tub to a bench before the door, and, her skirts tied up, she did the washing.

Joe Teal slipped into the cabin with a bottle of berry wine sent by his mother, having covered the four miles like a hound and yet breathing softly; and he refused food and quietly disappeared.

By afternoon the washing hung from every overhead pole in the cabin, beneath which she had to duck to make a meal and tend young Tom. The closeness of this living crossed her and made her more and more irritable. This was her mood when a straight, thin and whiskered man in a dark suit so old and hard-used that it had a green cast to it stepped from a horse before her door and cheerfully announced himself.

"I am Reverend White, ridin' my circuit," he said. "Sister Teal said you were here. Boy's better? This, I guess, is Caroline, and I've struck you at washin' time and you won't like me for it."

She didn't. It offended her enormously to bring him into this room with its crowded furniture, and its damp clothes scraping the top of his gray head. But he was a minister and she was courteous to him, by nature respecting his profession. She went hastily around to make up a meal which, because of its poor showing, further depressed her. He ate and he talked and he was full of good spirit.

"Husband be back soon? It's a long ride to Vancouver. Sister Teal mentioned he was after millstones. A miller by trade ?"

"He's got knowledge of it," said Mrs. Mercy.

"He'll make out, he'll do well. He's got good land, good water power—he's had the best choice before the multitude come. There's no land like it for richness." He gave her a passing glance and went back to his food. "A little rain, of course. There's the gift it's got—water to make things grow. I recall the harshness of Northern winters."

"I pine for cold weather," she said.

"That's natural, but another year here and you'll not hanker for home and friends. You'll have them here."

"Will they ever come?"

"By the thousands," said Reverend White, "and if you bend your ear, sister, you can hear the tramplin' of their feet now. It's destiny. That winter wheat planted in the field ?"

"Yes."

"The rain that troubles you will bring that wheat on fat and heavy. The rain is your bread and butter." He looked at the wine bottle on the table; she felt shame that he should see it and wondered what his thoughts were.

"That's Sister Teal's elderberry, I recognize. No medicine like it for your son."

"Could I offer you some, Reverend?"

He said, "No," in a rather reluctant way and at once said it stronger. "No. Barely enough for him. Now then," he said rising, "it's twenty miles to the next family and I have got to ride." He laid a hand on young Tom's head, on Caroline's head, his hands blackened from the reins of the horse.

He was a minister, but he had none of that refinement about him which, in Indiana, sets ministers apart; he was a man before a minister, more like a millwright than anything else. He thanked her for the meal and rode downgrade to the meadow and out of sight. She was disappointed because he had neither asked anything of her spiritual condition nor had knelt with them in prayer.

She would have been surprised at the Reverend White. Passing around a point of the hill he came to a grove of oaks well beyond the cabin, here dismounting to kneel before a tree. He knew her story from Mrs. Teal, he knew her trials from the trials of other women before her and he knew, by her expression, the depth of her unhappiness. Knowing it, he prayed for her aloud, naming all the troubles she had undergone and all the excellences he saw within her. He listed them in a good round voice to God, stating her case as a lawyer might have done; and in the same voice he asked for a small amount of forgiveness, for a great deal of help. Then he rose, brushed his wet knees and rode into the gathering twilight toward a cabin twenty miles away. . . .

She milked, fed the pigs, and gathered the eggs and locked in the chickens after counting them. After Caroline had gone to bed she got her basket and pulled the rocker to the fire—all the long day waiting for this restful moment—and settled there with thread and patch cloth. For a moment the redness of her hands drew her attention and she let them lie while she became aware of the scratches upon them. She remembered that her grandmother's hands had been like this, but not her mother's; for her grandmother had gone through the same drudgery while her mother, marrying the village merchant, had lived a calm life.

She might have married a merchant, too, and her days would have been as pleasant as her mother's. All day long the voices of the town would be around her, leaving no room for lonesomeness, and she would belong, she would dance, she would go to church. She had not let herself think too much of Bob Burglon—that was a kind of unfaithfulness; but now she let him come into her mind; his courtship sent its sweetness through her as she recalled it.

It was hard to know, sometimes, what put one man above another and why John Mercy, so abruptly coming into her life, had made Bob Burglon seem no longer right. It had been clear enough then. She looked closely at Bob Burglon, she looked closely at her husband—and she said silently, "No more of that," and put it out of her head. The fireplace light at last made her eyes tired and she went to bed. . . .

She was up still earlier next morning and by daybreak had finished the never-changing chores. Now she brought in from the shed the slabs of cedar bark young Tom had cut, and began pounding the cedar fiber free, at last having a pile of it and a great mound of fluff around her. She brought out a loom, tacking on the stringy cedar twine as warp, and began the tedious hand job of running the woof through; by noon she was sorry she had begun and grew cross when young Tom became hungry. "Caroline, fix his big stomach something."

She hated to waste time, and by two o'clock, having had no meal herself, finished the cedar mat, threw it on the floor before the doorway and was done with it. But for a moment she studied it and thought: *Why, it's not bad,* and saw how she could do better next time. She was in haste; everything piled up on her. From the shed she got a venison joint, and put it into the deep skillet. She made a pie, and at proper time laid onions and potatoes and parsnips around the baking venison. Twilight came on, she turning rapidly from one piece of work to another.

She changed young Tom's bed, washed his face; she did Caroline's hair and was momentarily happy with her daughter's prettiness; and then at last she did her own hair and tied on a new apron. It was full dark by that time; standing at the open doorway she listened for the sound of Mercy's wagon to rise from the far deep quiet of the night. She began to worry, to see the rivers he had to cross, the Indians who went back and forth through this country in their roving bands. Young Tom said, "It's way past suppertime."

"You can wait a little longer," she said; then, in the distance beyond the meadow, she heard Mercy's call. "It will be just a little while," she said. She looked at them, adding, "We will not say we've been troubled, mind you." She looked from one to the other. "I want you to know that there's always trouble, and each one has got to stand his own, or everybody'd always be crying. Your father's got his, and bears them, and we'll bear ours."

He circled the wagon into its place beside the cabin, seeing his wife and daughter framed in the doorway's gushing yellow light. He said, "That's a pretty sight. Everything well?"

Mrs. Mercy said, "We got along."

"I said eight days—and eight days it was."

"You can thank the Lord as much as your own guessing," she said. He unyoked and led away the oxen and came slowly back, walking with a weary man's loose knees. He got something from the wagon and said to Caroline, still standing in the doorway, "Magpie," and saw young Tom in bed. "What's here?"

"He had a cold," said Mrs. Mercy, "but it's all right now. We'll eat when you've washed." She looked at him, knowing he had spared no strength to be back on time; he met her glance and a sparkle got into his eyes and he said, "Well, then, I've not been been missed?"

"Don't be foolish, Mercy. It's not right to beg for sentiment." She watched him reach into the package he carried, laying out a clustered chunk of transparent rock candy, and a string of Hudson Bay beads. "Candy, from London, for the kids. Beads for you. Pretty things."

She looked at them, she didn't touch them, she didn't meet Mercy's eyes. Her manner was brisk, almost impatient. "I hope you didn't waste money on me. You know I don't wear trinkets. They will do for Caroline," she added and turned to bring the roast to the table.

He sat heavily on the rocker and got out of his boots, into his slippers. He washed and combed his hair and took his place at the table. When his family had come about it, he looked at them, one by one, and dropped his head.

"For the food, for a safe return, and for the health of this family, Lord, thanks, Amen." He raised his head, a steady faintly austere benevolence coming to his face. "No trouble, then?"

"Nothing to speak of," said Martha Mercy.

Suggested Further Reading

WORKS BY HAYCOX

The Wild Bunch. Boston: Little, Brown, 1943.

Bugles in the Afternoon. Boston: Little, Brown, 1944.

The Earthbreakers. Boston: Little, Brown, 1952.

Best Western Stories of Ernest Haycox. New York: Bantam Books, 1960; New York: Signet, 1975.

WORKS ABOUT HAYCOX

Bold, Christine. *Selling the Wild West: Popular Western Fiction, 1860-1960.* Bloomington: Indiana University Press, 1987.

Cawelti, John G. *Adventure, Mystery and Romance: Formula Stories as Art and Popular Culture.* Chicago: University of Chicago Press, 1976.

Etulain, Richard. *Ernest Haycox.* Boise State University Western Writers Series Number 86. Boise, Idaho: Boise State University, 1988.

Ben Hur Lampman

A well-known writer for the Portland *Oregonian*, Ben Hur Lampman (1886-1954) got his first taste of the newspaper trade as a boy working around his father's print shop in North Dakota. He later married Lena Sheldon, a New Yorker teaching school in the Dakotas, and they moved to Gold Hill, Oregon, where he printed a weekly newspaper from 1912 to 1916. His writing got him a job with *The Oregonian* where he wrote nature essays and editorials for many years. Although he is best known for his essays on fishing and on the pleasures of nature, his story "The Pack beyond the Fire," included here, and appearing in *The Oregonian* for June 30, 1940, was called by one New York editor, "the best short story of the year."

The Pack beyond the Fire

There were five of them, as though they might be a family, crouching close to the fire—a woman with feral alertness in her young eyes, and with a child at her breast; a man in his prime, who searched the darkness with constant and roving gaze; a stripling whose beard was beginning to curl. The fifth was an old, old man who crouched in the very ashes for warmth, incredibly wrinkled and hirsute. His faded, contemplative look was fixed on the heart of the fire. A darkness of forest was outlined against the sky save where, as the slope rose, the dark ruins of an ancient city lifted angular and desolate against the lonely stars. There was no speech between them until a sudden clamor, fiercely eager, fearful, broke the silence. The two younger men looked to their weapons, but casually, and tossed more branches on the fire. The woman drew nearer to it, clutching the child. "The dogs!" they said together. But the old man stirred not nor spoke at all.

Into the firelight there came leaping, and glancing backward, a lean fugitive stranger, breathing sharply. The clamor broke out again beyond the edge of the firelight, rose and waned, became the soft padding of feet, and low snarlings and whimperings. "I killed one," said the stranger. "But there are too many of them here, and it is not good country for hunting." The mate of the woman nodded. "We know that it isn't," he said. "They have driven the game away and they are bold with hunger. We came here for iron." The firelight lifted and eyes shone in the darkness, flashed, blazed and were gone. "There are more of them than ever before," said the stripling, "and they grow bolder. They caught our tame one and killed him."

The stranger looked from one of them to another and long at the old man, still staring into the heart of the fire. "It is strange," he said, "that he should live to be so very old. I have not seen an older one of us, and I have been wherever people are, from the sea to this place where I had thought were none." He spoke as casually as though the old man were not there. The silence became utter. Then far away the clamoring broke forth again. "They are gone," said the stripling. "How old is he?" the stranger asked. "How might one say?" the woman answered softly. "He has always been with us, and he was old as this, my mother used to say, when she was a girl." They shook their heads to marvel at it.

The stripling stirred the fire. "Old as he is," he said, "he is not always like this, sitting staring. For sometimes he remembers and he talks to me. It is delight to listen to him then, though he does not remember clearly enough to suit me, and he can answer but few of my questions." The half-moon had risen above the forest, and they heard the wild dogs hunting to westward of the ruined city. "Tomorrow we shall surely find iron," said the woman's mate. "But what does he remember?" urged the stranger curiously. Before the stripling could answer the old man lifted his look from the fire, and the white beard stirred about his withered lips. "I remember," the old man said, and quite clearly, "when all the dogs were tame."

Suggested Further Reading

WORKS BY LAMPMAN
Here Comes Somebody. Portland: Metropolitan Press, 1935.
At the End of the Car Line. Portland: Binford and Mort, 1942.
The Wild Swan. New York: Thomas Y. Crowell, 1947.
A Leaf from French Eddy. Portland: Touch-Stone Press, 1965.

Walt Morey

Best known as the author of *Gentle Ben*, the story of a boy's friendship with a giant bear, Walt Morey (1907-1992) has written many stories and books about animals and adventures in wild settings. He has lived most of his life in and near Portland, after a childhood following his carpenter father and his mother around the Northwest to various job sites. He worked in sawmills and on construction jobs and was a prizefighter before becoming an author. He started by writing for men's "pulp" magazine market, but later, after urgings from his wife, who was a schoolteacher, he began writing stories for young people. "Timber Top" is one of his early stories, published in 1941 in *Argosy* magazine.

Timber Top

He stood in the middle of the corduroy road, his worn suitcase in his hand, and he could see the camp, dark under the trees, a black belt of river, and the upward rush of the Olympics.

Danny Harmon was big, man big, but his eighteen years were in his face, in the fear that swelled suddenly within him. He'd thought, you swung an ax, pulled a saw, and you were a logger. Now he wasn't sure. This wasn't anything like the two-hundred acres of stumps and second growth at home. This was the real thing. Maybe he couldn't make the grade with these men. Maybe. . . .

He hunched his big shoulders in the worn mackinaw and went up the hard-packed trail, across the cleared space to the door of the single lighted building. He stopped there, for a minute the knob was a cold ball under his palm. Then he said to himself: "What the hell!" But it didn't help.

He opened the door and went in.

He went through a long room with a plank floor under his feet, plank tables and benches, the dining—no—the mess hall, to a door at the far end.

The cook shack. He'd known it would be like this, but not so big. A great iron stove in the middle of the floor, walls lined with pots and pans hanging from nails, the smell of cooked food and grease thick as a swamp fog.

The cook—he must have been the cook, for he was short and fat and wore a greasy apron—said: "So th' stage was late agin."

Dan tried to think of something a logger would say, that would show he'd been around and knew the answers. But all he said was: "I—I'm Dan Harmon, the new faller," and hoped the greenness didn't show.

The cook said: "Hungry, Danny?"

He wanted to say: "Don't call me Danny; they did that at home. I can do a man's work; I'm not a kid any more." He said: "No, I'm not hungry." And he hadn't eaten since noon. "Where do I sleep?"

"First bunkhouse, last bunk on th' left."

The bunkhouse was black dark inside, there were the steady sounds of men's breathing, someone's rasping snore, and the air was close and warm and used. He felt his way down a bunk-lined aisle, and finally his outstretched hand struck the wall. He slid his suitcase under the bunk, undressed in the dark and crawled between heavy blankets. He lay there staring wide-eyed into the darkness, feeling the hunger chew at his stomach. It must have been hours later the wind came up and moaned through the trees, and listening to it, he slept.

He turned out with the rest in the wan light of a single globe and fished his suitcase from under the bunk. He felt the impersonal eyes of the man across the aisle on him as he opened it and began to dress. His overalls were there, stiff and new, stagged-off in correct logger style, a cheap work shirt, and a pair of calked boots. Fifteen dollars those boots had cost, and he thought again, that was a lot for a farmer boy to spend on a pair of shoes.

He was the last to leave the bunkhouse, the last into the mess hall. Every head came up as he stepped through the door and the battery of eyes was like a weight slammed against him. For a moment they held him there, tongue frozen to the roof of his mouth. Then he slipped into a place a pair of wide shoulders made for him. Somewhere a voice said: "Hell! he's only a kid. How d'ya' like that, Mike?"

The wide-shouldered man said quietly: "Push that stuff this way, Brady; we eat, too."

He got through breakfast somehow, only lifting his eyes once, then he saw the man across the table grinning.

He walked the half mile to work with the man at the table—his name was Joe—and Nick, the woods boss who was short and barrel-chested.

The operation was just like pictures he'd seen. A steaming donkey with spar pole and highline stretching across the hills, and a sidetrack with half a trainload of logs. There he found Big Mike, his partner, and he looked big and tough as his name. Dan was surprised his own eyes were on a level with Big Mike's cold, black ones.

Big Mike sneered: "A school-boy logger," and spat on his hands. "Take hold of that saw."

It was good to feel the saw tear its way through tough wood and bark, see the chips fountain across the ground from his swinging ax. This was logging. This was a man's work. And Big Mike was pouring it on: a single glance around at the steady even pull of the rest showed him that.

But he just bent his back and put his big shoulders behind it and the first hour wasn't bad. The second he began to tire and in the third the blisters came, round, watery lumps that swelled under his hot palms. From there on it was plain hell. But when the donkey whistled for noon and he straightened his aching back he'd held his own.

Joe came and ate his lunch beside him on a log and said: "How'd it go?"

He said: "All right," and kept the palms of his hands turned down.

But it wasn't all right in the afternoon. By the end of the second cut his hands were on fire, just to touch the handle of the saw almost made him yell. And Big Mike kept pouring it on. He gritted his teeth, kept his head down so Big Mike wouldn't see his face, and pulled.

He didn't know how long that lasted. The pain had crawled through his arms and shoulders and settled in his stomach when he felt the saw handle go slick in his hands. It was stained red, the inside of his fingers were red. The blisters had broken.

A minute later Big Mike dropped the saw, reached for his ax. Dan got his own, lifted it and started to swing, but his fingers refused to tighten, and the slickness under his palms finished it. The ax shot from his grasp, Big Mike yelled as it cut a silvery arc above his head and dropped in the brush.

He froze there, numb with horror until Big Mike rushed around the tree, fists swinging. Dan had never in all his life hit a man, but he did now. He shot his right fist out instinctively to stop Mike, and it did, landing jarringly against his black stubble jaw. Then Big Mike's weight crashed him to the ground.

Everything was a crazy blur after that. Big Mike's fists almost caved his ribs, and a jerked-up knee shot the breath from his body in a sickening rush. Dan fought in a mad frenzy then, and he never knew where or how often he hit Big Mike.

But suddenly Big Mike's weight was snatched away. Dan saw him when he jumped to his feet. Big Mike was getting up ten feet away, and Joe was standing over him, spread-legged, arms swinging at his sides in a way anyone could understand.

Then the whole falling crew was milling around. Mike was yelling: "Get 'im outa here before I kill 'im! Get 'im out, quick!"

And Nick was shoving him back, saying to Dan: "Sorry, kid, we got loggin' t' do. Your check'll be ready t'night."

So this was the end, and all his plans and dreams were gone. He was turning away when Joe's quiet voice said: "He can work with me. Whitey can go with Mike. Okay, Whitey?"

"Sure."

Nick said: "Well—if ya wanta. . . ."

Big Mike growled: "Just keep th' fool outa my way." Then the gang melted back to the woods, and he went with Joe. And Joe kept looking at him until he said: "I could'a stayed with him only—only my hands. . . ."

Joe tossed him a red handkerchief: "Wrap it around th' handle, it'll make a cushion."

Dan burst out savagely: "Quit treating me like a baby. I can pull my weight."

"Don't be a fool," Joe said, and took hold of the saw.

Dan tried, the handkerchief helped, but his fingers refused to tighten on the handle. He only went through the motions. Joe did the work.

He couldn't sleep that night. His palms were on fire and he lay with them turned up on the covers and thought how grand it would feel to plunge them into the clear, cold spring at home.

Sometime later he heard the creak of a bunk, feet padded down the aisle and out the door. Minutes later they were back, a dim shadow bent over him and Joe's hoarse whisper said: "Dan, hold out your hands."

Joe's fingers groped for his, then something infinitely cool and soothing trickled into each hot palm. "Spread it around," Joe whispered. "It's special stuff I carry for my own hands."

He felt Joe's weight on the edge of the bunk, and after a minute: "Why'd ya' come, Dan? Ya' coulda got a job in town just as easy."

Dan shifted uncomfortably, and all the things that had sent him here, came back. The logging tales that had become part of him. The two hundred acres of stumps and brush at home, where he'd lain on sunny days, remembering the stories he'd heard, dreaming of the great stand it once had been. How he'd rebuilt in his mind's eye that logging operation complete with horse, oxen and brawling two-fisted men.

He said: "I—I had to come." The rest would have sounded kiddish put into words.

But it didn't when Joe said it. "That's how it was with me. My old man was a logger. I knew how to fall a tree and break out rollways before I knew my ABCs. And Paul Bunyan was greater than Washington and Lincoln rolled into one. I was a full-fledged faller at sixteen and figured that made me a man. I guess when a thing's in your blood there's nothing else you can do."

Dan said: "I know."

"But why come here? This's a fly-by-night that's cashin' in on high prices."

"I didn't know." Dan stopped, trying to bring Joe's face out of the darkness. "What're you doing here?"

Joe's low laugh sounded queer in the silence. "Ever watch a rock roll downhill? Watch how it bounces here and there lookin' for a place to light? That's me. I've had good jobs, from whistle punk to camp super. I've worked in a hundred camps. Maybe I'm lookin' for a good place to light. I dunno. But that's why I'm here. This was openin' up and I needed a job. But I won't stay." He stood up suddenly. "Here, put some more on your hands. We can't gab all night."

After Joe had gone he lifted his hands to his face, thought of Joe leaving the bunkhouse, coming back. Plain olive oil from the cook shack. He thinks I'm a kid, he thought bitterly. Thinks I can't do a man's work.

The pain in his hands was almost gone when he heard Joe's steady breathing. Joe who talked quietly, whose confidence fit him like his shirt. Who'd been a faller at sixteen and had logged in a hundred camps. Joe, who knew why a man had to go to the camps. Dan remembered then that he hadn't thanked Joe.

He learned to log in the weeks that followed. Learned to make his cut, to handle a springboard, to match Joe's smooth flow of power along the saw. He learned to hate, too, for he hated Big Mike. Big Mike who kept pouring it on with a cutting, sarcastic humor that left him helpless to fight back. Who called him Joe's kid until the whole camp took it up.

He learned to ride the log train to town on Saturday night. Learned what it was like to walk the streets of Harbor a hundred strong to the rolling bite of their calks. He'd been one of them that first night as he huddled at Joe's shoulder with a half dozen others at the end of a car of logs. The rest of the camp was strung along the train, there was laughter and talk, and somewhere a heavy voice sang:

I eat when I'm hungry,
I drink when I'm dry.
If a tree don't fall on me
I'll live till I die.

For this was celebration night. Saturday night. A warm feeling swelled in him until it was too big for his chest to hold.

He was one of them when they pushed through the ancient doors of the Broken Dollar and lined the battered bar. He ordered beer with the rest, was lifting his glass, watching his reflection in the mirror of the back-bar when Big Mike's voice rumbled from the end of the room:

"Better watch yuhr kid, Joe. He'll be tearin' th' town apart in another hour."

He stood there, stiff, helpless, anger boiling in his throat as laughter ran the bar, and careless jabs that cut like a knife were tossed his way.

He forced himself to finish the drink, to stand there an age-long minute afterward, then he turned blindly to the door.

Joe was beside him in less than half a block. After a few steps he said: "They're nice guys, but they gotta play, an' th' youngest in camp's gotta take it."

"I suppose you took it?"

"Maybe not quite as bad."

Dan whirled: "Sure," he snarled, "and I'll tell you why. Nobody made a fool outa you. Nobody babied you; said do it this way, do it that way. Nobody followed you around giving advice until you couldn't think for yourself."

Joe said: "I guess you're right, Dan," and turned away. Dan went down the street into another, found an empty booth and ordered a drink. He ordered more drinks. Joe found him there, and he wasn't sure just how he got back to camp.

Next morning he tried to tell Joe how he felt.

Joe said: "I started at sixteen. Come on, there's a tree over here been waitin' for us a hundred years."

When they went to town after that he stayed with Joe, became more than ever Joe's kid. And Joe never lined the bar with the rest. He sat in a booth against the wall, drank sparingly, while his sharp eyes roved the room, the men that came and went through the swinging doors.

Then one day they did a fast job on a big one. It was close to the whistle, and for the first time Dan felt the full sweep of Joe's power across the saw, and matched it. When the tree snapped, the grave thunder had echoed away, there was still five minutes to go.

Joe said: "Twenty-eight minutes. That was loggin', Dan."

But he didn't know how good until nights later Big Mike looked down the table, said: "Me an' Whitey 're enterin' th' fallin' contest at th' Splash th' Forth. We dropped a four-footer in thirty minutes t'day." His black eyes found Dan's: "That's fallin', school-boy."

Dan turned to Joe, fought down his anger and asked in a voice the whole room could hear: "We fell one that big the other day. What was our time, Joe?"

Joe shrugged: "Don't remember," and went on eating.

"It was twenty-eight minutes, Joe. Remember? Twenty-eight minutes."

Big Mike scowled: "Half rotten, eh, kid?"

Joe's head snapped up: "It was solid as your head."

"Maybe you an' your kid oughta enter, too."

What followed was something torn from an ugly dream.

There was Joe's: "I log for money. Not to show off in front of a crowd."

And Big Mike's: "So, th' two-fifty to th' winnin' crew ain't money, huh? What's th' matter? Scared t' get beat, or scared of th' crowd?"

Silence. And Joe's eyes leaped down the table. Charged, oppressive silence. And Dan knew Big Mike hated Joe too.

There was Joe's words dropping into the hush: "What sort of a crack is that, Mike?"

"You figure it out."

Noise blossomed again, voices called along the tables: "Come on, Joe. You can do it. What're you waitin' for?" Joe's face had gone white, a muscle jerked in his cheek. Then there was his nod, his harsh: "Okay, we'll be there."

Later Dan said: "It's my fault, Joe. I thought I was showing Mike up. I—I won't enter."

"You tryin' to back out?"

"No. I—"

"Then can it. We're gonna pin Mike's ears back—maybe do better. Ya know, we make a good showin' they can't call ya Joe's kid any more."

"I wasn't thinking of that."

But he thought of nothing else in the days that followed. And, finally, when the day came, hot and still and breathless, and they went down on the log train he was tight as a drum-head. Big Mike was expansive, spending his end of the winners' purse already. Whitey wore a confident smile, and Joe was grim and silent. And Joe didn't break that silence until they had dropped off the train in the yards and the rest of the gang was hurrying uptown ahead.

He stood watching the long line of a freight creep out of the yards, and when he spoke there was a lift to his voice, a light in his eyes.

"We could hop her and be two hundred miles away by night, God knows where. Th' hell with Big Mike, th' hell with their Splash."

Dan said: "It'd look funny if we dropped out now."

Joe looked at him, not seeing him: "Yeah. Yeah, I guess it would." But he kept scowling at his feet as they went uptown. Finally he said: "How about hoppin' a freight with me tonight? We can draw our pay right after th' meet, get down in th' yards and be gone in an hour.

"I'll show ya' real loggin', Dan. Highlines a mile long. Skidroads and Cats and rafts worth a million dollars. I'll show ya' where ya' can walk on th' river for ten miles and never get your feet wet, th' logs are that thick. What do ya' say? Wanta go?"

Dan said: "I'd like to, Joe. I'd like to."

"Good." Joe smiled, and it was the first real smile Dan had seen in days.

They had built a long line of bleachers along the river bank and it looked as though half the people in the state were jammed into them. A newsreel camera was set up at the water's edge, and the man cranking it swept the crowd and the river where a swarm of pleasure crafts shuttled back and forth before the stands. Firecrackers made constant explosions, and the bleachers were alive with balloons and flags and the tense boil of noise that always marks a Fourth-of-July crowd.

Joe said: "I hear they ran a special train from Portland." His sharp eyes roved the bleachers. Even after the sports began he seemed to find more interest there than on the water.

And there were more water sports than Dan had dreamed there could be. There were Indians in long, brightly painted war canoes in a flashing mile-long race. There were bucking contests, log rolling, walking a greased pole. A dozen loggers put on a battle royal on a barge in the middle of the river, spilling each other into the water until but one, the winner, was left. There were boat races, swimming races, and a man dove from the top of the bridge tower.

The sun was swinging down the western sky in a hot, white ball that made him sweat just standing there, when two tugs towed a huge barge to the middle of the river with a dozen thirty-foot logs fastened upright around its rim.

Joe's taut voice said: "This's th' last. Th' fallin' contest. Let's go."

A launch took them out. Twenty-four men in calked boots and stagged-off overalls who were strangely silent, even to Big Mike. Dan thought, suddenly, if he'd only kept his mouth shut that night he could be up there in the stands enjoying this, part of the crowd, the noise. Joe sat beside him staring at his feet, his face stiff.

He didn't look up even when they climbed the steps to the barge.

Glistening tools were spread out beside each upright log. A crosscut, two axes, two pairs of springboards. Joe squatted beside the tools, examined them. His hand trembled as he reached for an ax. Dan knew how he felt. His own heart was pounding around in his chest like a lot of loose bolts in a can.

A man in white shirt and pants, with a megaphone in one hand, a revolver in the other, yelled to the crowd on the bank.

"The cuts will be made from springboards ten feet in the air. They will start with the gun and go until the last man has finished. All right, boys. Get set!"

Dan caught up his ax, the cold sweat of his palms turned the handle slick and sudden panic gripped him as he visioned that day in the woods when the keen blade had cut an arc above Big Mike's head. Suppose it happened here, before thirty thousand people. . . .

Joe said: "Cut your notch plenty deep," and faced him across the tree, swinging his ax lightly in both brown hands.

Then the gun crashed.

Dan swung his ax with the full sweep of arms and shoulders, gripping the handle until his fingers cramped. Around them he heard the chunk of other axes, and waves of sound rolled across the water from shore.

They finished the first notch together, jammed in springboard, climbed up, swung their axes again. A dozen hard strokes, the second was set. Then they heard the first whip of a saw. As Joe leaned down, scooped up their own saw Dan glanced toward the sound. Big Mike and Whitey were beginning their under-cut. Six strokes ahead, he thought frantically, and it only took one to win.

His own work was ragged, jerky. Seconds were flying, bringing the sounds of more saws. Then Joe's quiet: "We're just fallin' a tree, Dan." Joe's smooth flow of power along the saw drove the panic away.

They finished the under-cut, chopped it out, dropped their axes to the deck of the barge and began the long cut through. The finishing cut, the hard cut. That took everything you had, and more too. That made him a logging man like Joe, Big Mike and the rest of the camp, or left him just Joe's kid. From there on it was a nightmare. The sound of the saw swelled to a whine and he had to let himself out all the way. It wasn't like falling a tree in the woods. The sun burned into his back, sweat poured down his face into his eyes, half blinding him, and he didn't dare let go of the handle to swipe it away. He blinked his eyes, shook his head, and Joe seemed to raise the pace.

Pain crawled across his shoulders, down his arms to his finger tips. Hot July air pumped into his laboring lungs until his throat was a dust-dry pipe. Minutes wore away, each an eternity, and still Joe kept the pace. Arms and shoulders went numb and he wasn't sure he was pulling his weight any more. But his arms swept back and forth before his smarting eyes, and the sound of the saw, the sound of the crowd made a hollow roar in his head.

He tried to think of Big Mike. How he hated Big Mike. But there was no room with his lungs on fire and pain like a knife in his back. He was letting Joe down, he did know that, quitting on Joe, proving he was only a kid. He tried to bring more to each pull on the saw, and there was nothing left to bring.

He didn't hear it snap when it started to go. He didn't see it plunge. But he did hear the thundering wave of sound that rolled up from shore. Then the saw was motionless under his palms, a fountain of water shot into the air before his eyes and cool drops spattered his face. Then he saw the log rolling beneath him, shaking green water and a blanket of suds from its brown back. And Joe, red-faced, his soaked shirt plastered to his heaving chest was grinning across the stump, his hoarse voice croaking: "We won, Dan! We won!" And back of Joe's voice was a great roaring—the voice of the crowd, hailing the victors. It was over; the job was done.

But he couldn't believe it until his eyes jumped to Big Mike and Whitey's log, just beginning to fall. Until the man in white shirt and pants pointed at them, yelling through the megaphone at the crowd. Then he just stood there, numbed arms hanging at his sides, afraid to step down to the next springboard and onto the float for fear his legs would crumble.

Seconds later the last log fell and he followed Joe down.

The crowd was streaming out of the bleachers when the launch took them back. Big Mike slouched in the stern, scowling darkly, had nothing to say and Dan was too tired to care.

Joe grabbed his arm as they stepped from the launch: "Let's get outa here. Get our dough and beat it."

They hadn't taken a dozen steps when the two grim men were before them. The big one laid a heavy hand on Joe's shoulder, said: "Just a minute. Aren't you Edward Brandon?"

Dan turned. "What's the idea, mister? This is—" Then he felt Joe's hand on his arm.

"Sorry, buddy," Joe mumbled, and tried to brush by.

But the big man swung him around, and Dan caught the silvery flash of a star. "Two years is a long time, Ed," the big man said in a cold voice. "You know the guy died."

Dan stood there, staring at Joe. He had changed—no, it wasn't that. He was still tall and dark and quiet. It was something else, a sudden droop to his shoulders, a hopeless resignation in eyes and voice. "All right," he said. "Yes, I knew he'd died. He fell over backward when I hit him. I had to hit him."

The big man smiled a little. "We remembered you were runner-up at the Lakeview Rodeo two years ago. We figured you'd show up at one of these sooner or later. Now, let's go."

They were turning away when Dan caught Joe's arm: "Joe—I—I. . . ." Words piled up in his throat, he was fighting to keep his voice steady when Joe said:

"It had to come, Dan. Forget it. You're a top logger now." Then he was gone, the pressure of his fingers on Dan's arm in farewell.

Dan stood there, the crowd milled around him, laughing, talking, and his own gang swarmed out of the stands yelling: "Dan! Hey, Dan!"

He turned, pushing blindly through the crowd, for he knew what they wanted. And later he'd meet them there. He'd line up at the bar with the best of them, there'd be back-slapping, drinking, and he'd be a top logging man. But right now he was Joe's kid and he couldn't let them see him cry.

Suggested Further Reading

WORKS BY MOREY
Gentle Ben. New York: Dutton, 1965.
Kavik, the Wolf Dog. New York: Dutton, 1968.
Run Far, Run Fast. New York: Dutton, 1974.
Year of the Black Pony. New York: Dutton, 1976.

WORKS ABOUT MOREY
"Morey, Walt(er Nelson)." *Something about the Author*, Vol. 51. Detroit: Gale Research Co., 1988, pp. 124-131.

Beverly Cleary

Beverly Cleary was born Beverly Bunn in McMinnville, Oregon, in 1916. Her early years were spent on a farm near Yamhill. Later her family moved to Portland, where she attended Fernwood and Gregory Heights elementary schools and Grant High School. Her early life is recorded in her fine autobiography, *A Girl from Yamhill*. She experienced some reading difficulty in her early years in school, which may account for her keen understanding of children with school problems, a frequent situation in her books. After overcoming her reading problems, she became an avid reader and resolved to write books for boys and girls when she grew up. She wanted to write stories which would be honest and funny, the sorts of stories which she loved in the "Our Gang" comedies at the movies, stories which were being lived in her life and the lives of her friends, but which rarely found their way into the usual sorts of children's books. Those who have read her stories know that she achieved her goal.

Her thirty-plus books have won many awards, including the Newbery Medal, the Laura Ingalls Wilder Award, and over 35 statewide awards. Her "Ramona" books, from one of which (*Ramona the Brave*) the following story is taken, have been the basis for a television series, as has *The Mouse and the Motorcycle*. She lives now in Carmel, California.

Owl Trouble

One afternoon late in September, when the air was hazy with smoke from distant forest fires and the sun hung in the sky like an orange volleyball, Ramona was sharpening her pencil as an excuse to look out the window at Miss Binney's afternoon kindergarten class, busy drawing butterflies with colored chalk on the asphalt of the playground. This had been a disappointing day for Ramona, who had come to school eager to tell about her new room, which was almost completed. Mrs. Griggs said they did not have time for Show and Tell that morning. Ramona had sat up as tall as she could, but Mrs. Griggs chose Patty to lead the flag salute.

How happy the kindergartners looked out in the smoky autumn sunshine! Ramona turned the handle of the pencil sharpener more and more slowly while she admired the butterflies with pink wings and yellow spots and butterflies with green wings and orange spots. She longed to be outside drawing with those bright chalks.

At the same time Ramona wondered what Beezus was doing upstairs in Mr. Cardoza's room. Beezus was enjoying school. Every time Beezus opened her mouth at home it was Mr. Cardoza this or Mr. Cardoza that. Mr. Cardoza let his class push their desks around any way they wanted. Mr. Cardoza—guess what!—drove a red sports car. Mr. Cardoza let his class bring mice to school. Mr. Cardoza said funny things that made his class laugh. When his class grew too noisy, he said, "All right, let's quiet down to a dull roar." Mr. Cardoza expected his class to have good manners. . . .

Mrs. Griggs's calm voice interrupted Ramona's thoughts. "Ramona, remember your seat."

Ramona, who discovered she had ground her pencil in half, remembered her seat. She sat quietly as Mrs. Griggs pushed a lock of hair behind her ear and said, as she had said every day since first grade had started, "We are not in kindergarten any longer. We are in the first grade, and people in the first grade must learn to be good workers."

What Mrs. Griggs did not seem to understand was that Ramona was a good worker. She had learned *bunny* and *apple* and *airplane* and all the other words in her new reader. When Mrs. Griggs read out, "Toys," Ramona could circle *toys* in her workbook. She was not like poor little Davy, who was still stuck on *saw* and *was*. If the book said *saw*, Davy read *was*. If the book said *dog*, Davy read *god*. Ramona felt so sorry for Davy that whenever she could she tried to help him circle the right pictures in his workbook. Mrs. Griggs did not understand that Ramona wanted to help Davy. She always told Ramona to keep her eyes on her own work. "Keep your eyes on your own work," was a favorite saying of Mrs. Griggs. Another was, "Nobody likes a tattletale." If Joey complained that Eric J. hit him, Mrs. Griggs answered, "Joey, nobody likes a tattletale."

Now Mrs. Griggs was saying, "If Susan and Howie and Davy were eating apples and gave apples to Eric J. and Patty, how many people would have apples?" Ramona sat quietly while half the class waved their hands.

"Ramona," said Mrs. Griggs, in a voice that hinted she had caught Ramona napping.

"Five," answered Ramona. She was bored, not napping. She had learned to think about school-work, and at the same time think about other things in a private corner of her mind. "Mrs. Griggs, when do we get to make paper-bag owls?"

Susan spoke without raising her hand. "Yes, Mrs. Griggs. You said we would get to make wise old owls for Parents' Night." Parents' Night was not the same as Open House. On Parents' Night the children stayed home while parents came to school to listen to teachers explain what the children were going to learn during the school year.

"Yes," said Howie. "We remembered to bring our paper bags from home."

Mrs. Griggs looked tired. She glanced at the clock.

"Whoo-whoo!" hooted Davy, which was brave of him and, as Ramona could not help thinking, rather kindergartenish. Others must not have agreed with this thought, for Mrs. Griggs's room was filled with a hubbub of hoots.

Mrs. Griggs tucked the wisp of hair behind her ear and gave up. "All right, class. Since the afternoon is so warm, we will postpone our seatwork and work on our owls."

Instantly Room One was wide awake. Paper bags and crayons came out of desks. The scissors monitor passed out scissors. The paper monitor passed out squares of orange, black, and yellow paper. Mrs. Griggs got out the pastepots and paper bags for those who had forgotten to bring theirs from home. The class would make owls, print their names on them, and set them up on their desks for their parents to admire.

The minutes on the electric clock clicked by with an astonishing speed. Mrs. Griggs showed the class how to make orange triangles for beaks and big yellow circles with smaller black circles on top for eyes. She told Patty not to worry if her bag had *Frosty Ice Cream Bag* printed on one side. Just turn it over and use the other side. Most people tried to make their owls look straight ahead, but Eric R. made his owl cross-eyed. Ramona tried her eyes in several positions and finally decided to have them looking off to the right. Then she noticed Susan's owl was looking off to the right, too.

Ramona frowned and picked up her black crayon. Since the owl was supposed to look wise, she drew spectacles around his eyes, and out of the corner of her eye, she noticed Susan doing the same thing. Susan was copying Ramona's owl! "Copycat!" whispered Ramona, but Susan ignored her by going over her crayon lines to make them blacker.

"Ramona, pay attention to your own work," said Mrs. Griggs. "Howie, it is not necessary to pound your eyes down with your fist. The paste will make them stick."

Ramona pulled her owl closer to her chest and tried to hide it in the circle of her arm, so that old copycat Susan could not see. With her brown crayon she drew wings and began to cover her owl with V's, which represented feathers.

By now Mrs. Griggs was walking up and down between the desks admiring and commenting on the owls, Karen's owl was such a nice, neat owl. My, what big eyes Patty's owl had! George wasted paste. So had several others. "Class, when we waste paste," said Mrs. Griggs, "and then pound our eyes down with our fists, our eyes skid." Ramona congratulated herself on her owl's nonskid eyes.

Mrs. Griggs paused between Ramona's and Susan's desks. Ramona bent over her owl, because she wanted to surprise Mrs. Griggs when it was finished. "What a wise old owl Susan has made!" Mrs. Griggs held up Susan's owl for the class to see while Susan tried to look modest and pleased at the same time. Ramona was furious. Susan's owl had wings and feathers exactly like her owl. Susan had peeked! Susan had copied! She scowled at Susan and thought, copycat, copycat! She longed to tell Mrs. Griggs that Susan copied, but she knew what the answer would be. "Ramona, nobody likes a tattletale."

Mrs. Griggs continued to admire Susan's owl. "Susan, your owl is looking at something. What do you think he's looking at?"

"Um-m." Susan was taken by surprise. "Um-m. Another owl?"

How dumb, thought Ramona. He's looking at a bat, a mouse, a witch riding on a broomstick, Superman, anything but another owl.

Mrs. Griggs suspended Susan's owl with two paper clips to the wire across the top of the blackboard for all to admire. "Class, it is time to clean up our desk. Scissors monitor, collect the scissors," said Mrs. Griggs. "Leave your owls on your desks for me to hang up after the paste dries."

Ramona stuffed her crayons into the box so hard that she broke several, but she did not care. She refused to look at Susan. She looked at her own owl, which no longer seemed like her own. Suddenly she hated it. Now everyone would think Ramona had copied Susan's owl, when it was the other way around.

They would call her Ramona Copycat instead of Ramona Kitty Cat. With both hands she crushed her owl, her beautiful wise owl, into a wad and squashed it down as hard as she could. Then, with her head held high, she marched to the front of the room and flung it into the wastebasket. As the bell rang, she marched out of the room without looking back.

All that week Ramona stared at the owls above the blackboard. Cross-eyed owls, pastewaster's owls with eyes that had skidded off in all directions, one-eyed owls made by those so anxious not to waste paste that they had not used enough, and right in the center Susan's wise and handsome owl copied from Ramona's owl.

If Mrs. Griggs noticed that Ramona's owl was missing, she said nothing. The afternoon of Parents' Night she unclipped the owls from the wire and passed them out to their owners along with sheets of old newspaper for wadding up and stuffing inside the owls to make them stand up. Miserable because she had no owl to stand upon her desk, Ramona pretended to be busy making her desk tidy.

"Ramona, what happened to your owl?" asked Susan, who knew very well what had happened to Ramona's owl.

"You shut up," said Ramona.

"Mrs. Griggs, Ramona doesn't have an owl," said Howie, who was the kind of boy who always looked around the classroom to make sure everything was in order.

Ramona scowled.

"Why, Ramona," said Mrs. Griggs. "What happened to your owl?"

Ramona spoke with all the dignity she could muster. "I do not care for owls." She did care. She cared so much it hurt, but Mrs. Griggs was not going to call her a tattletale.

Mrs. Griggs looked at Ramona as if she were trying to understand something. All she said was, "All right, Ramona, if that's the way you feel."

That was not the way Ramona felt, but she was relieved to have Mrs. Griggs's permission to remain owlless on Parents' Night. She felt unhappy and confused. Which was worse, a copycat or a tattletale? Ramona thought a copycat was worse. She half-heartedly joined the class in cleaning up the room for their parents, and every time she passed Susan's desk, she grew more angry. Susan was a copycat and a cheater. Ramona longed to seize one of those curls, stretch it out as far as she could, and then let it go. *Boing*, she thought, but she kept her hands to herself, which was not easy even though she was in the first grade.

Susan sat her owl up on her desk and gave it a little pat. Fury made Ramona's chest feel tight. Susan was pretending not to notice Ramona.

At last the room was in order for Parents' Night. Twenty-five owls stood up straight looking in all directions. The bell rang. Mrs. Griggs took her place by the door as the class began to leave the room.

Ramona slid out of her seat. Her chest felt tighter. Her head told her to keep her hands to herself, but her hands did not obey. They seized Susan's owl. They crushed the owl with a sound of crackling paper.

Susan gasped. Ramona twisted the owl as hard as she could until it looked like nothing but an old paper bag scribbled with crayon. Without meaning to, Ramona had done a terrible thing.

"Mrs. Griggs!" cried Susan. "Ramona scrunched my owl!"

"Tattletale." Ramona threw the twisted bag on the floor, and as Mrs. Griggs approached to see what had happened, she dodged past her teacher, out the door and down the hall, running as fast as she could, even though running in the halls was forbidden. She wove through the upper classes, who had come down the stairs. She plowed through the other first grade coming out of Room Two. She jumped down the steps and was out of the building on her way home, running as hard as she could, her sandals pounding on the sidewalk and crackling through fallen leaves. She ran as if she were pursued by Susan, Mrs. Griggs, the principal, all of Room One, the whole school. She ran from her conscience and from God, who, as they said in Sunday School, was everywhere. She ran as if Something was coming to get her. She ran until her lungs felt as if they were bursting with the smoky air. She ran until her sandals slipped on dry leaves and she fell sprawling on the sidewalk. Ignoring the pain, she scrambled to her feet and fled home with blood trickling from her knees.

Ramona burst through the back door, safe from Something. "Mama! Mama! I fell down!" she managed between gasps.

"Oh, poor baby!" Mrs. Quimby took one look at Ramona's bloody legs and led her into the bathroom, where she knelt and cleaned the wounds, dabbed them with antiseptic, and covered them with Band-Aids. Her mother's sympathy made Ramona feel very sorry for herself. Poor little misunderstood first grader.

Mrs. Quimby wiped Ramona's sweaty tear-stained face with a damp washcloth, kissed Ramona for comfort, and said, "That's my brave girl."

Ramona wanted to say, But I'm not brave, Mama. I'm scared because I did something bad. Yet she could not bring herself to admit the truth. Poor little Ramona with her wounded knees. It was all mean old Susan's fault for being such a copycat.

Mrs. Quimby sat back on her heels. "Guess what?" she said.

"What?" Ramona hoped for a glorious surprise to make up for her unhappy day. Ramona always longed for glorious surprises. That was the way she was.

"The workmen finished the new room, and before they left they moved your bed and the dresser and bookcase we had stored in the garage, and to-night you are going to sleep in your very own room!"

"Really?" This actually was a glorious surprise. There had been days when the workmen had not come at all, and the whole Quimby family had despaired of the room ever being completed. Ramona's knees hurt, but who cared? She ran down the hall to see the room for herself.

Yes, there was her bed in one corner, the bookcase filled with more toys than books in another, and against the wall, the dresser.

For the first time Ramona looked into her very own mirror in her very own room. She saw a stranger, a girl with red eyes and a puffy, tear-stained face, who did not look at all the way Ramona pictured herself. Ramona thought of herself as the kind of girl everyone should like, but this girl. . . .

Ramona scowled, and the girl scowled back. Ramona managed a small smile. So did the girl. Ramona felt better. She wanted the girl in the mirror to like her.

Suggested Further Reading

WORKS BY CLEARY
Henry and Ribsy. New York: William Morrow, 1954.
The Mouse and the Motorcycle. New York: William Morrow, 1965.
Ramona the Brave. New York: William Morrow, 1975.
A Girl from Yamhill: A Memoir. New York: Dell, 1988.

WORKS ABOUT CLEARY
"Beverly Cleary." In *Something about the Author*, vol. 43, ed. Anne Commire. Detroit: Gale Research Co., 1986, pp. 53-61.

Modern and Contemporary
Oregon Short Fiction

Bernard Malamud

Born in Brooklyn, New York, in 1914 to Russian Jewish parents, Bernard Malamud achieved wide fame as a writer before he died in New York City in 1986. As a young man, he taught English at Harlem High School and in evening classes while earning a master's degree from Columbia University. Afterward, he came to Corvallis, where he taught at Oregon State University from 1949 to 1961, when he left for Bennington College in Vermont. Although only one of Malamud's major novels, *A New Life,* is set in Oregon, his remarkable literary career was launched at Corvallis, where he published his first four books, and won five literary prizes, including the National Book Award. At his death he was working on a novel about the Nez Perce in the Northwest, recently published as *The People*, along with several previously uncollected stories. One of these stories is presented here. It could be set in Oregon.

Although known as a Jewish writer, Malamud saw himself as interested in a wider human spectrum: those who are not blessed by life, outsiders who are struggling to get along. In this sense, Oregon is much involved in Malamud's work. As Suzanne Clark says, his fiction "teaches us to include him in our list of Oregon writers not because he typifies a pure regional type, but because he represents the necessity of admitting strangeness into the history of our lives if we will be human. In his life and work he reminds us that the study of Oregon writers ought to be multicultural."

Riding Pants

After a supper of fried kidneys and brains—he was thoroughly sick of every kind of meat—Herm quickly cleared the table and piled the dirty dishes in with the oily pans in the metal sink. He planned to leave like the wind, but in the thinking of it hesitated just long enough for his father to get his tongue free.

"Herm," said the butcher in a tired but angry voice as he stroked the fat-to-bursting beef-livered cat that looked like him, "you better think of getting them fancy pants off and giving me a hand. I never heard of a boy of sixteen years wearing riding pants for all day when he should be thinking to start some steady work."

He was sitting, with the cat on his knees, in a rocker in the harshly lit kitchen behind the butcher shop where they always ate since the death of the butcher's wife. He had on—it never seemed otherwise—his white store jacket with the bloody sleeves, an apron, also blood-smeared and tight around his bulging belly, and the stupid yellow pancake of a straw hat that he wore in storm, sleet, or dead of winter. His mustache was gray, his lips thin, and his eyes, once blue as ice, were dark with fatigue.

"Not in a butcher store, Pa," Herm answered.

"What's the matter with one?" said the butcher, sitting up and looking around with exaggerated movements of the head.

Herm turned away. "Blood," he said sideways, "and chicken feathers."

The butcher slumped back in the chair.

"The Lord made certain creatures designed for man to satisfy his craving for food. Meat and fowl are full of proteins and vitamins. Somebody has to carve the animal and trim the meat clear of bone and gristle. There's no shame attached to such work. I did it my whole life long and never stole a cent from no one."

Herm considered whether there was a concealed stab in his words but he could find none. He had not stolen anything since he was thirteen and the butcher was never one to carry a long grudge.

"Meat might be good, but I don't have to like it."

"What do you like, Herm?"

Herm thought of his riding pants and the leather boots he was saving for. He knew, though, what his father meant—that he never stuck to a job. After he quit school he had a paper route, but the pay was chicken feed, so he left that and did lawn-mowing and cellar-cleaning, but that was not steady enough, so he quit that too, but not before he had enough to buy a pair of riding pants.

Since he could think of nothing to say, he tried to walk out, but his father called him back.

"Herm, I'm a mighty tired man since your momma died. I don't get near enough rest and I need it. I can't afford to pay a butcher's clerk because my take is not good. As a matter of fact it's bad. I'm every day losing customers for the reason that I can't give them the service they're entitled to. I know you're favorable to delivering orders but I need more of your help. You didn't like high school and asked me to sign you out. I did that, but you haven't been doing anything worthwhile for the past two months, so I decided I could use you in here. What do you say?"

"What am I supposed to say?"

"Yes or no, damn it."

"Then no, damn it," Herm said, his face flaring. "I hate butcher stores. I hate guts and chicken feathers, and I want to live my own kind of life and not yours."

And though the butcher called and called, he ran out of the store.

That night, while Herm was asleep, the butcher took his riding pants and locked them in the closet of his bedroom, but Herm guessed where they were and the next day went to the hardware store down the block, bought a skeleton key for a dime, and sneaked his riding pants out of his father's closet.

*   *   *

When Herm had just learned to ride he liked to go often, though he didn't always enjoy it. In the beginning he was too conscious of the horse's body, the massive frame he had to straddle, each independent rippling muscle, and the danger that he might have his head kicked in if he fell under the thundering hooves. And the worst of it was that sometimes while riding he was conscious of the interior layout of the horse, where the different cuts of round, rump, and flank were, as if the horse were stripped and labeled on a chart, posted, as a steer was, on the wall in the back of the store. He kept thinking of this the night he was out on Girlie, the roan they told him he wasn't ready for, and she had got the reins from him and turned and ran the way she wanted, shaking him away when he tried to hold her back, till she came to the stable with him on her like a sack of beans and everybody laughing. After that he had made up his mind to quit horses, and did, but one spring night he went back and took out Girlie, who, though lively, was docile to his touch and went with him everywhere and did everything he wanted; and the next morning he took his last twenty-five dollars out of the savings account and bought the riding pants, and that same night dreamed he was on a horse that dissolved under him as he rode but there he was with his riding pants on galloping away on thin air.

*   *   *

Herm woke to hear the sound of a cleaver on the wooden block down in the store. As it was still night he jumped out of bed frightened and searched for his riding pants. They were not in the bottom drawer where he had hidden them under a pile of his mother's clothes, so he ran to his father's closet and saw it was open and the butcher not in bed. In his pajamas Herm raced downstairs and tried to get into the butcher shop, but he was locked out and stood by the door crying as his father chopped the tightly rolled pants as if they were a bologna, with the slices falling off at each sock of the cleaver onto the floor, where the cat sniffed the uncurled remains.

*   *   *

He woke with the moon on his bed, rose and went on bare toes into his father's room, which looked so different now that it was no longer his mother's, and tried to find the butcher's trousers. They were hanging on a chair but without the store keys in the pockets, or the billfold, he realized, blushing. Some loose change clinked and the butcher stirred in the creaking bed. Herm stood desperately still but, when his father had quieted, hung the pants and tiptoed back to his room. He pushed up the window softly, deciding he would slide down the telephone wires to the back yard and get in that way. Once within the store he would find a knife, catch the cat, and dismember it, leaving the pieces for his father to find in the morning; but not his son.

Testing the waterspout, he found it too shaky, but the wires held his weight, so he slid slowly down to the ground. Then he climbed up the sill and tried to push on the window. The butcher had latched it, not knowing Herm had loosened the screws of the latch; it gave and he was able to climb in. As his foot touched the floor, he thought he heard something scamper away but wasn't sure. Afraid to pull the light on because the Holmes police usually passed along the block this time of night, he said softly in the dark, "Here, kitty, here, kitty kitty," and felt around on the pile of burlap bags, but the cat was not where she usually slept.

He felt his way into the store and looked in the windows and they too were empty except for the pulpy blood droppings from the chickens that had hung on the hooks. He tried the paper-bag slots behind the counter and the cat was not there either, so he called again, "Here, kitty kitty kitty," but could not find it. Then he noticed the icebox door had been left ajar, which surprised him

because the butcher always yelled whenever anyone kept it open too long. He went in thinking of course the damn cat was there, poking its greedy head into the bowl of slightly sour chicken livers the butcher conveniently kept on the bottom shelf.

"Here, kitty," he whispered as he stepped into the box, and was completely unprepared when the door slammed shut behind him. He thought at first, so what, it could be opened from the inside, but then it flashed on him that the butcher had vaguely mentioned he was having trouble with the door handle and the locksmith was taking it away till tomorrow. He thought then, Oh, my God, I'm trapped here and will freeze to death, and his skull all but cracked with terror. Fumbling his way to the door, he worked frantically on the lock with his numbed fingers, wishing he had at least switched on the light from outside where the switch was, and he could feel the hole where the handle had been but was unable to get his comb or house key in to turn it. He thought if he had a screwdriver that might do it, or he could unscrew the metal plate and pick the lock apart, and for a second his heart leaped in expectation that he had taken a knife with him, but he hadn't.

Holding his head back to escape the impaling hooks, he reached his hand along the shelves on the side of the icebox and then the top shelf, cautiously feeling if the butcher had maybe left some tool around. His hand moved forward and stopped; it took him a minute to comprehend it was not going farther, because his fingers had entered a moist bony cavern; he felt suddenly shocked, as if he were touching the inside of an electric socket, but the hole was in a pig's head where an eye had been. Stepping back, he tripped over something he thought was the cat, but when he touched it, it was a bag of damp squirmy guts. As he flung it away he lost his balance and his face brushed against the clammy open side of a bleeding lamb. He sat down in the sawdust on the floor and bit his knuckles.

After a time, his fright prevented any further disgust. He tried to reason out what to do, but there was nothing he could think of; so he tried to think what time it was and could he live till his father came down to open the store. He had heard of people staying alive by beating their arms together and walking back and forth till help came, but when he tried that it tired him more, so that he began to feel very sleepy, and though he knew he oughtn't, he sat down again. He might have cried, but the tears were frozen in, and he began to wonder from afar if there was some quicker way to die. By now the icebox had filled with white mist, and from the distance, through the haze, a winged black horse moved toward him. This is it, he thought, and got up to mount it, but his foot slipped from the stirrup and he fell forward, his head bonging against the door, which opened, and he fell out on the floor.

*   *   *

He woke in the morning with a cutting headache and would have stayed in bed but was too hungry, so he dressed and went down-stairs. He had six dollars in his pocket, all he owned in the world; he intended to have breakfast and after that pretend to go for a newspaper and never come back again.

The butcher was sitting in the rocker, sleepily stroking the cat. Neither he nor Herm spoke. There were some slices of uncooked bacon on a plate on the table and two eggs in a cardboard carton, but he could not look at them. He poured himself a cup of black coffee and drank it with an unbuttered roll.

A customer came into the store and the butcher rose with a sigh to serve her. The cat jumped off his lap and followed him. They looked like brothers. Herm turned away. This was the last he would see of either of them.

He heard a woman's resounding voice ordering some porterhouse steak and a chunk of calves' liver, nice and juicy for the dogs, and recognized her as Mrs. Gibbs, the doctor's wife, whom all the storekeepers treated like the Empress of Japan, all but kissing her rear end, especially his father, and this was what he wanted his own son to do. Then he heard the butcher go into the icebox and he shivered. The butcher came out and hacked at something with the cleaver and Herm shivered again. Finally the lady, who had talked loud and steadily, the butcher always assenting, was served. The door closed behind her corpulent bulk and the store was quiet. The butcher returned and sat in his chair, fanning his red face with his straw hat, his bald head glistening with sweat. It took him a half hour to recover every time he waited on her.

When the door opened again a few minutes later, it almost seemed as if he would not be able to get up, but Mrs. Gibbs's bellow brought him immediately to his feet. "Coming," he called with a sudden frog in his throat and hurried inside. Then Herm heard her yelling about something, but her voice was so powerful the sound blurred. He got up and stood at the door.

It was her, all right, a tub of a woman with a large hat, a meaty face, and a thick rump covered in mink.

"You stupid dope," she shouted at the butcher, "you don't even know how to wrap a package. You let the liver blood run all over my fur. My coat is ruined."

The anguished butcher attempted to apologize, but her voice beat him down. He tried to apologize with his hands and his rolling eyes and with his yellow straw hat, but she would have none of it. When he went forth with a clean rag and tried to wipe the mink, she drove him back with an angry yelp. The door shut with a bang. On the counter stood her dripping bag. Herm could see his father had tried to save paper.

He went back to the table. About a half hour later the butcher came in. His face was deathly white and he looked like a white scarecrow with a yellow straw hat. He sat in the rocker without rocking. The cat tried to jump into his lap but he wouldn't let it and sat there looking into the back yard and far away.

Herm too was looking into the back yard. He was thinking of all the places he could go where there were horses. He wanted to be where there were many and he could ride them all.

But then he got up and reached for the blood-smeared apron hanging on a hook. He looped the loop over his head and tied the strings around him. They covered where the riding pants had been, but he felt as though he still had them on.

Suggested Further Reading

Works by Malamud

The Natural. New York: Harcourt, Brace, 1952.

The Assistant. New York: Farrar, Straus, Giroux, 1957.

The Magic Barrel (winner of the National Book Award). New York: Farrar, Straus, Giroux, 1958.

A New Life. New York: Farrar, Straus, Giroux, 1961.

The Fixer (winner of the Pulitzer Prize). New York: Farrar, Straus, Giroux, 1966.

The Stories of Bernard Malamud. New York: Farrar, Straus, Giroux, 1983.

The People and Uncollected Stories, ed. Robert Giroux. New York: Farrar, Straus, Giroux, 1989.

Works about Malamud

Astro, Richard, and Jackson Benson, eds. *The Fiction of Bernard Malamud.* Corvallis: Oregon State University Press, 1977.

Clark, Suzanne. "Bernard Malamud as the Western Other." *Oregon English Journal* 13:1 (Spring 1991): 24-27.

Solotaroff, Robert. *Bernard Malamud: A Study of the Short Fiction.* Boston: Twayne, 1989.

Ursula Le Guin

Daughter of a noted anthropologist (Alfred Louis Kroeber) and writer (Theodora Kroeber), Ursula Le Guin, born in 1929, has been a long-time resident of Portland. She is the author of a number of celebrated books, including *The Left Hand of Darkness, The Farthest Shore, The Word for World Is Forest, The Lathe of Heaven,* and *Always Coming Home.* She writes essays and poetry as well as fiction. She has won many writing honors, including Hugo, Nebula, and National Book awards, the latter for *The Farthest Shore.*

Although Le Guin is known primarily as a science fiction and fantasy writer, her work goes beyond narrow perceptions of these labels to include personal, social, and environmental problems which are central to real human lives. The work which follows was winner of the Hugo Award for best short story, 1974. Her introductory remarks to the tale reveal just how deeply the moral human condition is a part of her mythical regions, in this case, a utopian land whose presumably favored status may suggest some version of Oregon. At least that idea may be hinted at in the story's title.

The central idea of this psychomyth, the scapegoat, turns up in Dostoyevsky's *Brothers Karamazov*, and several people have asked me, rather suspiciously, why I gave the credit to William James. The fact is, I haven't been able to re-read Dostoyevsky, much as I loved him, since I was twenty-five, and I'd simply forgotten he used the idea. But when I met it in James's "The Moral Philospher and the Moral Life," it was with a shock of recognition. Here is how James puts it:

> Or if the hypothesis were offered us of a world in which Messrs. Fourier's and Bellamy's and Morris's utopias should all be outdone, and millions kept permanently happy on the one simple condition that a certain lost soul on the far-off edge of things should lead a life of lonely torment, what except a specific and independent sort of emotion can it be which would make us immediately feel, even though an impulse arose within us to clutch at the happiness so offered, how hideous a thing would be its enjoyment when deliberately accepted as the fruit of such a bargain?

The dilemma of the American conscience can hardly be better stated. Dostoyevsky was a great artist, and a radical one, but his early social radicalism reversed itself, leaving him a violent reactionary. Whereas the American James who seems so mild, so naively gentlemanly—look how he says "us," assuming all his readers are as decent as himself!—was, and remained, and remains, a genuinely radical thinker. Directly after the "lost soul" passage he goes on,

> All the higher, more penetrating ideals are revolutionary. They present themselves far less in the guise of effects of past experience than in that of probable causes of future experience, factors to which the environment and the lessons it has so far taught us must learn to bend.

The application of those two sentences to this story, and to science fiction, and to all thinking about the future, is quite direct. Ideals as "the probable causes of future experience"—that is a subtle and an exhilarating remark!

Of course I didn't read James and sit down and say, Now I'll write a story about that "lost soul." It seldom works that simply. I sat down and started a story, just because I felt like it, with nothing but the *word* "Omelas" in mind. It came from a road sign: Salem (Oregon) backwards. Don't you read road signs backwards? POTS. WOLS nerdlihc. Ocsicnarf Nas . . . Salem equals schelomo equals salaam equals Peace. Melas. O melas. Omelas. Homme hélas. "Where do you get your ideas from, Ms. Le Guin?" From forgetting Dostoyevsky and reading road signs backwards, naturally. Where else?

Ursula Le Guin

The Ones Who Walk Away from Omelas

With a clamor of bells that set the swallows soaring, the Festival of Summer came to the city Omelas, bright-towered by the sea. The rigging of the boats in harbor sparkled with flags. In the streets between houses with red roofs and painted walls, between old moss-grown gardens and under avenues of trees, past great parks and public buildings, processions moved. Some were decorous: old people in long stiff robes of mauve and grey, grave master workmen, quiet, merry women carrying their babies and chatting as they walked. In other streets the music beat faster, a shimmering of gong and tambourine, and the people went dancing, the procession was a dance. Children dodged in and out, their high calls rising like the swallows' crossing flights over the music and the singing. All the processions wound towards the north side of the city, where on the great water-meadow called the Green Fields boys and girls, naked in the bright air, with mud-stained feet and ankles and long, lithe arms, exercised their restive horses before the race. The horses wore no gear at all but a halter without bit. Their manes were braided with streamers of silver, gold, and green. They flared their nostrils and pranced and boasted to one another; they were vastly excited, the horse being the only animal who has adopted our ceremonies as his own. Far off to the north and west the mountains stood up half encircling Omelas on her bay. The air of morning was so clear that the snow still crowning the Eighteen Peaks burned with white-gold fire across the miles of sunlit air, under the dark blue of the sky. There was just enough wind to make the banners that marked the racecourse snap and flutter now and then. In the silence of the broad green meadows one could hear the music winding through the city streets, farther and nearer and ever approaching, a cheerful faint sweetness of the air that from time to time trembled and gathered together and broke out into the great joyous clanging of the bells.

Joyous! How is one to tell about joy? How describe the citizens of Omelas?

They were not simple folk, you see, though they were happy. But we do not say the words of cheer much any more. All smiles have become archaic. Given a description such as this one tends to make certain assumptions. Given a description such as this one tends to look next for the King, mounted on a splendid stallion and surrounded by his noble knights, or perhaps in a golden litter borne by great-muscled slaves. But there was no king. They did not use swords, or keep slaves. They were not barbarians. I do not know the rules and laws of

their society, but I suspect that they were singularly few. As they did without monarchy and slavery, so they also got on without the stock exchange, the advertisement, the secret police, and the bomb. Yet I repeat that these were not simple folk, not dulcet shepherds, noble savages, bland utopians. They were not less complex than us. The trouble is that we have a bad habit, encouraged by pedants and sophisticates, of considering happiness as something rather stupid. Only pain is intellectual, only evil interesting. This is the treason of the artist: a refusal to admit the banality of evil and the terrible boredom of pain. If you can't lick 'em, join 'em. If it hurts, repeat it. But to praise despair is to condemn delight, to embrace violence is to lose hold of everything else. We have almost lost hold; we can no longer describe a happy man, nor make any celebration of joy. How can I tell you about the people of Omelas? They were not naïve and happy children—though their children were, in fact, happy. They were mature, intelligent, passionate adults whose lives were not wretched. O miracle! but I wish I could describe it better. I wish I could convince you.

Omelas sounds in my words like a city in a fairy tale, long ago and far away, once upon a time. Perhaps it would be best if you imagined it as your own fancy bids, assuming it will rise to the occasion, for certainly I cannot suit you all. For instance, how about technology? I think that there would be no cars or helicopters in and above the streets; this follows from the fact that the people of Omelas are happy people. Happiness is based on a just discrimination of what is necessary, what is neither necessary nor destructive, and what is destructive. In the middle category, however—that of the unnecessary but undestructive, that of comfort, luxury, exuberance, etc.—they could perfectly well have central heating, subway trains, washing machines, and all kinds of marvelous devices not yet invented here, floating light-sources, fuelless power, a cure for the common cold. Or they could have none of that: it doesn't matter. As you like it. I incline to think that people from towns up and down the coast have been coming in to Omelas during the last days before the Festival on very fast little trains and double-decked trams, and that the train station of Omelas is actually the handsomest building in town, though plainer than the magnificent Farmers' Market. But even granted trains, I fear that Omelas so far strikes some of you as goody-goody. Smiles, bells, parades, horses, bleh. If so, please add an orgy. If an orgy would help, don't hesitate. Let us not, however, have temples from which issue beautiful nude priests and priestesses already half in ecstasy and ready to copulate with any man or woman, lover or stranger, who desires union with the deep godhead of the blood, although that was my first idea. But really it would be better not to have any temples in Omelas—at least, not manned temples. Religion yes, clergy no. Surely the beautiful nudes can just wander about, offering themselves like divine soufflés to the hunger of the needy and the rapture of the flesh. Let them join the processions. Let tambourines be struck above the copulations, and the glory of desire be proclaimed upon the gongs, and (a not unimportant point) let the offspring of these delightful rituals be beloved and looked after by all. One thing I know there is none of in Omelas is guilt. But what else should there be? I thought at first there were no drugs, but that is puritanical. For those who like it, the faint insistent sweetness of *drooz* may perfume the ways of the city, *drooz* which first brings a great lightness and brilliance to the mind and limbs, and then after some hours a dreamy languor, and wonderful visions at last of the very arcana and inmost secrets of the Universe, as well as exciting the pleasure of sex beyond all belief; and it is not habit-forming. For more modest tastes I think there ought to be beer. What else, what else belongs in the joyous city ? The sense of victory, surely, the celebration of courage. But as we did without clergy, let us do without soldiers. The joy built upon successful slaughter is not the right kind of joy; it will not do; it is fearful and it is trivial. A boundless and generous contentment, a magnanimous triumph felt not against some outer enemy but in communion with the finest and fairest in the souls of all men everywhere and the splendor of the world's summer: this is what swells the hearts of the people of Omelas, and the victory they celebrate is that of life. I really don't think many of them need to take *drooz*.

Most of the processions have reached the Green Fields by now. A marvelous smell of cooking goes forth from the red and blue tents of the provisioners. The faces of small children are amiably sticky; in the benign grey beard of a man a couple of crumbs of rich pastry are entangled. The youths and girls have mounted their horses and are beginning to group around the starting line of the course. An old woman, small, fat, and laughing, is passing out flowers from a basket, and tall young men wear her flowers in their shining hair. A child of nine or ten sits at the edge of the crowd, alone, playing on a wooden flute. People pause to listen, and they smile, but they do not speak to him, for he never ceases playing and never sees them, his dark eyes wholly rapt in the sweet, thin magic of the tune.

He finishes, and slowly lowers his hands holding the wooden flute.

As if that little private silence were the signal, all at once a trumpet sounds from the pavilion near the starting line: imperious, melancholy, piercing. The horses rear on their slender legs, and some of them neigh in answer. Sober-faced, the young riders stroke the horses' necks and soothe them, whispering, "Quiet, quiet, there my beauty, my hope. . . ." They begin to form in rank along the starting line. The crowds along the racecourse are like a field of grass and flowers in the wind. The Festival of Summer has begun.

Do you believe? Do you accept the festival, the city, the joy? No? Then let me describe one more thing.

In a basement under one of the beautiful public buildings of Omelas, or perhaps in the cellar of one of its spacious private homes, there is a room. It has one locked door, and no window. A little light seeps in dustily between cracks in the boards, secondhand from a cobwebbed window somewhere across the cellar. In one corner of the little room a couple of mops, with stiff, clotted, foul-smelling heads, stand near a rusty bucket. The floor is dirt, a little damp to the touch, as cellar dirt usually is. The room is about three paces long and two wide: a mere broom closet or disused tool room. In the room a child is sitting. It could be a boy or a girl. It looks about six, but actually is nearly ten. It is feeble-minded. Perhaps it was born defective, or perhaps it has become imbecile through fear, malnutrition, and neglect. It picks its nose and occasionally fumbles vaguely with its toes or genitals, as it sits hunched in the corner far-thest from the bucket and the two mops. It is afraid of the mops. It finds them horrible. It shuts its eyes, but it knows the mops are still standing there; and the door is locked; and nobody will come. The door is always locked; and nobody ever comes, except that sometimes—the child has no understanding of time or interval—sometimes the door rattles terribly and opens, and a person, or several people, are there. One of them may come in and kick the child to make it stand up. The others never come close, but peer in at it with frightened, disgusted eyes. The food bowl and the water jug are hastily filled, the door is locked, the eyes disappear. The people at the door never say anything, but the child, who has not always lived in the tool room, and can remember sunlight and its mother's voice, sometimes speaks. "I will be good," it says. "Please let me out. I will be good!" They never answer. The child used to scream for help at night, and cry a good deal, but now it only makes a kind of whining, "eh-haa, eh-haa," and it speaks less and less often. It is so thin there are no calves to its legs; its belly protrudes; it lives on a half-bowl of corn meal and grease a day. It is naked. Its buttocks and thighs are a mass of festered sores, as it sits in its own excrement continually.

They all know it is there, all the people of Omelas. Some of them have come to see it, others are content merely to know it is there. They all know that it has to be there. Some of them understand why, and some do not, but they all understand that their happiness, the beauty of their city, the tenderness of their friendships, the health of their children, the wisdom of their scholars, the skill of their makers, even the abundance of their harvest and the kindly weathers of their skies, depend wholly on this child's abominable misery.

This is usually explained to children when they are between eight and twelve, whenever they seem capable of understanding; and most of those who come to see the child are young people, though often enough an adult comes, or comes back, to see the child. No matter how well the matter has been explained to them, these young spectators are always shocked and sickened at the sight. They feel disgust, which they had thought themselves superior to. They feel anger, outrage, impotence, despite all the explanations. They would like to do something for the child. But there is nothing they can do. If the child were brought up into the sunlight out of that vile place, if it were cleaned and fed and comforted, that would be a good thing, indeed; but if it were done, in that day and hour all the prosperity and beauty and delight of Omelas would wither and be destroyed. Those are the terms. To exchange all the goodness and grace of every life in Omelas for that single, small improvement: to throw away the happiness of thousands for the chance of the happiness of one: that would be to let guilt within the walls indeed.

The terms are strict and absolute; there may not even be a kind word spoken to the child.

Often the young people go home in tears, or in a tearless rage, when they have seen the child and faced this terrible paradox. They may brood over it for weeks or years. But as time goes on they begin to realize that even if the child could be released, it would not get much good of its freedom: a little vague pleasure of warmth and food, no doubt, but little more. It is too degraded and imbecile to know any real joy. It has been afraid too long ever to be free of fear. Its habits are too uncouth for it to respond to humane treatment. Indeed, after so long it would probably be wretched without walls about it to protect it, and darkness for its eyes, and its own excrement to sit in. Their tears at the bitter injustice dry when they begin to perceive the terrible justice of reality, and to accept it. Yet it is their tears and anger, the trying of their generosity and the acceptance of their helplessness, which are perhaps the true source of the splendor of their lives. Theirs is no vapid, irresponsible happiness. They know that they, like the child, are not free. They know compassion. It is the existence of the child, and their knowledge of its existence, that makes possible the nobility of their architecture, the poignancy of their music, the profundity of their science. It is because of the child that they are so gentle with children. They know that if the wretched one were not there snivelling in the dark, the other one, the flute-player, could make no joyful music as the young riders line up in their beauty for the race in the sunlight of the first morning of summer.

Now do you believe in them? Are they not more credible? But there is one more thing to tell, and this is quite incredible.

At times one of the adolescent girls or boys who go to see the child does not go home to weep or rage, does not, in fact, go home at all. Sometimes also a man or woman much older falls silent for a day or two, and then leaves home. These people go out into the street, and walk down the street alone. They keep walking, and walk straight out of the city of Omelas, through the beautiful gates. They keep walking across the farmlands of Omelas. Each one goes alone, youth or girl, man or woman. Night falls; the traveler must pass down village streets, between the houses with yellow-lit windows, and on out into the darkness of the fields. Each alone, they go west or north, towards the mountains. They go on. They leave Omelas, they walk ahead into the darkness, and they do not come back. The place they go towards is a place even less imaginable to most of us than the city of happiness. I cannot describe it at all. It is possible that it does not exist. But they seem to know where they are going, the ones who walk away from Omelas.

Suggested Further Reading

WORKS BY LE GUIN

The Left Hand of Darkness. New York: Ace Books, 1969.

The Lathe of Heaven. New York: Charles Scribner's Sons, 1971.

The Farthest Shore. New York: Atheneum, 1972.

The Wind's Twelve Quarters. New York: Harper and Row, 1975.

The Word for World Is Forest. New York: Berkley Publishing Company, 1976.

Always Coming Home. New York: Harper and Row, 1985.

WORKS ABOUT LE GUIN

Bucknall, Barbara, *Ursula Le Guin.* New York: Ungar, 1981.

Cummins, Elizabeth. *Understanding Ursula Le Guin.* Columbia: University of South Carolina Press, 1990.

Spivak, Charlotte. *Ursula Le Guin.* Boston: Twayne Publishers, 1984.

William Kittredge

Born in 1932 into a ranching family, William Kittredge grew up in the Warner Valley of Southeastern Oregon. He attended college at Oregon State University, where he tells, in his noteworthy book of essays, *Owning It All*, of being torn between the General Agriculture program and the writing classes of Bernard Malamud. The conflict continued until his thirty-third year, when he gave up managing the ranch and vowed that he would be a writer. He participated in the Writers' Workshop at the University of Iowa, then, in 1969, took a job teaching creative writing at the University of Montana, where he remains today, part of a remarkable creative heritage at Missoula, which includes such names as Harold G. Merriam, D'Arcy McNickle, A.B. Guthrie, Dorothy M. Johnson, Norman Maclean, Richard Hugo, Leslie Fiedler, Mary Clearman Blue, James Welch, and Annick Smith.

Native Cutthroat

Standing on the rim of the canyon of Denio Creek, Gus Eckert heard the undulating sound of four rifle shots, the first two quick, the last spaced a minute or so apart. He did not move until the last shot finished echoing. Someone shooting a deer. And while thinking that, sure it was nothing more, felt he had been himself attacked.

Porous volcanic rocks were embedded in the sandy ground at his feet. Along the canyon bottom, half in shadow, he could see aspen and willow already, early in October, turning color, their leaves a variety of shades between deep, flat green and yellow, beautiful and quiet. The streamcourse was also scattered with occasional pine, lumber trees isolated miles downstream from the timbered mountains where the creek began.

He began walking the canyon edge toward the break where the trail had gone down, and thought of the stream, water falling between rocks, swirling under a sod bank, places where trout would be hanging quietly, waiting. Gus had been looking forward to this trip since deciding on retirement and knew just which flies he would use and which holes he would fish and how he would work them. He wore hip-length wading boots and an old khaki shirt with bright patches of fresh cloth on the sleeves where his Tech Sergeant stripes had been, and carried a fly rod in its aluminum container and a landing net. A wicker creel hung over his shoulder.

The canyon, a few miles further downstream, opened into the valley where Gus had lived as a boy. His father, very old now, and retired, had worked as a herder for the large sheep ranch, the 7J, that headquartered by the creekmouth. The old man lived there yet, enclosed by the bare mountains, overlooking the swamp hayland and marshes and ponds edged by reeds higher than a man on horseback where water birds, Canadian geese and sand hill cranes and sometimes an avocet, wintered and hatched their young.

Once in the canyon Gus could see nothing beyond the rim. The sky was totally clear and pale, dusty blue-gray. The air was hot and still and the only sounds were his heavy breathing and the scrape of his feet, the rod case banging a rock, noises he really didn't hear.

Everything seemed slightly changed. He'd parked his new Ford pickup with its silver camper at the end of the rough desert road above the canyon. He'd traveled the road many times as a boy and now it was nearly gone, washed into trenches of gravel on the hillsides and grown up with brush across the alkali flats. The only people who come out here now, he thought, are fishermen, and not many of those. The sheep, since the building of the highway after the war, were trucked to the summer range, no longer trailed along this road by herders.

He rested and could see the abutment at the near end of the sheep bridge his father had helped build in the early 1920s, soon after coming from Germany. It seemed abandoned, like other things here.

As a boy Gus had ridden out in late summer to wait for his father to return from the range with the sheep. No one was ever certain when the old man would return, so Gus had come each day toward the end of August. He remembered riding an old blue-roan gelding, leaving the horse hobbled and grazing by the creek while he fished, sometimes stripping to swim in one of the pools above the sheep bridge or just lying quietly on his back in cool shallow water and watching the clouds. When it was evening and his father had not come, he would resaddle the horse and return to the valley.

Until the day that marked the end of his summer. On that day he would hear, from the road cut along the canyonside toward the bridge, the bell on the lead goat and a muffled bark from one of his father's dogs. The sheep, when he looked up, would be there browsing among the rocks and brush, would have come over the rim without his noticing. Later, after a time which made it seem the sheep and dogs were alone, his father's canvas-topped caravan trailer, an old wagon with a tent over the bed, would come into sight and start precariously down behind two aged mules. Gus stood now just above that road. It was nearly gone, covered by rockslides and brush.

Starting downhill again, Gus edged over a reef of crumbling lava boulders fallen from the shelf-like cliff of the rim and then through a thicket of dry mahogany brush. When he first heard the sound—something like the amplified buzzing of a locust—he was among juniper and rabbit brush.

He did not—for a moment—remember. Then he knew and stopped, balanced, his foot suspended above an embedded gray rock with pale green lichen traced in its crevices.

The snake, when he finally saw it among the shadowed remnants of silver grass under a clump of brush, was nearly ten feet away, its flat and triangular head hovering over a thick coil, gray and mottled and angry.

Scrambling uphill, slipping in loose dirt and gravel, Gus watched the reptile and wondered if he would be able to kill it without crushing the rattles, and was surprised that his first thought, even in the midst of quick fright, had been of that. He remembered killing snakes, stretching them out with a stick and smashing the head, saving the rattles in the way his father had shown him. It was a large snake, four or five feet long, and would carry ten or twelve rattles and a button. The old man would like that. He would grunt and carefully press them into the cotton-lined show box with the rest, the collection of his life-time, then look up and smile.

"Another one," he would say. "Someday they'll all be gone." He'd been killing snakes nearly fifty years, since first coming to this country, and still he could say things like that, and say them seriously.

Encumbered by his fishing gear, Gus moved down until he was level with the snake, then reached forward with the aluminum rod case, testing and probing.

The reaction was swift and violent, a strike against the metal Gus felt as a contact with flesh, throbbing and prolonged, as if the blow had been to himself, then a quick and smooth recoiling. Gus flicked a handful of dirt toward the snake, testing again, but this time the reptile remained static except for the wavering tail, hostile and ready, waiting in the gray shade for him to come closer or go away.

Gus was sweating now and a little sickened. His hands were soft and moist and trembled as he waited, attempting to draw himself to the task of killing. He could hear the creek water flowing among boulders in the canyon bottom, low and quiet and murmuring, and could sense from the light around him the sun close and brilliant in the dust blue sky, forcing heat into the stillness here below the rim.

He reached, without looking away from his snake, for a rock. And heard, above and behind him, discordant and out of pitch with the first, the sound of another.

Gus turned slowly and withdrew his hand and crouched and remembered old things he had heard about snakes traveling in pairs. Or in dens. They could be everywhere. He could only hear the second snake. It was somewhere close above him, out of sight.

He spun, fled down the hillside, and fell, landing on one shoulder and rolling onto his back, feeling the wicker crush beneath his weight. He lay a moment stunned, wondering if he were hurt, then sat up.

The creel was ruined. Since he could remember it had hung on the veranda porch of the unpainted four-room house where his father lived in the valley. The old man would be furious. Past eighty, crippled by age, unable to ever fish again, he would nevertheless be outraged by this clumsiness and waste.

Below, the rod case was undamaged. Gus climbed down to retrieve it. His shoulder ached and his palms were embedded with tiny weed thorns and his shirt was torn across the back.

He rested, picking out the thorns, no longer sweating so heavily or shaking. He remembered his father holding a snake with thumb and forefinger directly behind the head. The old man held the gaping fanged mouth out in front of his own face and laughed, let the writhing, tight twisting body circle his forearm, then slowly pinched until the back of the flat head was crushed. "There," he said. "That's how we do it." Then he cut the rattles from the twitching tail.

Gus began to climb back again, carefully working upward through the scattered brush, armed with a dry juniper limb and a large flat rock. He stayed as much as possible in the open ground between the brush clumps. The first snake was gone. There was no sound except his own, no warning.

They had escaped. Sweat ran in his eyes and burned and his shoulder ached. The reflecting sunlight was blinding. The snakes had to be coiled somewhere near, perhaps only a few yards away. He floundered uphill, thrashing angrily through the brush, breathless now and nearly exhausted, aware of nothing but the hillside and brush scratching at him, light and heat.

Then he had to rest and began to calm and realize the absurdity of what he was doing. The snakes could be coiled anywhere and strike quickly, as they warned, and their fangs would puncture and withdraw, leaving him to die alone in this heat, unable to climb the canyonside.

He could hear the creekwater flowing. The air would cool as evening came and the trout would begin to feed on the surface, splashing and rippling quietly. He rubbed sweat from his eyes and began to be appalled at the way he had been drawn toward the water.

"Retired," the old man had said, spitting in the homemade tin sink. As if he didn't understand, hadn't received the letters.

He had come here from Munich at the end of the old war. The good of Europe, he had told Gus, was gone, worn away by too many centuries of too many people. Too many wars and armies, centuries of killing. It was better here. Since coming to this valley he had never been away except to summer the sheep on the desert. His short thick hair had turned completely white and he was hunched forward by age until his head and neck were sunk between his shoulders.

The old man worked clumsily at fixing a pot of coffee, spilling the grounds and greenish dregs and sweeping them to the floor with the sleeve of his coarse-knit sweater. Gus remembered his mother knitting that sweater on winter nights when he was a child. During the years away, occasionally trying to remember his father, Gus had been able to recall only the deep animal smell of his clothing, the odor that seemed the strength of the man.

"So now what you got?" the old man asked, going slowly across to stoke the fire in the aged black cookstove. "Twenty over nothing."

"It was a living. Like the sheep." He had been secure and never hurried—drinking coffee in midmorning in the dark and ordered interiors of supply warehouses.

"A game for children."

"I got the pension."

His father snorted and went to pour the coffee and the talk stopped there. The old man wandered to raging about a fence west of the valley. "Fencing sheep," the old man said. "Thank God I'm old." Gus drank the coffee and didn't listen. He remembered his mother, the last time he saw her.

"A good man," she said. "Be a good man like your father. He was always the most gentle man." Once tall and erect with straight hair long and black over her shoulders, she had been stooped and nearly bald as she approached death. She had died nearly six years ago and been already buried when Gus arrived after flying from England.

"She was finished," his father had said. "There was no need for you to have come all this way because there's nothing to be done. She had life. It goes."

Gus remembered himself as a boy following his father, listening to stories of the old country before the war. They fished together and his father talked of his own father—Gus's grandfather—and of expeditions to Austria in his own childhood, walking trips to the private trout streams.

They, his father and grandfather, slept under down-filled comforters in three- and four-bedroom hotels high up mountain valleys and woke to find frost crusted on the windows and breath misting, washed in cold water and went directly to breakfast, from the table went warm and full out into the new morning where grass was frozen dark green and heavy, walked to the streams and fished the riffles as the sun appeared above the close mountains to the east. Fog hung just above the water, rainbowed by the sun, and Gus's grandfather, dead at Verdun, an officer in German artillery, gutted the fish as the morning ended and the current carried away the entrails and heads.

Gus's father spoke of touching the dead trout for the first time, when he was ten or twelve, and of their hard, clean feel. They were different than other fish, the old man said. Natives. Gus wondered then what difference there was. Fish were fish. He asked his father and the old man said there was no difference now, because Europe was ruined and the streams here were filled with planted fish from the hatcheries. Natives existed only in isolated places where men seldom went.

Gus had been stationed in Austria after the second war, but had never fished the streams, remembered only the rain on the countryside, houses perched in sunlight on the snow of the mountains, skiers walking the streets of Innsbruck toward the lifts. He had learned, talking to an old man in a tavern, that the fish in the private trout streams were not natives, were planted and had been since before his father was born. That was wrong and all of Austria was wrong. Gus had expected the country to seem familiar, but for some reason, listening to his father, he had imagined it all wrong. It was only another strange place, a foreign country. And now I'm here, he thought. He went to the stove and poured more coffee and listened to his father's voice mumbling on about the price of wool.

Standing in the evening shadows just upstream from the sheep bridge, Gus unscrewed the cap from the aluminum case and began setting up the rod, rubbing each ferrule on the side of his nose to oil it slightly. The bridge seemed mostly the same, three sagging pine logs between rock piers, covered with rough laminated boards, a way of crossing the sheep during the high water of early spring. His father had helped build it, pulled the logs into place with a span of four horses only a year or so after coming to the valley. Now it was rotting, unused, the old paths on either side grown up with brush.

In late summer, when his father brought the sheep, he always brought them in the afternoon so they could camp that night by the stream and fish. The old man was strong and rough then, his hands and face almost the color of his amber beard and the hair that reached almost to his shoulders after growing untouched all summer. They would fish the deep holes above the bridge and cook their catch over a fire of pitch and pine knots and then Gus would sleep beside the wagon, deep in the strong animal odor of the blankets his father shared with him. Before sunlight reached the canyon bottom they would stoke the smouldering fire and wash in creek water and stand warming while coffee brewed and chops fried and sputtered in the pan. After eating and throwing the scraps to the dogs they would break camp and start the sheep toward the valley.

Remembering, Gus cast a dry Renegade just above the bridge, eventually taking two small trout and stringing them together on a forked willow switch. After the second he changed to a white bucktail Rio Grand King for the evening rise. These were the same patterns he and his father had used. Each thing along the creek seemed familiar. The sawcut stump of a tree felled for use as a bridge stringer was rotten, but it was nearly as it had been when Gus and his father had used it for a table at their camp. His father had told him of cutting the tree. It had settled on his crosscut saw and he had spent nearly all of one day wedging the saw loose. "I was green then," the old man said. "But I learned."

The sun was gone and the canyon bottom was cooling. Upstream, held by damming boulders, was the first of the larger pools. Gus could see the white streak of a waterfall that dropped between boulders and scoured driftwood jammed around them by spring floods. Below, washed by the falling water, was a narrow pool of blackish deep water reflecting light cut by a dense aspen thicket. The still water on either side of the current was dimpled by feeding

trout, an occasional small fish breaking the surface and falling back. Gus watched the evening hatch of insects, the fish rising, then under the edge of an overhanging boulder near the head of the pool saw the swirled rise of a larger fish, a circle of ripples.

He quickly climbed around to the top of the boulders and driftwood. Aspen leaves, already frozen and yellowing, were close when he got into position to work the fly. His line tangled on a branch above his head as he tried to launch the first cast and he jerked it frantically loose, shredding leaves, then flipped the fly across the current and let it swing below, a white dart beneath the surface. That first cast brought just the interested nudge of an exploring trout. On the second cast he felt the sharp tug of a solid strike. A little rainbow fought clear of the water, leaping toward the shallow end of the pool. Then the line went slack.

Retrieving the fly, Gus saw that the hook had snapped off in the middle of its curvature, probably weakened when he had earlier snagged it on a rock downstream. He tied on a new fly, then lit a cigarette and waited for the fish to begin moving again. After a few silent moments he heard a gentle splash and dropped the new fly out into the current, letting it sweep downstream and across, out of the moving water, then bringing it back with a series of small tugs, keeping the white speck just under the surface, creating no wake. Then he dropped it directly beside the overhanging boulder beneath him, intending to flip it across the current and work it again.

The strike came at that awkward moment. He hauled back and held the line taut instinctively, letting the pole do the first work.

After the first splash there was only silence and the steady power beneath the surface, a throbbing on the line, then a heavy rush toward the shallow end of the pool and a series of smashing leaps that revealed a huge, glistening trout.

Gus slid from his awkward perch on the boulder, dropping into waist deep water and nearly falling, the freezing shock cramping his stomach. His boots were full and the water poured around him, dragging at his shirt as he braced his feet in the gravel and began to reel in. The line was slack and dead.

Cursing, he jerked the pole up and there was again the heavy power moving in deep circles near the center of the pool. The line cut a silver trail through the water and he couldn't move or control the fish as it began working toward the rough and moss-patched overhanging boulders and wedged driftwood. Gus rushed, floundering and nearly falling, to be there first and frighten the fish back, prevent that escape. They settled into the battle again, the fish circling the deepest water, out of sight, a force which was the imagined fish.

Gus's boots were dragging and tiring him and his right wrist ached from the cold. He wanted another cigarette and wondered what that would prove. His father would curse a man fool enough to smoke with this sort of fish on the line.

Ignoring that and somehow proud, even while knowing it was childish, Gus dug into his breast pocket, risking everything by this divided attention, and found the cigarettes and matches dry. He got a cigarette into his mouth and held the match book in his pole hand and attempted striking the paper matches. On the third try he got it, caught the light clean while the pole twisted in his hand. He dropped the matches into the water and was immediately sorry, thinking of the next cigarette.

The fish was glinting close to the surface. Now must be his move. He held the cigarette tight in his lips, letting the smoke burn his eyes, and took the landing net in his free hand and began to move toward the fish.

The bottom of the pool was small round gravel stones that rolled under his feet, sloping toward the deep center, and he almost went down, was nearly chest deep and beginning to feel the soft current when he slipped again and went under.

He held the pole above water, feeling his hands break water, fought the slippery bottom with his heavy boots, and wondered if this were to be the final wasting of his life.

Tumbling slowly over in the current he at last broke surface with his head and then was able to stand. Half the wet tobacco was in his mouth and he vomited yellow bile and finally, when the convulsion was finished, stood chest deep feeling the current that had saved him, mindless with cold and sickness, shaking with quick and weakening terror, gasping.

His vomit eddied downstream. The line was wrapped tight around his body, cutting into his side. The fish was a sliver glint only feet away.

Gus lunged with the landing net, missed, thought the fish gone, stood and saw it nearer, exhausted and undisturbed by this new thrashing. He stabbed again and was rewarded with the flopping weight that struggled in the net.

He carried it from the water and sat on the bank and shook, cold and exhausted and soaking, and felt the chill of evening and saw then how dark it had become. He laid the fish on grass at his feet. It was a huge stream trout, stippled along the sides, deep as a salmon, at least twenty inches and red beneath the gills, a native cutthroat.

The battle had taken longer than he had imagined, and in that time the light had gone and the trees and glinting stream and boulders, black and capped by the gray driftwood, seemed to merge. He lifted the fish and the feeble dying movements of the gills pumping, sensed rather than seen, and the occasional jerking undulations of the body as it died seemed part of himself, as if it were his own always present death coming now, sudden as light.

Frozen aspen leaves, dead and crisp and still, formed a pattern over his head and beyond he could see the rim as a dark edge against the blue-purple sky and toward the darker east, pinholes of starlight emerging. The stillness was complete, as if the cold rising and surrounding him was indeed death, and then the fish jerked and the peace was broken.

He laid the trout on sand beside the water and opened his knife and with one slow long stroke slit the belly open, releasing the entrails into the current.

Suggested Further Reading

WORKS BY KITTREDGE

The Van Gogh Fields. Columbia: University of Missouri Press, 1979.

We Are Not in This Together. Port Townsend, Washington: Graywolf Press, 1984.

Owning It All. St. Paul, Minnesota: Graywolf Press, 1987.

The Last Best Place: A Montana Anthology, ed. William Kittredge and Annick Smith. Helena: The Montana Historical Society Press, 1988.

Ken Kesey

Ken Kesey is generally recognized as the representative cult figure of the 1960s, especially after Tom Wolfe's 1968 bestseller about Kesey and his band of followers, *The Electric Kool-Aid Acid Test*, established Kesey as the Pied Piper of the hippie movement. Too often lost in this pop-culture perception of Kesey is his worth as a literary artist.

He was born in 1935 in Colorado, but his family moved to Springfield, Oregon, in 1946, where he attended Springfield High School. Upon graduation, he enrolled at the University of Oregon, where he was an accomplished wrestler and continued his interest in drama, and in writing, under the influence of Professor James B. Hall. Later, he was accepted into the graduate writing program at Stanford, where he studied with Malcolm Cowley, Wallace Stegner, and others. His fellow students included Larry McMurtry and Wendell Berry.

The publication of *One Flew Over the Cuckoo's Nest* in 1962 launched Kesey into fame. *Sometimes a Great Notion*, in 1964, was another success. Both books were made into Hollywood films in the 1970s, *Cuckoo's Nest* winning five Academy Awards. After a series of adventures, Kesey returned with his family to his farm in the Pleasant Hill area near Springfield, where he continues his creative activities. The story which follows is early work from his college days.

The First Sunday of September

It was Sunday and the sea was bad. They accepted that. But on Sundays the beer houses were closed and those who did not have a bottle stashed on their boats had no other choice but to go to church, and this they complained of before they accepted. They had learned to accept and respect the commandments of the sea for they know the sea's wrath firsthand; God's wrath could never really be more than words from the pulpit or stories from the Book.

At ten minutes to eleven the ones without bottles stepped over the sides of their boats. If they were married their wives followed, silent and pleased to be going to church for once. They wore slacks and white shirts and dark dresses, made limp by the thick perspiring air of the docks and never pressed except by the weight of other garments stored above. They left their boats and walked up the docks, like dark solemn birds lined out on a floating log, uncomfortable out of their element. The more fortunate lounged with their bottles at the scales by the fish-house, and waited for the pious little line to move stiffly past.

"Oh haw haw!" Mack yelled and waved his bottle. "It's a goddam funeral goin' past, I swear if it isn't! Why that's just real sad. I'm sorry, Mr. Anderson. My deepes' consolances, Mr. Petersen. Sure, look at 'em, a sad thing indeed. Did you ever see a more mournful flock? Who could it be for now, this funeral? Marv Oleson? No, he was never round an' they had his funeral at sea. Ivan? Ah no, not poor dear Ivan. He's drunk behind the fish-house."

The other loungers stomped the dock and laughed with him. They sat in a line and leaned against the sunny side of the fish-house: Crabby Joe, who always thought to have a bottle laid by, and Red Talbot with the blanched eyebrows who didn't go to church anyway, bottle or no. Little Donald and his cousin-wife laughed and crossed themselves. Jean Messner and his six unnamed brothers laughed. Olaf the cod man laughed and shouted in his stew pot tongue. Mack went on, encouraged.

"Sure, here's ol' Pop Weaver an' his missus. Mama, that preacher will faint dead away when he sees you bring Pop through that church door. Dead away, I swear it."

"A bit of God an' the Book never done no man no harm, Mack," Pop Weaver said, and saw his little wife's quick, pleased, agreeing nod. Mama Weaver had all the respect in the world for the ways of the sea, but she was glad when one of these rough fall Sundays came along to let her dress up for church.

Mama Weaver was a small woman but she boasted she was able to outdo any of the men in just damn near anything. Her face was brown and weather-etched like her husband's. Her hair was white-grey and very curly, like the foam on a rough sea, and her hands were as big as a man's. Her only son had been killed years before when he had tried to row in across the bar from their out-anchored boat. "Damn carelessness, plain damn foolishness," she always said when anyone mentioned the boy's death, "He was old enough to know better."

The line of churchgoers petered out at eleven o'clock and they could be heard tuning up inside the church. The loungers leaning against the fish-house became quiet. When they drank, now, they turned away from the tall church windows and shielded their bottles with their backs. The metal-staved hymns that rolled from the church and rumbled down the docks like metal-staved barrels might have made them uneasy—a few tried to think that it was that, and promised silently that on the next Sabbath, the rough sea permitting, they might also go to church—but most of them knew it was not the hymns or the church at all because those singing in church probably felt just as uneasy. It was not the hymns; it was the sound of the sea a mile out.

Down the dock ramps, below the fish-house and the church, the fishing boats lay moored and felt the sound from a mile out. They rocked and rubbed the docks with their rubber tire bumpers, waltzing their troller poles back and forth to the undeniable tune of the sea. It was this tune that made the men and their wives uneasy. They looked down from the fish-house at the waltzing decks, or up through the church windows at the waltzing tips of the troller poles thrust waving like a leafless forest in the wind. They heard the mile-out tune and gauged the waltz. It was September.

September already, and by the fish-house or in the church the fishermen heard the already September sea, heard it rolling a mile out, could hear the dreary *clangdang* of the pitching bell buoy a mile out to sea saying, "fall's comiiing, comaaang, comiiing. . . ." Fall, and then the hardtime, blowtime, raining, Oregon seacoast winter. Salmon would soon be pigeon-holing rivers and streams all along the west coast, the same rivers and streams they had traced out four years before. After four years of mystery, the salmon were back: twenty pounds of fresh red meat. For three months the fishermen had followed the run from Port Orford to Astoria and back, and in a few more weeks the run would be gone. The fish would re-enter the rivers and fight back up over the rocks and rapids to that certain sandy shallow where they would deposit their milt and eggs, and then thrash out their lives in the place they had started, up the Long Tom or the Willamette or the Columbia, scarred and hooknosed and looking as angrily at their death as they had at their fate in the sea.

The fishermen watched the troller waltz and heard the tune and gauged: about three more weeks, at the most four, to make their season of money; money to last until May when the first Chinook rolled back into the waters. If the money lasted, they lived easy on their boats and scraped and painted and puttered with their motors and carved weird, useless plugs. If the money did not last they stood in line at the employment office for a shovel or an ax or a job cutting huckleberry sprays for florists.

Three, at the most four weeks more; thirty times across the bar after fish and thirty times back, they would cross a narrow stretch of surf that was bad and getting worse each day, risking a boat so important, because it was their home as well as their job and their future, that it seemed more a risk than their lives. They felt a personal grudge toward the sea that continually threatened to claim all they had, and a personal fear of each wave. They felt as always the respect for the sea's commandments. They felt the sea's hate, the almost animal hate of being contained, penned with mountains and shores. And in turn they hated the sea's hate as all men do who dare to take their living from a mile out. They hated the sea's hate, but the sea they respected and loved. And the three or four more weeks that they feared they anticipated as well.

On the docks Little Donald sang:

If all them young ladies was fish in the river
I'd be a shark, and I'd tickle their liver.

Oh, roll your leg over, roll your leg o-over
Roll your leg over the man in the moon.

And Mack laughed his three-block laugh.

And from the white chipped house-of-the-lord, aged, crumbling in the sea air, the metal-staved voices rolled:

"Holy, ho-lee, ho-o-lee. . . ."

And by the scales Olaf the cod man grinned and clasped his hands over his head in the sign of victory, and said, "Ole! Hay, dat's me, you bat!" as he did whenever he heard the song.

At that moment out on the bar the very sound they were trying to drown out with laughter or prayer caught one of the tourist's sport boats. The waves whipped the boat crossways and rolled it like a paper toy. All eighteen feet of it drawing twenty inches of water, had chanced a bar and a sea along with twelve foot skiffs and twenty foot sports cruisers—tourist boats—on a bar that a forty-foot commercial troller drawing six feet of water with a ton of cement in the hold to keep it upright wouldn't go near, even on a Sunday without a bottle.

Little Donald sang louder:

My father was the keeper of the Eddystone light
And he slept with a mermaid one fine night. . . .

And Mack shouted, "Oh haw, with a stinkin' mermaid. Ohaw haw!"

And the brassbound, barrel-staved:

The winds and the waves will obey thy will,
Peace, be still. . . .

One of the men from the eighteen-foot sport boat was drowned. Another was mashed into the jetty and his collar bone was broken. The man with the broken collar bone was from Bend; the man that drowned was an insurance broker from Salem. The sea did not know either one.

That afternoon, with church over and dinner eaten, the men who had gone to church changed back into their working clothes and joined the group by the scales, all duty to the Sunday God done. They shared the bottles and joked about the eighteen-foot tourist's skiff that drew only twenty inches of water, out on a September bar.

It was low tide and still ebbing and on the pilings around the docks the barnacles tickled and sizzled in the sun. Town boys stood on the dock and tried to spear the big perch flashing past. The gulls and the black, long-necked ducks flew down to the bar and found it too rough to dive for a meal, and flew back to the scales to pick at the trash.

One of the town boys was swimming. He stroked back and forth within the moorage, showing off to no one in particular. He was a logger's son, with long hair and sideburns. His nose had been broken.

"Hey ho," Mack shouted, "We got us a seal with sideburns. Hey seal, can you play the gittar while you swim?"

The boy did not answer.

"Hang your clothes on a hickory limb," Little Donald sang, "but don't go near the water."

"Can swim you kid back to the *Dixie Lee* and forth?" Olaf the cod man said, "Aye joost bat you can't."

The boy did not answer. He frowned and stroked back and forth keeping his head carefully from the water, to preserve his hair.

"Bet you can't make it to the *Dixie Lee* one way, boy," Pop Weaver said.

The boy looked at the black and green troller seventy-five yards up river and didn't answer.

"Aye bat you can't a dollar," Olaf the cod man said.

"Fact," Pop said winking around, "I bet an old woman could beat you up there an' then swim back just for exercise."

"Sure, sure she could," the boy had to say, treading water now.

"Oh haw, by God, we got us a race."

Ivan sat up. "Who's racin'?"

"Ivan here's in the race. Who else? Who else is gonna challenge our little seal down there?"

"Aye joost try, by got!"

"Olaf's in the race! Hey, Olaf's racin'. Who else, who else?"

People began to step from their boats to the docks and walk to the scales. Some tourists edged in.

"Pass the hat! Pass the hat! We'll have a purse for this race. Make it worth somethin'. Seal, this is a bigtime event. You better go up on the dock an' rest."

The boy did not say anything. He treaded water and looked up the river to the rocking boat.

Little Donald looked around at the women in the gathering crowd. "Those who don't have any shorts can't race. Got to have shorts on. Women here."

"Shorts only. No shorts you don't get to enter. Oh haw!" And Mack passed his turtle-palmed hand among the tourists for money. The tourists looked at the shell-hard face and the shell-hard hand and dropped in quarters and dimes. "Come on, come on an' cough up. You're about to see our sturdiest men risk their lives in the ragin' tide against Sealo, the sideburned seal!"

"I don't know," the boy said, nervous now with the people. He lifted himself onto the docks and stood there glaring. "Where's this old woman you were talking about?"

"Pop, get Mama up here. Tell her she can win a big purse, big stakes. Tell her it's a command performance. Oh haw haw!"

"Mama," Pop Weaver yelled down to the *Destiny*, "Mama, come up here."

From the cabin of the *Destiny*, Mama's small white-grey head poked up. She was still wearing her churchgoing clothes. "What the hell you want?" she called.

"We want you to race this seal boy here, Mama," Mack yelled back.

"Swimmin'?"

"Sure, swimmin'. What else you think? Get on your swim suit, them without shorts can't enter."

"Pop?" Mama asked.

"Just up to the *Dixie Lee*, Mama. There's a purse."

"Well, okay," she said, "I'll be right up."

In a few minutes she appeared in a black suit. Her arms and neck were browned deeply, but the rest of her body was almost grey, white-grey like her hair. She had none of the dimply skin most women get at the backs of their legs past forty. By the time she got to the scales there were five men stripped to their shorts standing beside the boy. They stood without saying anything, not yet ready for the race to start.

The men by the scales wanted to make more of it; it was too good to let end so soon. When the race started it couldn't be stopped and brought back for more entertainment. It would be over. On the docks below, the contestants waited for someone to start it, grinning at each other. The boy looked sullen. The air around the pilings was heavy, like a roll of thick, rancid fat. One of the men looked at the water pitching in the moorage and said, "Water's pretty rough." And from the jetty point a mile out they could hear the waves crashing over the rocks with a deep sound, "rough, roughhh, roughhhh!"

"Look out, look out!" Ivan yelled and fell in, clothes and all. His legs were still on the dock but his front quarters were stroking wildly in the water. Little Donald hauled him back onto the dock.

"Van, you're disqualified for jumpin' the gun an' for bein' drunk. Go sit down."

"Jus' as well," Ivan said, "Can't swim a stroke."

They stood, five fishermen, brown of arm and neck, the boy, and the old woman. They stood on the dock and looked toward the *Dixie Lee*. They tried to laugh at Ivan. They tried to maneuver him into falling in again. They tried to get more to enter the race. It was finally the boy who asked to get it over with.

"All right, all right, what's your big hurry?" Mack said, then looked around him. "Okay then. Just go up to the *Dixie Lee*. First to touch it wins. Now. Everybody ready?"

"Christ yes, I'm freezing standing out here," the boy said.

"All right. On your mark, get set, *go!*"

They jumped into the swelling water and began swimming into the ebb. The boy took the lead, grimly stroking, pulling into the stream. A few yards behind him Mama stroked smoothly, stroke-five-and-breathe, the stroke of an experienced distance swimmer.

At halfway they were the only two left in the race; the five others had turned back with the ebb for the docks. The boy still fought the tide. Behind him the woman's head followed smoothly, easily floating on the dark water, like a clot of foam blown by the wind. She swam on her side now, relaxing. She was talking to the boy.

The crowd could see her talking, and quieted to hear what she said. It became very still on the docks. In a sudden, strange calm, as if a mile out the bell had hushed the surf for a moment and was listening too, the people lining the dock could hear the boy's choppy breath and Mama's voice:

"Don't fight it, sonny. Don't fight the water. You can't make it. Get on your back an' head for shore. Don't fight it."

The crowd sensed the boy's fear more than they witnessed it. The boy did not seem to be in any trouble; he continued on hard against the tide, bound against it. He wasn't swimming as strongly as he had been when he started but he didn't look tired. Yet they sensed it.

At the last Mama tried desperately to reach him before he went under. He had not thrashed or called out, he had continued on against the tide, toward the *Dixie Lee* twenty yards ahead of him. They did not know if he was trying to reach the *Dixie Lee* because it was closer than the dock, or if he was still racing, choosing to fight the sea and drown in it rather than be beaten by a grey-headed old lady.

The crowd ran down the docks and some of the men kicked off their shoes and swam out to Mama.

"Not here! Not here! The tide would wash him back that way!" She dived under and when she came up she yelled at the crowd on the docks. "Run, damn it, don't just stand there! Back that way! Look for him comin' past!"

She swam hard downstream with her face in the water, leaving the men thrashing behind her in their wet clothes. She dived again. The men crawled from the water back onto the docks. The crowd stood silently and watched the old woman dive. She dived until she was exhausted, then, as if she had set a certain amount of time to look even though she knew she wouldn't find the boy, she treaded water and drifted toward the docks. Pop helped her in with a towel. Her body appeared even greyer than before. They all watched her chattering and crying. Pop was the only one who spoke.

"He's probably clean out to the jetty by now, Mama. Lodged in the rocks with the crabs pickin' on him."

"Who was he?"

"Some logger's kid. From the mountains."

"He shoulda knowed better, then," she said. "God help him." She sat down and began to shiver. "God help him," she repeated.

On the high docks, by the scales, above the waltzing trollers, Mack looked at the coins in his turtle-shell palm, tossed them underhand out into the swelling water. They fell, flashing, into a dozen widening circles at the spot where the boy had dived.

"Hadn't somebody better get the police? Or the coast guard?" one of the tourists said.

"Yeah. Yeah, go ahead." Mama said.

"And tell his parents? And tell the preacher?"

"Sure, go ahead."

When the coast guard arrived in their buoy-tender the fishermen had all left the docks and gone to their boats. Only some tourists remained, telling the late comers how it had been to see a person drown. The gulls and the black, long-necked ducks flew down to the bar and the sea was rougher than before.

Suggested Further Reading

Works by Kesey

One Flew Over the Cuckoo's Nest. New York: Viking Press, 1962.

Sometimes a Great Notion. New York: Viking Press, 1964.

Kesey's Garage Sale. New York: Viking Press, 1973.

Kesey. Edited by Michael Strelow. Eugene, Oregon: Northwest Review Books, 1977.

Sailor Song. New York: Viking Press, 1992.

Works about Kesey

Porter, M. Gilbert. *The Art of Grit: Ken Kesey's Fiction.* Columbia: University of Missouri Press, 1982.

———. *One Flew Over the Cuckoo's Nest: Rising to Heroism.* Boston: Twayne Publishers, 1989.

Tanner, Stephen L. *Ken Kesey.* Boston: Twayne Publishers, 1983.

Don Berry

Minnesota-born, Don Berry left home at fifteen and later spent two years at Reed College where he was influenced in his craft by teachers Lloyd Reynolds and Dorothy Johansen. After a period of apprenticeship, during which he wrote science fiction, Berry published *Trask*, in 1960. *Trask* has become the definitive historical novel of the Oregon coast. It was followed by *Moontrap*, set in the Willamette Valley at about the time of the Whitman massacre, and *To Build a Ship*, a sequel to *Trask* set in the Tillamook Bay country. Berry also has written a notable history of the Rocky Mountain fur trade, *A Majority of Scoundrels*.

Berry, like his former Portland housemate Gary Snyder, has been strongly influenced by Zen Buddhism. The reader may find the intense Zen exploration of the self and the physical world at the heart of all of Berry's novels, as the following section from *Moontrap* shows. Though he is not primarily a short fiction writer, except for his apprenticeship stories, he is included here because no collection of Oregon fiction would be complete without an example of his work.

A Trap for the Moon

The stillness of dusk; a time almost perfectly neutral, a suspension, filled with the promise of depth and solitude in the night to come. The old man gathered wood, enjoying the changing shapes of his camp in the changing light, seeing how one tree began to recede into shadow and another, by contrast, move forward for his attention. He moved quietly in the warm grayness, picking up a stick here, a larger slab there, and carrying them two or three at a time back to his rocky little point. It was an inefficient way to get wood together, but he didn't mind. He liked to spend the calm expanse of dusk in a calm manner; it was insanity to do anything else.

He did not need much wood, and there was not only the question of the fire, but a question of timing. He thought he was going to like this little camp very much, and he wanted things to go properly. It was most satisfying for him to finish laying the fire and have it ready to light at the precise moment in the growing darkness when it seemed to him that he needed a little more light. It was, in the end, perfectly unimportant. But there was a certain contentment for a man in feeling that he has well suited his actions to the changes of the world around him.

It was a kind of contentment the old man had not felt for a while now, ever since he got mixed up with the man-ugliness of the settlement. There it always seemed that he was running counter to something, always conscious of conflict, of tension. He couldn't let the world take him along, because of the noise and stink of the man-world. He shrugged as he kindled the fire, and put the thought away from him. It was over, now. This was not the place to be worrying about it.

He filled his little cup half full of water, dropped in a couple of tiny pieces of flaky white suet from the pack. He put the cup by the fire where it would boil quickly and got a handful of the jerked deer. The jerky was in flat sticks like a hardened leather, eight or ten inches long. He broke a few of them in half and stood them on end in the cup. They were still too long, and stood up out of the cup like a fistful of bark. When the water neared the boiling stage, he turned the strips end for end, to let the other half soften a little.

When he was finished it was a little softer. Not much, but enough to make a difference—and he had a cup of weak broth to drink. It was not like fresh meat, but it was better than no meat at all. He chewed on the rubbery strips and watched the orange and gold reflections of his fire ripple in the water, almost as though a tiny sun were burning just beneath the surface.

Slowly the balance of light changed. The western sky grew dark, and in the east was the pale glow of the rising moon, not yet visible above the trees. The old man put one last stick on the fire to last until he was asleep. He made a half-hearted attempt to clear away some of the larger rocks before he rolled up in his blanket, but he knew it wouldn't make much difference. If you got rid of the rocks you had the holes they left. It was better to try to fit yourself around the worst spots.

With the setting of the sun the night had become pleasantly cool. He took off his moccasins, which were still wet from the wading. The dust he had collected on the slope had formed a fine silty layer of mud inside. He rinsed them out carefully, scrubbing away the soapy-feeling layer. Ruefully he noted that the hole in the right sole had grown considerably from the rough pounding down the rocky slope. He stuck his little finger through the hole experimentally, then shrugged. He washed his feet and put the moccasins back on to prevent them from shrinking up so badly in the night they could not be worn tomorrow.

He pulled the blanket over him, tucked the edges under and rolled over to his side. He could see both the fire and the reflection of it in the tiny inlet beside him. He glanced up at the light and eerie glow that preceded the appearance of the moon, and realized there would be a time in the night when the great disk would be overhead in the space between the trees, directly over the river. Then he would be able to see both the moon and its reflection in the still inlet. It would be pleasant, but would not happen for a couple of hours. He thought he would like to wake up for it, to see two moons at the same time.

A fly or something buzzed near his ear, and he sleepily swatted at it, hoping it was not a mosquito. Mosquitoes were a damned nuisance. They said the ones that buzzed weren't the ones that bit you, but the buzzing ones were the ones you swatted. It didn't seem fair, but he supposed it was probably true. There was nothing to guarantee that things would be fair. He wondered vaguely if a mosquito could see the end of its own nose.

He wakened without being startled, and at first could not understand why. Then he realized he had promised himself a look at the overhead moon, and it was the sudden increase of light that had brought him out of sleep. It was almost directly above, framed between the wall of trees that edged the river. The night was very clear, and the markings on the face of the brilliant disk were sharp and distinct. For the thousandth time the old man tried to make some

sense of them, tried to make them fit into a comprehensible pattern, tried to see the man in the moon. He never could. Everybody else saw the man in the moon, and a dozen times people had tried to explain it to him, but he never could see it. To him there were gray patches, and he was perfectly familiar with their shape; but he could not make pictures out of them. It was the moon, with its uniqueness, and resembled nothing but itself. It was sufficient.

He glanced over at the reflection in the inlet, where the moon's twin wavered luminously in the darkness. The inlet was not as calm as it had appeared. The reflection lengthened and shortened and occasionally broke, distorting the perfect symmetry of the brilliance that hung overhead. He wondered if it would be possible to make it hold perfectly still, and be the perfect, flawless duplicate he had seen in his mind when he had thought about it before. In an odd way it seemed possible to him that in the reflection he might be able to see the pictures, even though he could not see them in the moon itself.

The more he thought about it, the more it seemed to be a good idea. He had always wanted to see the man in the moon. He unwrapped himself from the blanket. His fire was still glowing faintly, and he threw on one of the pieces of wood he'd been saving for morning. As it flamed up and lit a small circle he surveyed the problem.

The mouth of the inlet was only about eight feet wide, and there was already a fallen log damming part of it. One end of the log rested up on his bank, and he thought if he could get that end into the water across the mouth it might do the job. It was too heavy to lift, but he thought he could pry it off with a lever of some kind. He looked around the edges of the fire circle until he found a windfall about six inches through at the base.

He dragged it back to the fire and hacked off a few of the more troublesome branches. With the lever he waded to the river side of the log and thrust the thick end beneath, wedging it in the stones of the bottom. He heaved up, but the end of the lever slipped and the log dropped back to the bank. He took a more secure purchase and tried again, and this time it worked perfectly. The end of the log rose from the bank and slid down the lever with a great splash to lie directly across the mouth of the inlet.

The splash completely destroyed the moon's image, scattering it in wild ripples and flecks of brightness that darted on the surface. He climbed back up on the bank and squatted on his heels to wait for the disturbance to die down and the whole image to return. When the ripples had settled, he found the reflection still wavered and moved. There was undoubtedly a current coming in from somewhere, probably around the end of the log, where it did not fit perfectly against the bank.

He sighed, and gathered up some stones and twigs to dam the gap. He had to go back into the water to do it, and his legs were getting cold. He packed the sticks and rocks into the open space, sealing them in with mud. It would wash away, but it might last long enough to get the moon still for just a moment. There was not much to packing the end, but when he had finished the improvised dam he had to wait again for the ripples to subside so he could see if it had worked.

It had not been enough. The reflection still wavered and distorted itself. The current must be coming in under the log itself. It was more complicated than he had expected, building a trap for the moon.

He went back into the water again. Patiently he began to wedge stones at the bottom of the log, filling spaces between larger ones with smaller ones, and scraping up gravel from the bottom to dam whatever holes he had left. He worked as quickly as he could, but plugging most of the eight-foot length still took him almost twenty minutes.

When he got back to the bank and looked in the water there was no image at all. The moon had passed over the clear space above and was behind the trees again on its slow and certain journey to the other side of the world.

Suggested Further Reading

WORKS BY BERRY

Trask. New York: Viking, 1960; rpt. Sausalito: Comstock Editions, 1969.

A Majority of Scoundrels: An Informal History of the Rocky Mountain Fur Company. New York: Harper, 1961.

Moontrap. New York: Viking, 1962; rpt. Sausalito: Comstock Editions, 1971.

To Build a Ship. New York: Viking, 1963; rpt. Sausalito: Comstock Editions, 1977.

WORKS ABOUT BERRY

Love, Glen A. *Don Berry.* Boise State University Western Writers Series, Number 35. Boise, Idaho: Boise State University Press, 1978.

Percival Everett

As recently as 1940, there were only about 2,000 African Americans in Oregon. They were unwelcome during the pioneering and homesteading period, and the Ku Klux Klan activities during the 1920s further discouraged their settlement in Oregon. As a result, there have been few black writers in Oregon, until recently.

Percival Everett, in this story from his collection, *The Weather and Women Treat Me Fair,* gives us a rare glimpse into the black experience in Oregon. Everett was born in Florida in 1956. He received his bachelor's degree at the University of Miami, then studied at the University of Oregon and at Brown University, from which he received his master's degree in 1982. He has worked as a jazz musician, a ranch hand, and a high school teacher. His ranching experience is put to good use in this story set outside Portland. He taught in and directed the Graduate Creative Writing Program at the University of Kentucky, Lexington, from 1985 to 1989, and now teaches at the University of Notre Dame.

Cry About a Nickel

Clouds hung like webs in the firs and a fine mist wet the air. Blackberry thickets sprawled wide and high, most of the berries withered past picking. Back home, on an autumn morning like this, we might be sharpening knives and boiling water to butcher a hog. But here I was in the wet Cascades. I pulled my pickup to the side of the road and got out. I looked down the steep slope at the Clackamas River tumbling at a good clip over and around rocks. I made my way down a path to the bank and found it littered with fishermen, shoulder to shoulder, casting lures and dragging them past a great many large fish just sitting in a pool as if parked in a lot. Being sincerely ignorant I figured I was running little risk of sounding so when I asked the man nearest me—

"What kind of fish are those?"

The man let his eyes find me slowly and his smile was a few beats behind. "Why, they're steelhead."

"They don't seem to be very interested," I said.

The man turned back to his line and said nothing.

I watched a bit longer, then climbed back to the road. In South Carolina fishing was done quietly, in private, for creatures hidden from view. At least a man could say, "Aw there ain't no fish here." But this seemed like premeditated self-humiliation.

A boy at the house told me I'd find his father in one of the stables. I wandered into the near one, didn't see him, but I caught a mare nosing around her hock. I found a halter on a nail outside her stall and put it on her, tied her head up.

"What're you doing there?" a man yelled at me.

"She was nosin' around her hock and I saw it was capped and had ointment on it. I raised her head up so she wouldn't burn her nose."

"What do you know about capped hocks? Who are you?"

"Are you Mr. Davis?"

"Yeah. I'm waitin'."

"Name's Cooper. I heard you had a job open."

"What do you know about horses?"

"I know enough to tie a horse's head up when I'm trying to blister her."

"Where're you from?"

"Carolina."

"North?"

"No, the good one."

Davis rubbed his jaw and studied the mare. "We don't get many blacks around here."

"The horse said the same thing."

"Five hundred a month. Includes a two-room trailer and utilities."

Davis had twenty-three horses, most pretty good, and a lot of land. He rented rides to hunters and to anybody who just wanted to get wet in the woods.

The first thing was to clean out the medicine chest. The box was full of all sorts of old salves and liniments and I just had to say aloud to myself, "Pathetic."

Davis had stepped into the tack room without me noticing. "What's pathetic?" he asked.

I sat there on the floor, thinking oh no, but I couldn't back off. "All this stuff," I said. "Better to have nothing than all this useless trash."

He didn't like this. "What's wrong with it?"

I looked in the box. "Well, sir, I appreciate the fact that this thermometer is fairly clean, but better to have a roll of string in the chest than keep this crap-crusted one on all the time. This is ugly."

"So, you've got a weak stomach."

I shook my head. "You've got ointments in here twenty years old. Why don't you grab the good stuff for me. Where's the colic relief? You've got three bottles of Bluestone and they're all empty."

He didn't look directly at me, just sort of flipped me a glance. "Fix it," he said and left.

There were no crossties, so I had to set up some for grooming. I was currycombing a tall stallion when Davis's son came into the stable.

"Hey, Joe," the kid said.

"Charlie."

"Mind if I help?"

I looked at the teenager. It was really a question. As a boy, I would have been required to work the place. "I don't know," I said. "Your father might think I'm not earning my pay. Don't you have other chores?"

"No."

I didn't understand this at all. I looked around. "I tell you what. You comb out the hindquarters on Nib here and then dandy-brush his head. I'm gonna shovel out his stall real quick."

The boy took the comb, stood behind the horse, and began stroking. "No," I said and I pulled him away. "Stand up there next to the shoulder, put your arm over his back, and do it like that. So, he won't kick the tar out of you."

Charlie laughed nervously and began working again. I shoveled at the stall and watched him. He was a nice boy. I couldn't tell if he was bright or not, he was so nervous. I stopped and listened to the rain on the roof.

"Does it ever stop raining?" I asked.

"One day last year."

I laughed, but he just stared at me. Then I thought he wasn't joking. "You're not saying—" Before I finished he was smiling.

"How'd you learn about horses?" he asked.

"Grew up with 'em. You don't spend much time with the animals?"

"Not really."

"People say that horses are stupid." I fanned some hay out of my face. "And they're right, you know. But at least it's something you can count on."

Then Davis showed up. "Charles."

The boy snapped to attention away from the horse and, glancing at the currycomb in his hand, threw it down. "I asked Joe if I could help, Daddy."

"Get in the house."

The boy ran from the stable.

"He's a good boy," I said.

Davis picked up the comb and studied it. "I'd appreciate it if from now on you just sent him back to the house."

"All right." I leaned the pitchfork against the wall and moved to take the horse from the crossties. "He's got a bunch of chores in there to take care of, does he? Homework and stuff?"

"Yeah."

Davis looked around at the stable and at the horses, at the stallion in front of him. "The other stables look this good?"

"Gettin' there."

It was a full-time job, all right, and I went to bed sore every night. Finally, I took a weekend off and drove the hour to Portland. I got a hotel room downtown on Saturday and tried to figure out what I was going to do all day. I went to the zoo and a movie, ate at a restaurant, watched bizarrely made-up kids at Pioneer Square, saw another movie, shot pool at a tavern, and went to bed. I dreamed about women. You work ranches and you talk about women and you talk about going to town to get yourself a woman, but you end up watching movies in dark rooms and shooting pool with men.

After a big breakfast at the hotel restaurant, I headed back to the ranch. The weather in Portland had been nice and, to my surprise, the sun was out all during my drive home. I parked by my trailer. Charlie was splitting wood over beside the house. Seeing him doing this made me feel good. I went inside and stowed my gear. There was a knock.

"Come," I said.

Davis came in. He had a bottle with him and a couple of glasses. "How was your trip?"

"Oh, it was a trip."

"Mind if I sit?"

I nodded that he was welcome and watched him fill the glasses. "You like bourbon?"

"You bet."

"Here you go." He handed the drink over.

I took it and sat with him at the table. He knocked his back and I followed suit. He poured another round.

He cleared his throat and focused on me. He had already had a few. "You're all right, Cooper." He leaned back. "Naw, I mean it." He sipped from his glass. "You want to hear how I lost my wife?"

I didn't say anything. I just looked at him.

"Killed herself."

I had a headache.

"Know what she died of?"

"A sudden?"

He frowned off my joke. "She took pills. She was an alcoholic and a diabetic and a Catholic. All three, any one of which is fatal alone."

"I'm sorry," I said.

He drank more. "They said she was manic, too." He looked out the window at the sky which was growing overcast. "Charles is a good boy."

"He's quiet."

"That's my fault, I guess."

"That's not a problem."

"He's small, you know."

I just looked at him.

"I don't have a lot of patience. I don't have a lot of friends either. I guess the two go together."

"I reckon."

"Tell me something, Cooper. What do you think of a man who can't talk to his kid?"

I swirled my whiskey in the glass and held his eyes.

"I've got a temper. A bad one."

I nodded.

"You want to hear what happened at Charlie's school last year?"

"To tell the truth, no, I don't."

Davis pulled a pack of cigarettes from his shirt pocket and fumbled his way through lighting one, blew out a cloud of blue smoke and coughed. He stood and went to the window, watched as his son split wood. "Look at him. He could do that all day. He's small, though."

I polished off my drink.

"You think I'm crazy."

I shook my head. "No, I don't."

"Well, I ain't crazy. He ain't right." He was hot and I was beginning to think he *was* touched. "Don't tell me how to run things!"

"Sure thing."

I didn't know what he was talking about.

He snatched up his bottle and walked out.

I fell on my bunk and looked at the ceiling. I wanted to pack up and leave, but I needed the job and I wasn't the sort to leave a man in a lurch. He had a mare ready to drop and a couple of horses with thrush real bad. I didn't like what I had seen in Davis's eyes. He was slow-boiling and soon there wouldn't be anything left to scorch but the pot.

I fixed some grits and scrambled eggs and sausages and sat down to dinner by myself. An evening rain came and went and I could see the fuzzy glow of the moon behind the clouds. I felt bad for little Charlie. Funny, I hadn't thought of him as small before, but he was. I felt sorry for him and I didn't know why. I wasn't about to get involved, though. My mother had a number of hobbies, but raising fools wasn't one of them.

A couple of days later, four fellows rented horses and went into the hills for elk. I knew when they rode out that all they were going to get up there was drunk. They didn't deserve the weather that day. It was almost hot when they came back. I was trimming hooves. Charlie was in the stable with the pregnant mare.

"Wooowee," said one man, "what a day."

"That was fun," said another, groaning and trying to work a kink out of his back as he climbed down. "That was more fun than huntin' coons."

They all dismounted and I took the horses. They'd ridden the animals hard right up to the end and they were sweating like crazy.

I called Charlie over. "Take these horses out and walk 'em around, get 'em cool." As he stepped away, I yelled for him to loosen the girths. His dad had let up a little and he was freer to hang about and help.

The men lined up along the fence and watched Charlie in the corral. "Ain't he pretty?" I heard one of the men say. I thought he was talking about a horse, but another spoke up.

"Hey, I heard about that locker-room business," he said.

"Oh, this was the boy?"

"Yeah."

I stepped out and saw that Charlie was ignoring them pretty good. They said a few more things and I got fed up, started toward them.

"Looks like we got the nigger riled," one said.

I stopped at the crack of a rifle shot. Davis was out of his house and just yards from the corral.

"You boys paid?" Davis asked.

The leader, more or less, put his hands up and laughed a little. "Yeah, we paid."

"Then get along."

"Okay, Davis. We'll get along. Nice boy you got there." The man chuckled again. They got into their car and left.

Davis watched them roll away. "Charles," he said. "Go on inside."

I caught Davis by the arm. "Hey, just let him forget about it."

He pulled away, didn't even look at me.

I watched him disappear into the house. Things were becoming a little more clear. More reason to ignore it. My motto: Avoid shit.

It was raining real good when I came back from the grocery store. As I swept around the yard I saw Charlie standing by the tree behind the house. I parked at the trailer, got out of my truck, and went inside for lunch. I finished my coffee and shivered against the chill in the air. Outside, I found it warmer than in the trailer. I started to go check the horses when I noticed that Charlie was still standing by that tree. I went to him. At twenty yards I could see that he was tied to it.

"What's the story?" I asked, looking around.

The boy just cried and I was pretty damn close to it myself. Rain dripped from his hair and ran down his face.

"Your father do this?" I was looking at the house, but I knew Charlie was nodding. "Why? Did he say why?" I was hesitant about untying him. I thought Davis had flipped and might be waiting at a window to blow my head off. I shouted as I reached for the rope. "Davis! I'm untying the boy! Okay!" I undid the knots and led the kid back to the house.

Davis was sitting in a chair in front of the fireplace. He looked really spaced out. "Hey, Davis, you all right?"

He said nothing.

"I brought Charlie inside here."

"I heard you." He leaned forward and poked at the burning logs. "He wouldn't tell me who they were."

"He's a strong boy," I said.

"You could call it that." He sat back again. "Earl Pryor has a mare ready, wants to breed her with Nib. Be over tomorrow."

"I'll have him ready. What time?"

"Said eight-thirty. Maybe I should have Charlie watch."

"For the love of God, Davis, stop and think. Listen to yourself. Charlie's a good kid who got beat up—think of it like that. It's none of my business, but—"

Davis cut me off. He stood and faced me. "You're right. It's none of your business and you don't know what the the hell you're talking about."

"Charlie didn't do anything."

"Pack up, drifter."

I looked at him for a second, but I'd heard him right. "Okay. Fine. But listen up, you're gonna drive that boy away and for no good reason."

But he wasn't listening. He was at his desk. "I'm paying you for this month and next. Fair enough?"

I looked across the room at Charlie. He had settled on the sofa and was looking out the window. Davis waved the check in front of me. I wanted to tell him what he could do with his goddamn money, but I didn't. I didn't look at his face. I just took the check, went to the trailer, and started packing.

I kept waiting for a knock on the door; Charlie coming to say goodbye or Davis coming to tell me to have that stallion ready in the morning. But there was no knock. I climbed into my pickup and drove away.

Suggested Further Reading

WORKS BY EVERETT

Suder. New York: Viking, 1983.

Walk Me to the Distance. New York: Ticknor and Fields, 1985.

Cutting Lisa. New York: Ticknor and Fields, 1986.

The Weather and Women Treat Me Fair. Little Rock, Arkansas: August House, 1987.

For Her Dark Skin. Seattle: Owl Creek Press, 1989.

WORKS ABOUT EVERETT

"Percival Everett," *Contemporary Authors,* Vol. 129, ed. Susan M. Trosky. Detroit: Gale Research, 1990.

Jim Heynen

Born in 1940 on a farm in Iowa, Jim Heynen graduated from Calvin College in Michigan and later earned a master's degree at the University of Iowa and a Master of Fine Arts degree at the University of Oregon. He studied Sioux Indian life and language in South Dakota before making the Northwest his home, where he writes poetry and nonfiction as well as short stories. He has taught creative writing at the universities of Iowa, Oregon, Alaska, and Washington, as well as Lewis and Clark College in Portland. Heynen's stories are very short, often fable-like glimpses of the everyday wonders of life, particularly rural life.

Who Kept One Hand in Her Pocket

There was a lady who kept one hand in her pocket. When she was in the garden, weeding, one hand was hidden in her pocket. When she was feeding oats to the chickens, she scattered the grain with one hand and kept the other in her pocket. In church. In the store. Wherever she was, one hand was always in her pocket.

The boys wanted to know why this was so. They asked people, but no one else knew either. So they made a plan, a trick to make her pull her hand out. They decided to lay a string where she walked and trip her with it as she passed by. When she was falling, the hidden hand would spring from the pocket to keep her from striking her face on the ground. Then they would run out to help her get up—but really to get a look at the hand.

They started talking about what they would see. Surely it was more than a withered hand. The lady must be hiding something better than that. A large black pearl, one of them guessed. Or a rose carved from ruby. Or something so pretty that they would never guess what it was.

The boys laid out the string one day but when the lady passed by they weren't able to pull it and trip her. They got too scared thinking that if they saw what the lady had hidden, she might give it to them. And if it was as beautiful as they thought, they might have to walk around the rest of their lives with one hand in their pockets, hiding what they had discovered.

Suggested Further Reading

WORKS BY HEYNEN

How the Sow Became a Goddess. Lewiston, Idaho: Confluence Press, 1977.
The Man Who Kept Cigars in His Cap. St. Paul: Graywolf Press, 1979.
You Know What Is Right. San Francisco: North Point Press, 1985.
One Hundred Over 100. Golden, Colorado: Fulcrum, 1990.

Molly Gloss

A fourth-generation Oregonian, Molly Gloss was born in Portland in 1944, where she grew up and graduated from Portland State in 1966, and where she lives today. She has published a number of short stories and a fantasy novel, *Outside the Gates*, which has also been translated into Spanish. Her most recent novel, *The Jump-Off Creek*, formed around the journal of a pioneer woman, won the Pacific Northwest Booksellers Award for excellence in 1990, and also received the 1990 H. L. Davis Book Award for Fiction from the Oregon Institute of Literary Arts. "The Doe," a powerful story in its own right, will also be recognized as a reworking of William Stafford's "Traveling Through the Dark," perhaps the best-known poem of modern Oregon.

The Doe

Kate took the river highway to Astoria and then went slowly down the coast searching for a vacancy in that long strand of villages facing the sea. The weather was poor and because of that she'd hoped to find the weekend crowd diminished a little. Instead it was encamped. Where the highway curved up the seaward face of Neahkahnie Mountain, there were oyster-colored clouds breaking like surf against the cliffs, and below, at Garibaldi, the rain hung like a beaded curtain in a doorway. But everywhere, for fifty miles along the coast, the decent rooms were taken. Finally, in twilight the color of pewter, she doubled back to Nehalem and turned inland into the knobs of the coast range—the slow road home. The fourth annual Kate-needs-some-time-alone weekend was now officially a washout. And by this time she was almost too stale to care.

The road sliced a clean, curving furrow through the timber. There were no other cars and the margins of the road were black and wet and featureless and Kate didn't see the doe until afterward. There was a pale watercolor of movement against the near trees, only that, and the sound when it struck the car, a padded sound like the one you'd make smacking your open hand on a seat cushion, and there was a jumbled minute, or part of a minute, getting the car in hand, skating on the wet pavement, and then she was sitting still in the darkness beneath the eaves of the trees. Under the palms of her hands, through the steering wheel, she could feel the car still quaking, or her hands quaking, and she managed after a while a sort of protest—"God *damn!*"

In the pulse of the emergency parking lights she walked back along the edge of the road. The doe lay flat against the gravel shoulder, waiting, watching Kate with dark, brittle-bright eyes. The rain beaded in the wooly hairs of Kate's coat, on the lenses of her glasses, on the smooth khaki-colored hide of the deer. She stood back a little beneath the trees, staring, hunching her shoulders against the wetness, and in a little while, when she could, she said, "I've never killed anything in my life," offering the words out loud so they seemed an explanation, and an apology. The doe's eyes, watching her, were flat, depthless, shining. In a bit Kate stooped to touch one smooth brown shoulder. Beneath the tips of her fingers the life sign was a soundless and simple tremble.

"I won't hurt you," Kate said, and didn't hear the irony until afterward. She sent the flat of her hand sliding across the big curve of belly where, *ah God,* the unborn fawn's timid heartbeat released the first of her tears. She squatted where she was, scrunched up small with her hands drawn back, to her lap, rocking a little on her heels, staring out to the curve of the road and the ditch running brown and fast with the rain and the trees climbing up the hillside behind in a black palisade. Damn. Ah, damn. Swearing without focus or purpose. Damn. Damn. Damn.

She sorted through the possibilities. The first, the worst one, unspeakable and horrifying, she cast out. The rest seemed vaguely melodramatic, wagging not-quite-real happy endings, but she squeezed her eyes shut and grabbed one. If there was someone else here, one of them could stay beside the doe, protect her, with road flares and blinking taillights, while the other went for help. For a vet. Or someone. She had simply to be patient and wait for a car to stop. She had simply to wait.

So she set flares along the road, spurting their red jets into the darkness, and she pulled the soccer blanket from the trunk and put it carefully over the doe until only the heartbreakingly patient face and the long brittle ankles showed above and below the fringe. Then she stood beneath the trees with her hands pushed in the pockets of her coat and her face turned out to the road shining in the rain. The doe lay quiet, indifferent or resigned, and no one came. She's in shock, Kate decided. There's no pain when you're in shock, is there? So she waited.

It was only when headlights struck the far trees that she remembered her own vulnerability and she went quickly back along the edge of the gravel to the car, locked herself in, and then rolled the window down enough to wave one hand out, signalling.

The car slowed cautiously at the flares and then finally stopped beside Kate. In the light thrown from the dashboard there were two very young faces, the boy showing brushy stripe of eyebrows and wide mouth and the girl a round face, honey-colored hair. The girl cranked her window down but it was the boy, leaning across, who said, "Broke down?"

Kate leaned her chin toward the open space in the window "No, my car is fine, I guess. But I *could* use some help. I've struck a deer. Would you know if there's a vet back in Nehalem?" She gestured vaguely toward the doe. "I think she's in shock. Maybe if one of us could get help for her . . . ," turning up the last word to make the whole thing a question. To leave room for other options. Or refusals.

The girl made a quick, splintered little sound of grief, fluttered one hand toward the doe . "Oh Jake, look, a deer." The boy turned his face to where she pointed.

In a moment, with his wide mouth pulled out stiff now, he said, "She's not dead?" and at Kate's dismal shake of head he flipped on his own emergency lights and left the car, bunching his thin shoulders as he crossed through the rain to the doe.

Kate spoke to the girl across the wet space between the cars. "I'm sorry if I've ruined your evening," offering, too, an apologetic half-smile.

The girl's round face was solemn, forgiving, faintly inattentive. "It's okay," she said, while her eyes followed the boy.

Kate watched him, too, twisting to peer through the smeared rear window. His hands reaching to touch the doe, were slender and tentative and, watching him, Kate betrayed herself with a despairing thought: *He is too young.*

The boy stayed with the doe quite a while, touching her carefully, thoroughly, and then for a moment simply squatting as Kate had done, staring out to the trees with the rain beading shiny in his hair. Finally he came back to Kate. He ducked his chin slightly before he said, "I think she's carrying a fawn." The girl made a wordless outrushing sound, pain or dismay, and the boy glanced briefly round to her with a helpless shrugging of his eyebrows.

In a moment Kate pushed out the little plea she had readied. "I don't know how badly she's hurt, but maybe she can be helped, or at least maybe the fawn could be saved."

In her own head the words whined with a childish and thin sound of urban naivete, and now she began to feel the first prickly edges of a kind of embarrassment. The boy ducked his chin slightly, as he had before, with that look of shyness or discomfort, and fixed his eyes on a point in the trees somewhere behind her.

"I hate to say it but I don't think there's much chance. You'd never get anybody out tonight, not for something like this," with a slight gesture of his head toward the doe. "And I think she must be in a pretty bad way or she'd be moving more, maybe trying to get up or something."

In the red light between the cars he displayed a smooth and very young face, but Kate had lost that earlier sense of his helplessness, of his beardless innocence. She didn't feel, what, twenty years older than him? Instead, simply on the strength of his one forthright statement (or maybe just on the strength of his masculinity) she found she was sliding toward a feeling of dependence and deliverance. It was easy to give up the tidy little happy ending now that someone else had come.

For the moment he seemed to wait, as if Kate, having struck the deer, should be the one to say out loud the one thing that seemed unavoidable. And finally, past a closed throat, she managed: "I guess the poor thing should be put out of her suffering," tacking around at the end to leave a faint and rueful question mark.

The boy made a wordless sound, pained, agreeing, then nothing more; in the silence Kate began to feel fresh despair. Something else, too, leaking in under the edges. Impatience?

"Do you have a gun or anything like that?" the boy asked finally.

Kate shook her head. And watching his grave eyes beneath their ledge of brows, found she could not bring herself to suggest a stone. The silence seemed thick and cottony and dingy with gloom. I can't, she said with her silence. I'm sorry but I just wouldn't be able to do it. It will have to be you. I'm sorry. Seeing now, in a sudden wash of anguish and guilt that this had been the reason for waiting. Someone else will have to do it.

"Well, I've never had to do anything like this before," the boy said, glancing gingerly toward the doe and then toward the girl, with that characteristic ducking of his chin. "But I can't see letting her lay there and suffer." He lifted both hands in a sudden sharp-edged gesture of resolve. "I'll get your blanket," he said, "and then you can just go on if you want. I'll take care of it."

His face had become very pale and hard, all of its adolescent smoothness gone jagged. He ducked his chin again and walked very stiffly through the rain to the place where the doe waited. Kate watched him retrieve the blanket. He bunched it against his chest with both arms so his shoulders were a bow, a long turned-in curve. He came and stood beside her a moment, looking out at the trees from his stiffened face, and into the silence made a sound of sour amusement. "My mom just bought me a 'Save the Whales' tee-shirt," he said, and managed to make his words say something else, something complex and only dimly relevant. He pushed the blanket to her through the window and where he brushed her hand the touch was chill and wet. He went through the rain to his car and said something to the girl and then went to stand looking at the doe with his hands fisted in his pockets. He stood with his shoulders tucked in tight and protective.

Kate looked away, looked out at the indifferent darkness of the trees. At the edge of her view she could see the girl in the other car holding herself very stiffly, her pale round face staring straight out through the windshield, straight out to the road while she waited for the boy. Kate began to shake again, thought, *Someone else will have to do it,* and remembered with not much surprise that she'd said that once already, with a different intent.

She unlocked the car and walked back through the rain, through the cool and unburdening rain, to stand beside the boy.

"She doesn't act as though she's in pain," Kate said, offering him one of her own earlier self-deceptions.

There were down-turned puckers at the corner of his mouth, as though weights hung there dragging. "No," he said. "She doesn't."

She said, "I'd feel so much better about this if we at least tried to get her some help." She had already begun to feel cool and controlled, floating detached from her earlier feelings as if they had happened to someone else, as if she'd heard the story second-hand. It was unexpectedly easy to get the right tone of voice, imploring, apologetic. "Since she doesn't seem to be suffering, I just hate to give up without making an effort to save her."

The boy's thin shirt was dark across the shoulders where the rain had soaked through. The ends of his hair dribbled wet down inside the collar. "I don't think there's a vet in Nehalem," he said in a moment, but she thought she could hear a softness, a loosening there at the edge of his voice.

"Then we could call the State Police," Kate said. "Or the Fish and Wildlife people, or the Humane Society, or the SPCA." Her whole list of happy endings. Then she waited for the boy, who stood watching the doe from that frighteningly young, frighteningly splintered face. Finally he made a sound of surrender or relief, a sigh.

"I guess it wouldn't hurt to try a couple of people," he said. And then, with his face turned carefully toward the trees, "If worse comes to worst, we can get my girlfriend's dad to come out," adding in a moment, "He goes elk hunting every year," as a clear little footnote.

Kate said, "Yes, if worse comes to worst," while her eyes watched the doe.

The boy shifted his weight, patted his pockets. "Have you got a piece of paper? I'll draw you a little map to get to my girlfriend's house."

She made a slight gesture of dismissal "You know where you're going. I'd only get lost and you'd be waiting here. I want you to go."

He gave her a doubtful look of objection. "I don't know if you should wait here alone."

"I'll lock myself in the car."

He looked from her to the doe, shifted his feet again, uncomfortable. "She lives between Nehalem and Manzanita," he said. "I might be an hour, maybe more, if I have to go get her dad. That's kind of a long time for you to wait. Kind of a long time to leave the doe like that, too."

"It's all right," Kate said. "It will be all right."

He looked at the doe again and then down the sloping curve of asphalt running red-beaded in the shine of taillights. Finally his shoulders moved indistinctly, a shrug, or a shrugging off. "Okay," he said, with another sound, a faint sigh. "I'll be back as quick as I can," and he crossed the road to his car.

The windows were black and wet and lustrous, like facets of gems. The girl showed her face within one, a pale image smiling a melancholy encouragement, and then the boy stirred the car. Inside the cones of headlights each rain bead seemed to fall singly, with a solitary glare. And Kate, watching the two of them out of sight behind the bending of the road, watching through melting scald of tears, felt at once as encapsulated as those separate drops of rain.

Still, she did not wait. She went a little way into the trees to find a rock, a big flat slab, lying wet among leaves, and pried it from the earth with scrabbling fingernails, pried it out silently, with a sort of fierce impatience. Then she held it against her hips with both hands and went back down the slope to the place where the doe waited, put the rock carefully on the ground and then went back to the car for the blanket, shaking it out smooth over the doe again, and after a moment drawing the edge up over the doe's face, over those pleading eyes, those bright and dying eyes.

She knelt carefully beside the rock. It was bright and slick with rain, hard and cold and wet against the inner curve of her hands.

You'd better not wait. You'd better do it right now. Don't think about it any more.

She wiped her palms against her thighs, one harsh downward stroke, and touched the stone again.

"You'll be better off this way," she said, for the doe and for herself, pushing the words out loudly to the edges of the trees, shaping the words carefully and clearly with her stiff pleated mouth.

She lifted the great stone, swinging it up in a shivering arc to her chin and then quick, blind, fierce down, *Ah God, God*, rocking back sightless with a wordless outcry of agony and release and completion.

Suggested Further Reading

Works by Gloss
Outside the Gates. New York: Atheneum, 1986.
The Jump-Off Creek. Boston: Houghton Mifflin, 1989.

Raymond Carver

Raymond Carver (1938-1988) was born in Clatskanie, Oregon, where his father worked in a sawmill, and grew up in the Northwest among working-class people like those found in his stories. He went to high school in Yakima, married young, fathered two children, and worked at a series of low-paying jobs until his writing began to receive attention. After this, he taught and lectured on writing at a number of colleges and universities. He is one of a few modern writers credited with reviving the short story as a literary form. His stories and poetry have won numerous awards, including the O. Henry Award, a nomination for the Pulitzer Prize, and a National Book Award in fiction for *Will You Please Be Quiet, Please?* Carver's stories are often set in his native Northwest, but, as in the story which follows, there is usually little reference to place. Still, his work is anchored in the reality of human relationships. The fear and isolation of modern lives, even between mother and son, lend this story an ominous universality.

Why, Honey?

Dear Sir:

      I was so surprised to receive your letter asking about my son, how did you know I was here? I moved here years ago right after it started to happen. No one knows who I am here but I'm afraid all the same. Who I am afraid of is him. When I look at the paper I shake my head and wonder. I read what they write about him and I ask myself is that man really my son, is he really doing these things?

He was a good boy except for his outbursts and that he could not tell the truth. I can't give you any reasons. It started one summer over the Fourth of July, he would have been about fifteen. Our cat Trudy disappeared and was gone all night and the next day. Mrs. Cooper who lives behind us came the next evening to tell me Trudy crawled into her backyard that afternoon to die. Trudy was cut up she said but she recognized Trudy. Mr. Cooper buried the remains.

Cut up? I said. What do you mean cut up?

Mr. Cooper saw two boys in the field putting firecrackers in Trudy's ears and in her you know what. He tried to stop them but they ran.

Who, who would do such a thing, did he see who it was?

He didn't know the other boy but one of them ran this way. Mr. Cooper thought it was your son.

I shook my head. No, that's just not so, he wouldn't do a thing like that, he loved Trudy, Trudy has been in the family for years, no, it wasn't my son.

That evening I told him about Trudy and he acted surprised and shocked and said we should offer a reward. He typed something up and promised to post it at school. But just as he was going to his room that night he said don't take it too hard, mom, she was old, in cat years she was 65 or 70, she lived a long time.

He went to work afternoons and Saturdays as a stockboy at Hartley's. A friend of mine who worked there, Betty Wilks, told me about the job and said she would put in a word for him. I mentioned it to him that evening and he said good, jobs for young people are hard to find.

The night he was to draw his first check I cooked his favorite supper and had everything on the table when he walked in. Here's the man of the house, I said, hugging him. I am so proud, how much did you draw, honey? Eighty dollars, he said. I was flabbergasted. That's wonderful, honey, I just cannot believe it. I'm starved, he said, let's eat.

I was happy, but I couldn't understand it, it was more than I was making.

When I did the laundry I found the stub from Hartley's in his pocket, it was for 28 dollars, he said 80. Why didn't he just tell the truth? I couldn't understand.

I would ask him where did you go last night, honey? To the show he would answer. Then I would find out he went to the school dance or spent the evening riding around with somebody in a car. I would think what difference could it make, why doesn't he just be truthful, there is no reason to lie to his mother.

I remember once he was supposed to have gone on a field trip, so I asked him what did you see on the field trip, honey? And he shrugged and said land formations, volcanic rock, ash, they showed us where there used to be a big lake a million years ago, now it's just a desert. He looked me in the eyes and went on talking. Then I got a note from the school the next day saying they wanted permission for a field trip, could he have permission to go.

Near the end of his senior year he bought a car and was always gone. I was concerned about his grades but he only laughed. You know he was an excellent student, you know that about him if you know anything. After that he bought a shotgun and a hunting knife.

I hated to see those things in the house and I told him so. He laughed, he always had a laugh for you. He said he would keep the gun and the knife in the trunk of his car, he said they would be easier to get there anyway.

One Saturday night he did not come home. I worried myself into a terrible state. About ten o'clock the next morning he came in and asked me to cook him breakfast, he said he had worked up an appetite out hunting, he said he was sorry for being gone all night, he said they had driven a long way to get to this place. It sounded strange. He was nervous.

Where did you go?

Up to the Wenas. We got a few shots.

Who did you go with, honey?

Fred.

Fred?

He stared and I didn't say anything else.

On the Sunday right after I tiptoed into his room for his car keys. He had promised to pick up some breakfast items on his way home from work the night before and I thought he might have left the things in his car. I saw his

new shoes sitting half under his bed and covered with mud and sand. He opened his eyes.

Honey, what happened to your shoes? Look at your shoes.

I ran out of gas, I had to walk for gas. He sat up. What do you care?

I am your mother.

While he was in the shower I took the keys and went out to his car. I opened the trunk. I didn't find the groceries. I saw the shotgun lying on a quilt and the knife too and I saw a shirt of his rolled in a ball and I shook it out and it was full of blood. It was wet. I dropped it. I closed the trunk and started back for the house and I saw him watching at the window and he opened the door.

I forgot to tell you, he said, I had a bad bloody nose, I don't know if that shirt can be washed, throw it away. He smiled.

A few days later I asked how he was getting along at work. Fine, he said, he said he had gotten a raise. But I met Betty Wilks on the street and she said they were all sorry at Hartley's that he had quit, he was so well liked, she said, Betty Wilks.

Two nights after that I was in bed but I couldn't sleep, I stared at the ceiling. I heard his car pull up out front and I listened as he put the key in the lock and he came through the kitchen and down the hall to his room and he shut the door after him. I got up. I could see light under his door, I knocked and pushed on the door and said would you like a hot cup of tea, honey, I can't sleep. He was bent over by the dresser and slammed a drawer and turned on me, get out he screamed, get out of here, I'm sick of you spying he screamed. I went to my room and cried myself to sleep. He broke my heart that night.

The next morning he was up and out before I could see him, but that was all right with me. From then on I was going to treat him like a lodger unless he wanted to mend his ways, I was at my limit. He would have to apologize if he wanted us to be more than just strangers living together under the same roof.

When I came in that evening he had supper ready. How are you? he said, he took my coat. How was your day?

I said I didn't sleep last night, honey. I promised myself I wouldn't bring it up and I'm not trying to make you feel guilty but I'm not used to being talked to like that by my son.

I want to show you something, he said, and he showed me this essay he was writing for his civics class. I believe it was on relations between the congress and the supreme court. (It was the paper that won a prize for him at graduation!) I tried to read it and then I decided, this was the time. Honey, I'd like to have a talk with you, it's hard to raise a child with things the way they are these days, it's especially hard for us having no father in the house, no man to turn to when we need him. You are nearly grown now but I am still responsible and I feel I am entitled to some respect and consideration and have tried to be fair and honest with you. I want the truth, honey, that's all I've ever asked from you, the truth. Honey, I took a breath, suppose you had a child who when you asked him something, anything, where he's been or where he's going, what he's doing with his time, anything, never, he never once told you the truth? Who if you asked him is it raining outside, would answer no, it is nice and sunny, and I guess laugh to himself and think you were too old or too stupid to see his clothes are wet. Why should he lie, you ask yourself, what does he gain I don't understand. I keep asking myself why but I don't have the answer. Why, honey?

He didn't say anything, he kept staring, then he moved over alongside me and said I'll show you. Kneel is what I say, kneel down is what I say, he said, that's the first reason why.

I ran to my room and locked the door. He left that night, he took his things, what he wanted, and he left. Believe it or not I never saw him again. I saw him at his graduation but that was with a lot of people around. I sat in the audience and watched him get his diploma and a prize for his essay, then I heard him give the speech and then I clapped right along with the rest.

I went home after that.

I have never seen him again. Oh sure I have seen him on the TV and I have seen his pictures in the paper.

I found out he joined the marines and then I heard from someone he was out of the marines and going to college back east and then he married that girl and got himself in politics. I began to see his name in the paper. I found out his address and wrote to him, I wrote a letter every few months, there never was an answer. He ran for governor and was elected, and was famous now. That's when I began to worry.

I built up all these fears, I became afraid, I stopped writing him of course and then I hoped he would think I was dead. I moved here. I had them give me an unlisted number. And then I had to change my name. If you are a powerful man and want to find somebody, you can find them, it wouldn't be that hard.

I should be so proud but I am afraid. Last week I saw a car on the street with a man inside I know was watching me, I came straight back and locked the door. A few days ago the phone rang and rang, I was lying down. I picked up the receiver but there was nothing there.

I am old. I am his mother. I should be the proudest mother in all the land but I am only afraid.

Thank you for writing. I wanted someone to know. I am very ashamed.

I also wanted to ask how you got my name and knew where to write, I have been praying no one knew. But you did. Why did you? Please tell me why?

Yours truly,

Suggested Further Reading

WORKS BY CARVER
Will You Please Be Quiet, Please? New York: McGraw-Hill, 1976.
What We Talk about When We Talk about Love. New York: Alfred A. Knopf, 1981.
Fires: Essays, Poems, Stories, 1966-1982. Santa Barbara: Capra Press, 1983.
Cathedral. New York: Alfred A. Knopf, 1984.
Where I'm Calling From. New York: The Atlantic Monthly Press, 1988.
Carver Country (with Bob Adelman). New York: Charles Scribner's Sons, 1990.

WORKS ABOUT CARVER
Saltzman, Arthur M. *Understanding Raymond Carver.* Columbia, SC: University of South Carolina Press, 1988.
Gentry, Marshall Bruce, and William L. Stull, eds. *Conversations with Raymond Carver.* Jackson: University Press of Mississippi, 1990.

Ellen Howard

Ellen Howard was born in 1943 and grew up living with many relatives in a big house in Portland. She attended the University of Oregon in the early 1960s and later graduated with honors from Portland State University. She worked in libraries and offices until, at age forty, she achieved her lifelong dream of being a writer, when she published her first book, *Circle of Giving*. Since then, she has written a number of books for young people, including some which deal with sensitive issues, such as child abuse in *Gillyflower*.

Ellen Howard is a descendant of Oregon pioneers. Her mother and grandmother were storytellers, and the following story of a young girl's coming of age may have been inspired by her grandmother's stories of early life in Oregon. In "Blood of the Lamb," young Edith, after her mother's death, has gone to live with her married sister, Alena, who has her own family. Alena's husband, John, is a grim, Calvinistic figure who rules with an iron hand.

Blood of the Lamb

"Blooming" was what they called it then. Blooming, as a rosebud, chaste and white, turns toward the sun, unfolding to reveal the full-blown rose. In those days, girls, like rosebuds, were thought to come to womanhood thus—purely, gracefully, in beauty.

Edith did not remember blooming. She remembered the bright stain on her drawers and the fear . . . and the shame. She remembered. . . .

She stood on the landing of the girls' stairway that summer day and watched through the diamond-paned window as the hired man led the mule across the barnyard. She wished he would hurry—she felt so ill—but he moved slowly, matching the deliberate pace of the mule. John was not at home, Edith thought, or he would step livelier. She leaned her aching head against the glass of the window, hoping for coolness. The glass felt clammy. If only the window opened. It did not.

"There is a generation that are pure in their own eyes and yet is not washed from their filthiness," John would quote as, each evening, he locked the door of the staircase that led to the girls' room. Edith did not understand why pillow fighting was sinful, but she knew it must be. Since the evening John had found Vernon playing with them in their room, Vernon and even little Ira had been forbidden to use the girls' stairs. The window on the landing was nailed shut and the door to the yard, the only entrance to their attic room, was locked each night. The boys' room was at the other end of the attic with its own separate stair. John was particular about what he called "proprieties."

There was, for instance, this business of going to the privy. To go toward the privy when a boy or man was watching was immodest, said John. Yet it was so hard to find a moment when the yard was empty. Several times, weeping, little Lettie had wet her drawers waiting for a chance. But Alena only shushed her fearfully and took her upstairs to change her underthings.

If only the hired man would hurry, Edith thought. Her limbs and belly felt heavy with pain. She looked out once again at the dirt yard between the house and the barn. No one was in sight except for the shuffling man in overalls and the reluctant mule going at last around the corner of the barn.

Edith moved, as quickly as her swimming head allowed, down the stairs and out the door into the thick afternoon heat. She walked—she dared not run, it wasn't ladylike—away from the square gray clap-board house. Her boots kicked up puffs of gray dust. Her upper lip beaded with perspiration. The high collar and underarms and band of her waist were wet against her sticky skin. Even her drawers chafed wet between her legs. She stepped into the shade of the plum orchard with relief. It was not much cooler—the trees stood still and parched—but here the sun did not beat so mercilessly on her pounding head. She slowed, knowing she was hidden from view of the house.

The privy was unpainted, a one-holer, utilitarian, unprepossessing. As Edith opened the door, its smell assaulted her. Her stomach lurched and she began to breathe through her mouth to avoid the stench. She fastened the door carefully, turned and lifted the lid. The blue bottles buzzed frenziedly as she gathered up her skirts and fumbled for the buttons that fastened her drawers to her camisole. Her thighs and belly ached. She settled on the splintery wooden seat, holding her petticoats out of the way.

It was then that Edith saw the stains. The coarse white cotton of her summer drawers was smeared with blood. She stared at it in horror. Where had it come from? Fear rose in her in sickening waves. She could not pull her eyes away from the smears of red. The buzzing of the flies, the pounding of her heart roared painfully in her head. She sat, clutching her skirts, hunched forward on the seat, and looked and looked at the stains.

Long moments passed before she began to breathe again, before her heart slowed and an empty weakness in her knees and stomach replaced the first terror. Little by little she began to think, to hold her thoughts carefully still as she stilled her trembling knees. I must be hurt, she thought, but how?

Her thoughts darted back to the morning, spent in the kitchen with Alena, making jam. "Before it gets too hot," Alena had said. It had been too hot by ten o'clock, too hot to stand over the cookstove stirring the blueblack shining jam. "But we have to finish," Alena had sighed, perspiration dripping from her nose and chin as she built the fire still higher. "I told John we'd finish the blackberries today."

Could the heat hurt me? Edith wondered. I must look to see where I am bleeding. She swallowed hard and forced her eyes from the drying stains on her drawers. She could not look between her legs. She never had looked at herself—there. Or touched, especially not touched. She did not know how she knew, but she knew that to touch herself—there—was a sin. Not just immodest, but a sin. Even thinking about—that part—was a sin.

She tore a page from the mail-order catalog which hung by a string on the wall and wiped carefully between her legs. The paper was bloody. The sight of it filled her with a familiar sickening shame. "Shame," she could hear John thundering in her mind, as he thundered when the children laughed out loud, when Alena kissed the baby, when Vernon sang as he worked. "Shame" was his pronouncement on every show of affection or joy.

"But John," Alena would sometimes protest. "'Make a joyful noise before the Lord. . . .'"

John would seem not to hear. "'Delight is not seemly for a fool,'" he would quote and Alena would fall silent, head bowed before her husband's scornful gaze.

Edith forced herself to think. What must I do? She longed suddenly for her mother. She remembered a large, strong hand holding her small one. She remembered the close, cozy warmth of being held and rocked while a clear, soprano voice hummed a tune above her cuddled head. She remembered—and her mind veered away from the memory—the scent, the sick, heavy sweetness of lilies, the cold white face, eyes closed against her crying, "Mama, Mama!" And, "Kiss Mother goodbye, Edith," someone said, but Mother wasn't there in the box on the parlour chairs. That still mouth didn't whisper "shush." Those stiff white fingers didn't reach up to smooth Edith's hair as Mother's would have done.

Edith thought of Alena. Alena had said, crying, "I will be your mother now, Edith," and in the years since their mother's death, Alena had tried. But she had children of her own, Vernon, Lettie and Ira. No matter how Alena tried, she was a sister, not a mother, and there was always John between them. "Do not slobber over Edith, Alena," he commanded. "'Life is real and life is earnest' and the sooner children know it, the better for them." John did not approve of softness. "You are soft, Alena," he told his young wife. "'He that spareth his rod hateth his son; but he that loveth him chasteneth him. . . .'" Edith could not tell Alena about the blood. Alena was John's wife and a wife was bound to tell her husband all. Edith felt her heart sink with the heavy knowledge of what John would say. The blood was God's punishment for her iniquity.

Still hunched on the privy seat, Edith began to rock backward and forward silently.

Edith scarcely remembered the dazed journey back to the house and the hiding of her bloodstained underwear. But she remembered vividly how, in the days that followed, she had searched her conscience for her sins. God was just, she knew. "Everyman must die for his own sin . . . ," the Bible said. What was hers? Was it her delight in Vernon's rebellion?

Vernon loved to sing—not just hymns as God-fearing folk did, but frivolous tunes like "Buffalo Gals" and "Old Black Joe." "'The song of the drunkards . . . ,'" John said. Edith could not help exulting when, face still streaked with angry tears, Vernon defied his father's switch, by singing through clenched teeth,

"Buffalo Gals, won't you come out tonight,
Come out tonight, come out tonight. . . ."

The Bible said that he that loveth his son, chasteneth him, Edith thought, but it didn't say how the son would feel.

Perhaps it was her disobedience. There had been the Sunday John had seen her running after a butterfly in the yard.

"Edith!" his voice had broken the stillness of the heavy afternoon. She paused in mid-flight, her heart leaping with fear at his call, and the butterfly she was chasing fluttered out of sight. "Confine yourself to a walk, Edith," he said his voice hard and loud in her ears. "Remember it is the Sabbath day and keep it holy." She did not answer him, only stood, head hanging, while his voice beat against her. "If you cannot behave yourself in a seemly manner, you will have to come in," John said from the doorway.

Her lips were stiff. "Yes, sir," she said. The screen door slammed.

Edith walked on with dragging steps, past the barn and through the field to the crest of the hill. There, looking over the fields, she stopped. Nothing stirred. The sun weighed heavily on her shoulders and on the top of her head. The molten, slick gray sky glared without relief.

And then she felt the breeze. It came from nowhere, touching her damp forehead as Alena might have done, encouraging and comforting her. It lifted her skirts gently from her sticky legs, and cooled and lightened them.

It was the breeze that had done it, Edith thought. She had lifted her head and for one long uncertain moment, she looked back at the house. She knew John stood at the door, looking out at her.

But the breeze touched her face, as softly as Alena's hand, encouraging her. Turning abruptly, flinging back her braids, Edith rose on her toes like a dancer, paused, and plummeted down the hill into the hollow below.

"'An evil man seeketh only rebellion; therefore, a cruel messenger shall be sent against him,'" John had read from the Bible that evening at prayers. Was the blood her cruel messenger?

Perhaps vanity was her greatest sin. Edith loved bright colors, luscious textures, shine and sparkle. She hated the plain serviceable cottons of her ill-fitting dresses—too big the first year, made with 'room to grow,' and too small the next. She hoarded treasures in Mother's little Chinese basket, itself a treasure trimmed with tassels and blue beads. Was it so great a sin to love them, she wondered, counting over in her mind the rose-colored ribbon, the little gold brooch, the pansy she had pressed between the pages of Mother's Bible. "'Lay not up for yourselves treasures upon the earth . . . ,'" John said.

Edith moved through the long hot week in a daze. Her head pounded constantly with her fear and her guilt. The sickly sweet scent of lilies seemed always in her nose. Her back pained and her head spun dizzily. "You've gotten so clumsy lately, Edith. You certain you're all right? I've never known you to break a dish before," Alena said.

An old petticoat, torn into strips and folded into clumsy bandages staunched the flow of blood. Stealthily she washed them in her basin as best she could, and hung them, still stained, to dry behind her dresses in the curtained-off closet. Each day was preoccupied with the difficulties of tending to her hurt in secret. "Edith seems ill," Alena worried, putting a cool hand to her forehead. John's piercing gaze seemed to see through Edith's clothes. She waited numbly for discovery. "I will not have malingerers, Edith," John said.

Edith knew she was dying. She remembered the bloody foam on Mother's lips, the stained handkerchiefs and the wracking coughs of the days Mother had lain dying. She waited for weakness to overtake her. But, instead, the bleeding lessened. One morning the petticoat pad was unstained. She could not believe it. She was getting well!

Edith threw on her clothes with a lightened heart. She noticed for the first time a pleasant breeze stirring the curtains at her window. A meadowlark sang. Even the old iron stove, waiting for its blacking that morning, looked beautiful to Edith when she came into the kitchen. She began to hum, "I Walk Through The Garden Alone," as, enveloped in a ragged old apron of Alena's, she smeared on the blacking when the breakfast dishes had been cleared away.

The stove was shining, black and clean, and Edith was polishing the silvery handle of the oven door when she heard Alena's voice from the doorway.

"Edith, I'm so sorry. I just found these."

Edith turned, squatting on her heels, and looked up at the stained underdrawers in her sister's hands. The hymn died on her lips. Her smile drained away. Sickness rose in her throat, choking her. She opened her mouth, but no sound came.

"Edith, Edith," Alena was saying. "Edith, it's all right. I should have told you, but you seemed so young yet. I didn't think. . . . Edith, it happens to all of us. It means you are a woman . . . just something you must bear. But you needn't be frightened, dear. Oh, Edith, don't. Don't look like that."

Alena ran to her sister, who squatted still, unmoving before the stove. She gathered her, thin and trembling, into her arms and pressed her smooth head against her. "Edith, Edith," she crooned. "It's all right, dear. Don't worry. It's all right." She rocked her slowly, pressing her lips to Edith's hair. "It's all right."

Edith remembered lifting her face to look up into Alena's blue eyes. Her throat was constricted with terror, and she did not know her lips were forming a single soundless word. Alena looked down at her and saw the fear and shame and pain in the name on Edith's lips. She clutched Edith more tightly, straining her fiercely to her breast, her arms a strong circle about her. Edith felt the comforting pressure of her sister's arms and breathed in her clean warm smell.

"John need not know, dear," Alena whispered.

The tightness in Edith's chest loosened. She drew a long, sobbing breath and began to cry.

Suggested Further Reading

WORKS BY HOWARD

Circle of Giving. New York: Atheneum, 1984.

When Daylight Comes. New York: Atheneum, 1985.

Gillyflower. New York: Atheneum, 1986.

Edith Herself. New York: Atheneum, 1987.

Her Own Song. New York: Atheneum, 1988.

Sister. New York: Atheneum, 1990.

The Chickenhouse House. New York: Atheneum, 1991.

WORK ABOUT HOWARD

"Howard, Ellen, 1943-" In *Something about the Author,* vol. 67, ed. Donna Olendorf. Detroit: Gale Research Co., 1992, pp. 93-95.

Craig Lesley

Craig Lesley, born in The Dalles in 1945, grew up in Baker, Pendleton, Madras, and Hermiston, the kinds of places in which his two widely-praised novels, *Winterkill* and *River Song,* are set. Both works deal with Native Americans caught up in the vortex of present-day white America, while attempting to reclaim some sense of familial and communal tradition. Lesley spent his early summers working on Oregon ranches and for the Deschutes River Guide Service. He graduated from Whitman College, and later earned a master's degree in English from the University of Kansas, and a Master of Fine Arts degree from the University of Massachusetts. He now lives in Portland and teaches at Clackamas Community College in Oregon City.

Mint

Most people start brushing their teeth or pop one of those red-and-white striped mint candies into their mouths without thinking much about what went into the flavoring. Well, there's peppermint oil, of course, but other things, too: lots of sweat, boot grease, sheep and goose dung. (The farmers turn them loose in the fields to eat the quack grass.) And there are odd items such as a pitchfork and a lunch bucket or two. After three weeks of working mint harvest, the crew gets a little crazy, and someone tosses things through the chopper blades, just to see what comes out. All you get from a lunch bucket are metal filings. A pitchfork produces filings and shavings.

I know pitchforks because I used to be a stomper, and a pitchfork was my tool-of-trade. The stomper rides in the back of the mint truck, a special kind of dump truck, and stomps the mint stems and leaves after they have been run through the chopper. It's important to spread the mint around evenly and pack it down tight. The corners are tricky, because you have to duck around the chopper's boom. During the first few hours each day, your sinuses run constantly because of the menthol; your eyes sting, too, even behind the safety goggles.

The stomper, truck driver, and chopper driver make a team. Right away, the stomper works out signals with the chopper driver. He relays them to the truck driver, who pulls the truck up a little or drops back, snugs closer to the chopper or gives it some room, so the chopped mint coming through the boom piles in different parts of the truck bed, saving the stomper a lot of pitchforking.

Hank Stone was my favorite truck driver the summer I'm talking about, the summer of the accident. Everyone in Madras loved Hank, because he had starred as forward for the White Buffalos. People still remember those 22 second-half points in the state championship against Coquille. Hank was working mint harvest for pin money, even though he had a full-ride scholarship to Oregon State starting that fall.

Grady Price was one of the drifters who followed the harvest. Originally from Modesto, or so he said, and his old Buick Roadmaster had California plates. He looked like a lot of men who pass through—about 40, field clothes and coveralls, large lumpy hands that come from working with machinery. But he drove that old Fox chopper as if he came out of the womb clutching a steering wheel, keeping it lined right on the windrows of mowed mint and hardly ever jumping a corrugation. And those old Foxes were cranky, too, not like your new Cases or Massey Fergusons. Grady claimed that nothing held them together but baling wire and cussing, and we used a lot of both that summer.

Stomping in the truck bed I watched Grady hunched over the chopper's wheel, his dark suspenders making an X across his back. On windy days, he'd tug his stained gray cap lower and tuck his head down like a turtle. I never knew how he caught all my hand signals—he hardly ever looked back—but some days it went so smoothly, I quit using the pitchfork and just stomped and grinned, the mint flakes sticking in my teeth. Grady tagged me with the nickname "Boots" when he saw how stained my boots got from the green mint.

The three of us usually ate lunch together, resting in the shade of the chopper. Grady brought corned beef sandwiches with the meat sliced thick as two of his fingers. When he had finished eating, he wiped the crumbs from his pants and started telling stories about other harvests or California. I knew most of them weren't true, but I enjoyed them anyway because they helped pass the time.

"We're lucky to be working day shift," Grady said one day about a week into harvest.

"Too cold at night," Hank agreed.

"You could turn on the truck heater," Grady said. "But it's cold for a chopper jockey. And Boots would freeze in the truck bed with the damp mint pouring in." He paused a moment. "Damn dangerous, too."

Hank winked at me, our signal that one of Grady's stories was coming.

"Over to Nyssa," Grady said, "one old wino stomper got to nipping on the jug one night, just to warm up, but he fell asleep in the back of the truck and got buried under the mint. The driver figured that the wino had taken off to town so he and the chopper man stomped that load down best they could, threw a tarp over it, and ran it into the still. Cooked that old bastard right up with the mint."

"I'll bet that warmed him some," Hank said, grinning and pulling on his black-and-orange OSU cap.

Grady scowled at him. "More than he reckoned. The next day the straw boss had us boys go through the dumped mint slugs real careful-like with pitchforks, until we found him. He was puckered up and all shrunk down to mummy size."

"No kidding," Hank said. "You see him yourself?"

"It's good as gospel," Grady said. "They wound up burying him in a child's casket."

Out of earshot, Hank started calling Grady "Baloney Joe," but I figured he was just a lonely guy shooting the breeze to impress a couple kids.

And when Grady learned I was hitching to work, he offered me rides. He was staying close by at the Juniper Motel; so it wasn't any real trouble, and I liked the way he kept that old Buick Roadmaster. "Mint condition," he used to say and chuckle at his little joke.

He'd come by just after 5 so we'd have time to make a quick stop at Maw's Bakery before heading out to the fields. Mr. Maw would let us in the back door, and we'd stuff ourselves with jelly rolls and doughnuts, washing them down with coffee. While we ate, Mr. Maw would keep working, standing at the big fryer, turning the doughnuts with a wooden spoon, or rolling out bread dough on a long table, the flour up to his elbows. The bakery smelled like fresh dough and cinnamon, and I tried to remember those smells later, when I was knee-deep in chopped mint, my nose running steadily.

Sometimes before we'd go, Grady walked around the bakery looking at the mixers, tapping the stainless steel bowls with his forefinger. He'd peer through the large oven's little window at the baking bread and nod. "Nice place," he'd say to Mr. Maw. "Very nice." And Mr. Maw would smile and touch two fingers to his baker's hat as a kind of agreement.

On Friday nights, I'd scrub and scrub to get the mint smell off, then head to the teen dances on the second floor of the VFW hall. Hank was always there, too, wearing a red shirt with silver threads through it and a double-buckled white belt about as thin as a shoelace. He danced with all the popular girls, even Sandy Swanson, whose parents had the only swimming pool in town. Things came easy like that for Hank.

One night I left the stag line early and started home when I saw Grady's Buick parked outside the Recreation Tavern. He was inside shooting pool. Maybe it was the light, or the way he held his face as he concentrated on the shots but he looked different—wary and somehow sad. I've seen that look on other men, now that I'm older, but back then I didn't know what it meant. Still, I felt awkward, as if I was intruding on something personal, so I just slipped away before Grady saw me.

The next morning Grady was late, and we didn't stop at Maw's. "I guess I had a wonderful time," he said. "I woke up broke and remember getting so damn drunk, I was eating matches thinking they were bar pretzels."

It was no party-time when we got to the field, either. The thick mint was damp with night dew, and the chopper blades were dull; so the mint kept clogging the chopper's throat. Grady disengaged the chopper a few times, climbed off and went around in front, kicking at the slugs of mint and pulling away the tangled stems. "Damn night crew must have run the ditch bank to screw up these blades so bad," he mumbled.

I scrambled out of the truck bed to help out with the pitchfork.

"Work harder, you guys," Hank yelled from the truck window.

"Thinks he's too good to get out and help," Grady said.

"Only room for two, anyway," I said.

We had to take a long lunch break so Grady could pull the chopper blades and sharpen them on the grinder in the machine shop. Grady concentrated on those blades, the sparks flying off the grinder, and he got that same look, even behind the safety goggles. I thought maybe he was sick from the drinking. When he finished sharpening, Grady switched off the grinder and sat down on the work bench. "Let's take five," he said.

He didn't say anything else at first—just took off the safety goggles and held them by the elastic band, spinning them slowly. "Mr. Maw has got a nice place," he said after a while. "A man needs that. A long time back, my wife and I had a nice place, too, there just outside Modesto. Combination wrecking yard and cafe."

"Sounds OK," I said. I was a little surprised to hear him mention a wife, since he hadn't before.

"It was fine," he said. "Amyx was real good with the customers."

"Funny name," I said.

"Her father counted on a boy real bad and felt he'd been crossed by God, so he tagged that X behind Amy. Always bothered her some—like a bad birthmark."

"Probably not much to a name," I said.

"She didn't let on, but I knew. Back then, we worked hard trying to get started. I was building up the wrecking business, bought my own tow truck. She was cooking special barbecue sauce for the cafe trade—even had the name picked out—Modesto Red. People in California like things hot because of the Mexican influence. She tried all sorts of special ingredients to doctor that sauce. Maybe she even put in some mint leaves."

"You can keep it then," I said.

"Things went along, and we found out she was pregnant. Damn, we got busy then, getting everything ready. I put the tow truck on 24-hour call. She kept cooking sauce, wanting to get it just right, and dreaming about the baby. She wanted to pay back her daddy and wished on it being a boy."

"Was it?"

He took off his gray cap, wiped his forehead, then replaced the cap. "Yes," he said, so quiet I hardly heard him. "But something happened during the delivery and the cord twisted around his neck."

I couldn't think of anything to say. Maybe he didn't want me to; so we just sat there a while longer. Then Grady shrugged his shoulders. "Amyx took it hard. I started working more and more with the wrecking yard—getting out my grief. But sometimes I'd come back from a tow or road repair and find the cafe locked, her sitting in the corner booth, drinking coffee and tracing little circles on the Formica table. One day, all I came back to was a note and empty closets. After that, I sold the truck and bought that Buick. Been following harvests now for 15 years."

By September, we all were pretty tired of mint and working 12 hours on, 12 hours off. I was getting anxious because high school was about ready to start up, and I hadn't done half the things over the summer I'd promised myself. Grady said he was going on to Hood River for the apples, just as soon as mint harvest was over. And Hank was already packing for OSU. Sometimes, he'd bring a basketball out of his car at lunch and show off his dribbling. "After Labor Day, you can wave bye-bye to the Kid," Hank told us.

He was grinning at me one morning when I took my pitchfork and started climbing in the truck bed. "You might be looking at a bonus, Boots, just for sticking through the harvest," Hank said. "You're senior stomper now, because Perkins got fired last night for running two geese through the hopper."

"The heck he did," I said.

"The heck he didn't," Hank said. "They were sleeping on the ditch bank with their heads tucked under their wings, and he grabbed them and tossed them into the chopper before they could even squawk. Crazy bastard!"

"Not much left of those geese, I suppose."

"A puff of feathers and a fine red spray," Hank said. "But someday, an old coot in Portland will unscrew his Pepsodent and have it honk at him."

The wind kicked up that morning, bringing the smell of rain, and I had to stomp harder to keep some farmer's profit from blowing across Jefferson County. The straw boss came out to gripe about the blowing mint, but Grady took my side and told him to put two stompers in back, if he wanted a better job. At lunch, Grady muttered about the clutch slipping, but when the straw boss asked him if it would hold through shift, Grady said he thought so.

We tried to keep out of the wind while we ate lunch, but the mint flakes kept blowing around, and we had to pick them off our food. Grady finished his corned beef sandwich and said, "The wind and the way that mint's blowing reminds me of a story. I'd finished wheat harvest over at Jordan Valley one time and was coming towards Burns at night, when the wind kicked up like this, only harder. Every so often, I'd see something green flutter across the headlights. That was strange, because it's desert there, no trees.

"But there's a long straight stretch of road with a bad curve at the end, and getting closer to that curve, I saw more and more green things swirl past. I slowed down and just beyond the curve was a brand new station wagon—flipped over—the lights shining at a cockeyed angle.

"The back hatch had popped open, and those green things were blowing everywhere. The ground was like a goddam golf course. When I got out of the car, I could see what they were—sheets of Green Stamps. Even the license plate said S&H. So I started picking them up—good as money, I figured. Planned to get a coffee pot and fishing pole.

"Suddenly, I heard a groan—scared me most to death—and then I saw a man about a hundred feet from the car. It was the stamp salesman, all right. He was busted up pretty bad, but even so, he had crawled all around trying to save those stamps. He was clutching sheets in both hands and lying on a bunch more, trying to keep them from blowing away. As I carried him to the car, he kept muttering, 'The stamps, the stamps. I'm responsible.'"

Grady paused. "Can you beat that? At death's door and trying to save those damn stamps." Even Hank was quiet, as Grady finished the story.

"When I unloaded him at the hospital, I realized I hadn't saved any stamps at all, but maybe it's just as well. I never figured to profit from anyone's bad luck. I hope that guy made it, but I never knew. I looked at the papers when I got to my next job just out of Bend, but there wasn't anything about it."

That afternoon it rained, little squalls that dampened the mint and caused it to choke the chopper, even though the blades were still sharp. Grady and I kept working out the slugs. I broke them apart with my pitchfork; he kicked and pulled at the tangled stems. Every so often, he'd glance up at the gray sky and mutter, "Spit some more."

I thought it might rain hard enough to get the mint real wet; then we'd have to shut down until it dried. But it rained by fits and spurts the whole afternoon, and we kept fighting the wind.

Just before the end of shift, I was finishing stomping a loaded truck so the driver could run it to the still. Grady and Hank had started loading another truck, and I planned on leaving that load for the night stomper, so I took my own sweet time finishing up. At the rate they were going, the truck would be only half full by quitting time. As I was tying down the flapping tarp to cover the load, I saw that old Fox lumber to a stop at the far end of the field and Grady climb off.

I smiled a little, because I had the pitchfork, and I knew it would take Grady a while to clear the slug from the chopper's throat. I finished tying the tarp, and the truck left for the still. Then I started walking slowly across the field toward the chopper. "Quitting time," I wished.

The chopper lurched forward and then stopped. I took a few more steps before I saw Hank jump out of the truck. He was yelling and waving his cap. I started running, because it hit me suddenly that Grady hadn't been driving the chopper when it jerked ahead.

Stumbling across corrugations, I ran as if in a dream, weighted by my boots and fatigue. I saw others running, too, and the straw boss' pickup bumping across corrugations toward the yellow farmhouse north of the field. Once, I tripped on my pitchfork and fell onto the hard earth, my wind gone. When I could breathe again, I scrambled up, dropping the pitchfork and running harder.

By the time I reached the cluster of men, someone had already looped his belt around Grady's right thigh and twisted it tight for a tourniquet. I stared at the stump, sliced clean as a steak in a butcher's case, the bone showing white.

Hank put his OSU cap over the stump. "We don't need him seeing that and going into deeper shock," he said.

I hunkered by Grady's head and started praying under my breath. After a while, he opened his eyes and tried to sit up, but Hank held him down. "Just take it easy," he said. "Everything's going to be OK."

Grady tried to kid at first. "Call damage control," he said. "What's the estimate?"

"Broken leg," Hank said.

Grady's smile got real tight then and he shook his head. "It's bad, huh?"

"Your right leg's gone," I said, and didn't look at Hank.

"That was my favorite," Grady said. After that, he kept very quiet, and I counted the minutes until we heard sirens. When they got close, and the ambulance was bouncing across the field, Grady handed me his car keys. "Bring that Buick up to the hospital," he said. "Just in case I want to take a spin."

After the ambulance left, Hank did a funny thing, and I always was glad he took me along. He climbed into the truck and nodded at me; so I jumped in beside him.

Hank drove to the end of the field and onto the blacktop, but instead of turning toward Highway 26 and the mint still, we went toward the Deschutes Canyon. We hit gravel and found a place where Hank could back that truck right up to the rimrock. Then we dumped out that half-load of mint and whatever was left of Grady's leg.

"Let the bastards dock us," Hank said. But we both knew they wouldn't. That evening, driving the Buick into town, I gagged when I passed the still and smelled the cooking mint.

They gave Grady a good hospital room. One window looked off toward Mount Jefferson, and you could see Grizzly Butte from the other. A lot of people sent flowers, too, considering he was a migrant. Both crews chipped in to buy Grady a nice radio, in case he got tired of watching TV. Hank and I gave it to him in person.

Grady pretended to give us heck for not bringing his boot. "That was a brand new pair—practically," he protested. "What good is one boot?"

We all laughed at that, and when we told Grady about dumping the half-load over the canyon, he laughed so hard he choked.

I parked the Buick right outside Grady's window and honked a couple times so he'd know. Quail ran across the hospital lawn and rustled in the junipers, and I realized hunting season was coming up. I told Grady I knew some good places to road-hunt, where he wouldn't have to do any walking, but he said he'd given up hunting.

After school started, I still got up to see Grady a couple times a week, taking him magazines, jelly rolls, that sort of thing. Hank had gone to Corvallis by then, so I guess I was the only regular visitor. But when I came for one visit, Grady waved a get-well card and handed it to me.

"Amyx," I said, reading the signature. There was no return address, but it was canceled in Modesto.

"Maybe I should look her up," he said. "Time to quit running."

I was puzzled by his laugh, until I got the joke. "Running." Then I laughed, too.

The Buick was gone one Sunday when I went to visit. A woman at the front desk told me Grady had checked out. His forwarding address was General Delivery, Modesto.

I found the orderly who had wheelchaired Grady out to the Buick. "How could you just let him drive off like that?" I said. "He's only got one leg!"

"Look," the orderly said. "My job is to get him to the lot."

A lot of years have passed by now, of course, but I never heard from Grady, even though I wrote several times and sent a Christmas card to Modesto. I don't see many of those old Buicks anymore, but when I do, I pull up real close, just to see who's driving. Grady and Amyx might have fixed up their place or gotten another. I'd like to think so. And maybe Grady will read this and get in touch. Stranger things have happened.

You've read about Hank's career at Oregon State, and he's still a legend around here, even after he got hurt playing pro ball. Now he sells real estate in Denver, flies his own plane back for the reunions. I mentioned Grady to him a couple of times, but he just shook his head.

I never worked another harvest, but after high school I sold implements at the county co-op, mostly the new Massey Fergusons. Whenever I demonstrated a chopper, I'd tell about Grady and point out the new safety devices. Maybe that talk helped a sale or two, but most of those farmers are right-minded old boys who know that nothing's foolproof when it comes to machinery. But I felt I had to tell the story, anyway; I don't believe Grady would mind.

There's something else I almost never tell, although I might tell Grady, if he were here. I used to wonder about my part in the accident, thinking that if I'd run right over to help out with the pitchfork, maybe Grady wouldn't have lost his leg. But then my arm would have been in there when the chopper kicked on. I've pretty much quit worrying about it, and I almost never dream of those old Foxes any more.

Still, even now when August comes around and I smell the cooking mint, I get to feeling restless and empty. Some nights I drive out to where Hank and I dumped the half-load. I sit there with the motor running quietly, the head lights shining across the darkness of the canyon. I put on the radio and twist the dial until I get Modesto, coming in like next door. Then after a while, I tuck my right leg up on the front seat and practice driving with just my left, tear down those country back roads, past the mint field—black at night—until just before dawn, when the first farmhouse lights wink on.

Suggested Further Reading

WORKS BY LESLEY
Winterkill. Boston: Hougton Mifflin, 1984.
River Song. Boston: Houghton Mifflin, 1989.
Talking Leaves: Contemporary Native American Fiction, ed. Craig Lesley and Kathryn Stavrakis. New York: Dell-Laurel, 1991.

Elizabeth Woody

Elizabeth Woody is known primarily as a poet, but she also writes fiction. She is a Native American of Warm Springs, Wasco, and Navajo background, and she studied writing at the Institute of American Indian Arts in Santa Fe. She now lives in Portland. Her poems have appeared in a number of collections and magazines. The story included here was published in a recent collection of contemporary Native American short stories, *Talking Leaves*, which includes other stories with Oregon and Northwest relationships, such as those by Gloria Bird, Tina Marie Freeman-Villalobos, and Kathleen Shaye Hill.

HomeCooking

The flat teeth of the morning sun chew at the blisters of the old, tar-papered house. In the garden that thrives under a cloak of sagging cheesecloth, the grasshoppers pose on the promise of a meal. Granma is framed in the kitchen window as the tongues of curtains remain out from the morning breeze. Even with the hollyhocks' colorful bonnets, up tight against the wall, the house can appear as barren as a piano without ivory. There is a swarm of colors about the screendoor, of calicos, tabbys, sylvesters and blackies. They mew for their meal, in a chorus. As I turn back the covers from my floor bed, I hear humming and a spoon scratching the sides of a pan.

Watching the swill of leftovers sop up the milk, Granma turns to take the pan to the cats, twenty-some wild ones. She is pleased to see me up so early and smiles a toothless greeting. "Hi honey, got to feed my livestock." She sings her good-morning, almost, in the sweet, high-voiced, rhythmic dialect of Warm Springs English, that sounds Indian. She is no bigger than five feet and no more than ninety-eight pounds. I see her hook the cats in her path expertly with her toes to flip them aside, with a dancer's grace, a certain harmless precision. I once had balked at Granpa's joke about putting up little goalposts in the yard, for Granma to improve her "cat-punting." That was some years ago. Now, I am oblivious to her harmless way of walking through the fur mass of cats that stay for the one meal and all the mice and grasshoppers they can eat in the garden.

As I settle at the table I think of the music my grandmother makes, that evokes some aspect of the world I had forgotten since the last visit. Like toads slurping up great moths at night, or the ripple and tumble of water over the rocks in the river, that is how her songs sound to me. I breathe in the sweet smell of old age that lingers after my mother's mother. The Nivea, the cleanliness of air-dried cotton, the oiled hair. I notice two rainbow trout on the counter and move to clean them.

She returns quietly, upon seeing me work to clean the plump trout, tells me, "You can fry up those fish. Someone brought them over real early. One relative, I don't know at all. All these kids look like strangers to me. I guess it's just old age that makes me forget how many of all you kids there are." She laughs a little as she looks to my response out of her eye-corners, sitting behind her coffee at the table.

"Oh, Granma," I say, catching her mood, tease back, "I know you have to remember me. If not for my family resemblance, but just for the trouble you took to wind me, catch me, to make me come inside from playing." I eye her, likewise with cornered eyes. I see her catch her coffee in her lips, in her effort to keep from spitting the liquid and by laughing encourage me. She responds quickly by saying that my mother could outrun her. Usually, she ends this comment on my mother's great speed in childhood, by saying that "she was just too tired to whip her for her naughtiness." Listening to the house groan in the ceiling, Granma changes the subject, to the building of our ranch house up Tenino Valley.

"Your Grandfather's people made that old ranch house over there. All from one tree. All the people came to do what they could. Pound the nails. Split the wood. The women butchered and barbecued the steers. Everyone helped then. They drug the tree there by horse team. Those days our people knew how to do everything for themselves. Not like nowadays, where we have to hire big shots to come in and boss us around."

The pan snaps from the wet skin of the fish as I begin to fry them up. I know that she did not witness the building of this ranch house. She has only merged her stories with my grandfather's, a merging they wanted, symbolized by the two cedar trees that they both planted, side by side, when they married. Saying to one another that these trees would grow together, like they would, inter-mingle their roots and branches as one, while still letting the winds of life blow between them. I say, to bring her back to the moment, "These are pretty trout, Granma . About as good as the ones we used to catch, that made Grandpa so mad when I was a kid."

Granma reaches up to arrange the folds of her navy-blue western bandanna on her head. It is folded, tri-cornered and knotted on top. She tilts her chin upward. "Oh, how he would get mad. He always said I had more luck than sense. I had a good dream about him last night. That he and I and Baby were fishing. Baby and I caught a fish and we were screaming, and then we were jumping up and down around it, squealing. Granpa said we were scaring away his fish; he always wanted the fish to just jump on his hook."

I laugh, "Granma, I must have been that baby. Sometimes, I wish that we had some poles, so we could fish. But then, we never did learn how to tie a good knot for the hooks. Oh, how we chased the grasshoppers for bait. You laughed so hard at me, jumping as hard as the bugs. We just had to sit down in the cheat grass and hold our sides and our dresses close to our legs, so the grasshoppers wouldn't jump on them. But what really got Granpa was the fish we caught and you would just flip them up in the air behind us. He said that was no way to treat a fish."

Granma, nodding her head, retorts, "We only used a pin and bait. He had to spend our money on the fancy lures, the steelhead poles. He had his science and some notion that he treated the fish better when he made some big game out of it. We just needed fish for our table, not the fireplace. Your Granpa was a good man, even though he had a soft heart about killing things, like the deer."

The heat intensifies outside and the "hotbugs" sing their legs into a zzzing without pause. Granma sips her coffee, intermittently stirs the spoon in her cup. She eyes the spiral and begins to dream, like she dreams during the day, between words.

These stories of old days are magical. I'm gullible and young enough to still believe in magic. The magic is this soft rumble of blood-life, laughter, our great heart under the land. I hear that great tree and the cedars breathe through this house, too, on occasion. Up the valley, I can see the mountain hold a cap of a cloud. That mountain is as storied as our lives. He walked, lived, and lusted after a young woman mountain, fought with Wy-East, for her, in a time way before the Changer came to have all this chaos beaded up into some monstrously big Dreamer design. The design I only sense from the perspective of a bead. Sometimes I dream of this. I see segments of this power hanging from the hands of old ladies as they dance at gatherings. When I told my boyfriend this, he just said I was too way-out for him. That's how he seems to be anymore. Despite all his singing, sweating, he's too heavy with war and struggle to see the story. Yet, love always seems to knock men down, to drag them back to these houses of magic. Just like love knocks us down and pulls us out to the sticks, to follow that guy anywhere he wants to go. Keep an eye on him, just in case something might take him away by terrible magic. Yes, the age of the Changer has passed, but the bloodline is still with us, and the inspiring thread of women's labor, the beads, the Great Transformer and the talk of love. The Beautiful Woman in Earth still whispers into the ears of her children.

"Owwww-witch!" I holler, as the grease sizzles on the skin of my hand. The fish get one last bite on me.

"Watch your cooking. You might just get as bad as me. I never got the hang of cooking on electric stoves. I always cooked on woodstoves or campfires, especially the first days I was married to your grandfather. We lived in a tent to put his brother through college, you know."

"Yeah, Gram, but I think it isn't your cooking abilities I inherited, but the old Dreamer brain. I wasn't thinking about the fish in the pan."

At this point she chuckles deeply, bobbing her head, which turns her bandanna a nudge-worth out of place. A meadowlark tinkles a song from the yard. She tilts her head, so her bandanna looks correct, and says, "He sings about

the rain that will come soon. Of course, in Indian, he makes his song. That's why it is so beautiful." She taps her finger on the neck handle of her eternal coffee cup. She waits, as she always waits, in a meditation. She waits through her chores. She waits as she waters the lawn with her green hoses, thumb holding the spray over the grass and shadows of juniper. She waits for her children to come and visit as I visit, answering her call for company.

As I pull out the enamel, shallow-bowled dishes, I remain quiet so as not to interrupt the thoughts I see about her, probably a prayer. She responds to me out of courtesy, since her thoughts linger over her long life, and the memories that are so rare and necessary.

I again think about the music I hear. I hear songs in my dreams. Which is unusual, since I do not know any songs, or even know Indian. I think of it as this, the music comes from the tapping of her finger, beating out the occasional soft song. The way a river sounds while we fish, and the sound of the life—dragonflies whirring, singing to me—the music mingles and makes these songs that sound through my dreams. Maybe I catch the hum of the mountain over there too. He's waiting, you see, to get involved with that fiery young woman he sees at the corner of his eyes. Mountain love is a real shaky, fired-up affair. They push up great hilly ranges, bed over the lakes, rub up against one another so wildly, that it takes years to cover up all that passionate rumbling and love talk. Once my grandmother said that her great-grandmother and aunt had to run their horses into a lake to cover themselves with wet hides to keep from getting burned. The water was so hot, it took all their courage to stay put. 1 believe that was the last rumble before the mountains curled up for a good sleep.

When I told one of my science teachers about this, he said that these stories are just myth, not fact, and that mountains don't love or even erupt anymore. I believed him until Mount St. Helens erupted. It erased all innocent belief in the fable of absolute science for me. Thank goodness, I had heard some "fact" about those mountains way before I entered school.

I give my grandmother her share of the fish, and she says, as she always says, "Oh, honey, that is too much. Put some back. I'm not company."

"Eat, Granma, we have plenty for many lifetimes over." I settle my "husky" body down to savor the fish. "You know I sure miss Granpa. I miss his whistling in the mornings. When you and him would cook together. You remember that?"

Granma retorts, "I have spent half of my life cooking for all of you. But it was your grandfather who could cook the best. He knew all the dishes of this and that. Just like he knew all that wild music. High-wy-ahn, I think it was called. He was a great singer as well as a great jokester. You tell a story as tall as he could, but I always thought you hung around him too much."

I smile, then say, "You both were pretty wild examples for me to follow. I think a lot about how you two would play in the kitchen, while you cooked what you called a farmer's breakfast, the potatoes, ham steaks, eggs. Between flipping over the food, you would dance to western music on the transistor radio, the jitterbug, the Charleston. Yeah, I remember how you two carried on while you thought I was still asleep." I smile thinking of how agile Granma was, dancing, diaper pins on her dress, blue tennis shoes toeing in and out. Granpa, twirling her around, in his sleeveless white undershirt, pants always neatly belted, with a smile wide in pleasure, watching Granma's face spin like a light in the morning dawn. Granpa had a grin so wide, it was as if it could go halfway around his head, especially when he had Granma going, or getting her aggravated from his teasing. Then he'd grin all the more while he sweet-talked his way back into her good humor.

"It seemed that you always ended up your dancing with a good fight, boxing, with your dukes curled over. You always won with your 'Appalachian apple cut' half a windup, a quick strike to Granpa's 'glass jaw.' Then you'd grab his pants seat and have him in your mercy. He'd holler, 'I give up honey! I give up, I'll marry you!'"

We both laughed a great laugh at the memory. Granma tucked the trout meat into a pooch in her soft cheek, tilted her chin toward me, and said in a quiet, matter-of-fact tone, "Your grandfather didn't marry me for my homecooking. I thought you always knew that."

Suggested Further Reading

WORKS BY WOODY
Hand Into Stone: Poems. New York: Contact II Publications, 1988.

WORKS ABOUT WOODY
Dancing on the Rim of the World. ed. Andrea Lerner. Tucson: Sun Tracks and the University of Arizona Press, 1990, pp. 245-49.

Juan Armando Epple

Juan Armando Epple was born in southern Chile in 1946, and grew up in Valdivia, where he also went to college. He later taught Spanish American literature at the Austral University of Chile. He came to the United States as an exile in 1974 and, after earning his master's and doctor's degrees from Harvard, joined the University of Oregon faculty in 1980. He recently won the grand prize in a Chilean national literary contest for his story, "La raiz del juego" ("The Rules of the Game"). Epple's short stories have been published in several languages. He is now working on a collection of his short stories dealing with the experiences of children in exile. "Los persas" ("Garage Sale People") portrays this experience as it relates to life in contemporary Springfield and Eugene, and to that peculiar American institution, the garage sale. The story alternates, in its telling, betweent hree family members, the mother (Marta), the daughter (Marisol), and the father (Dario). The story is presented here in both its English and original Spanish versions, for those readers who know Spanish and who may want a fuller sense of the experience of an exile from South America who now calls Oregon home.

Los Persas

Voy a dar una vuelta, dijo, y antes que alcanzara a preguntarle adónde ya estaba sacando el auto en retroceso, metiendo las ruedas en los lirios que él mismo se había encargado de trasplantar desde la casa que tuvimos en Springfield, antes de trasladarnos a Eugene. Los lirios son los más perjudicados cuando anda enrabiado o confundido con alguno de esos trabajos que le suelen encargar, y que empieza a escribir con entusiasmo pero luego deja de lado explicando que no puede agarrar bien el hilo.

La *typewriter* de mi *daddy* es como la *sewing machine* que tiene mi mamá, esa que compró usada en un *garage sale* y que a veces trabaja bien y otras se atasca. Cuando él escribe sin parar por una hora es porque está contestando una carta de uno de sus amigos, esos testamentos de diez páginas que les ha dado por intercambiarse por correo, reclama mi mamá. Y cuando escribe un ratito y luego hay un silencio largo en su cuarto es porque está pensando en algún problema, ¿como esos *homeworks* que nos da Miss Greenfield?, y ya sabemos que en cualquier momento va a bajar, va a dar una vuelta por la cocina destapando las ollas o va a pasar directamente al yard a regar sus tomates, diciendo que le sirve para concentrarse.

—Apuesto que tu papá quería ver el noticiero y tú le cambiaste el canal—le dije a Marisol, que ya se había instalado frente al televisor con un paquete de galletas y los discos de Def Leppard desparramados por el suelo, enchufada en uno de esos programas musicales donde los cantantes cambian de escenario a cada estrofa.

—No, él me dijo que hoy tenía que escribir algunas cartas. Además, el único programa que le interesa es el noticiario de las siete. Yo le fui a decir que por qué no aprovechaba de escribirle también una carta a la abuela y así la traíamos de una vez, aunque sea de visita. Entonces él se levantó del asiento y pumm . . . salió. ¿Crees que fue al *post office*?

Como no entiendo ni papá del fútbol americano, y no me hablen del béisbol, sin contar lo difícil que es agarrar el inglés de las películas (es como hablar masticando una papa, explica Marta, tratando de imitar alguna frase), la única forma de sacarle el cuerpo a las preguntas de Marisol es salir a la calle a calentar un poco los músculos. Aunque esta frase ya no me alcanza ni para metáfora, porque cada vez que me topo con un espejo veo que he seguido aumentando varias libras por año, y ya me están asomando las primeras canas. Es la edad más interesante del hombre, celebra Marta, aunque no deja de pasarme un dedo por la aureola de fraile que también se me va dibujando en la nuca. Además, cada vez que me decido a salir a correr me encuentro compitiendo con cientos de atletas que no sólo compran las mismas zapatillas Nike, sino que están convencidos de que Eugene es la capital mundial del *jogging* y hasta los más modestos se conforman con ganar la maratón de Nueva York. Al final he optado por entrenarme en la clásica silla de ruedas de este país, aunque sea para imaginar que vamos a descubrir nuevas rutas, deslizándome por calles rigurosamente diagramadas, con sus semáforos y policías de tránsito regulando el ejercicio, jurándole fidelidad a este auto que lucía tan imponente los primeros días, y que ahora se mueve a saltos, como un Pinto resfriado.

Cuando estaba aprendiendo a manejar y el Chino (que es de Antofagasta, y ni él sabe de dónde le cayó el apodo) me enseñó algunas técnicas básicas de mantención, como medir el aire de las ruedas, cambiarle el aceite, ponerle *antifreezing* al radiador, pensé que sería util agenciarme algunas de esas herramientas que él trae en el maletero de su convertible (este sí que es convertible, compadre, celebra pasándole una manga ostentosa al capot de los años de la cocoa, porque se convierte hasta en cama cuando se presenta la ocasión), me detuve una vez frente a uno de esos letreros que anuncian "Garage sale," buscando algo extra para equipar el auto. Con una curiosidad que poco a poco se fue convirtiendo en obsesión descubrí que los garage sales consistían en pequeños mercados familiares que los gringos instalan en el garage o el patio de sus casas, donde ponen a la venta objetos de segunda mano o incluso nuevos, traídos seguramente de sus safaris turísticos o de esas irresistibles liquidaciones de las grandes tiendas, y que acumulan en sus casas hasta que la pasión ingenua por la novedad los obliga a ofrecerlos por unos pocos dólares para dejar más espacio para otras adquisiciones. En las primeras salidas me dejé llevar por el entusiasmo, un entusiasmo a precio casi regalado por la variedad de artículos dispuestos en mesitas o depositadas como al descuido en los prados de tarjeta postal. Comencé a llevar a la casa inesperados trofeos que activaban una mirada entre compasiva y recelosa de Marta: un arado del tiempo anterior a la gasolina (esa parcela que tuvimos que vender apresuradamente en el Sur para poder salir a tiempo del país), litografías, anzuelos, marcos de retratos, una guayabera mexicana nueva, que usé hasta en pleno invierno, no tanto para imaginarme cómo nos habría ido en ese país si nos hubiera llegado la visa a tiempo sino para revivir las despedidas en la Bomba Bar, anotar las direcciones, repasar el lenguaje cifrado para comunicarnos noticias, y el gringo Hoefler mirando de reojo las sillas vacías, decidido a quedarse hasta el último por alguna secreta razón ancestral, y ahora un brindis por "El azote de Puebla", un par de pistolas Colt 45 en imitación de lata, de esas idealizadas en las novelas de cowboy de un tal Marcial Lafuente Estefanía, que resultó ser luego un español que decidió exiliarse en un rincón de su propio país y que pudo ganarse la vida escribiendo historias de un Far West que diagramaba con la ayuda de un mapa arrancado de un National Geographic Magazine, discos de Frankie Avalon o Los Cuatro Latinos, y esos best sellers que se devalúan tan rápido que hay que arrumbarlos en una caja a ver si alguien se los lleva gratis, *help yourself.* Suspendí mis compras de ocasión cuando, al volver una tarde con un maniquí escultural que merecía estar en mi oficina, encontré a Marta atareada arrumbando nuestros propios desusos en el garage, tratando de organizar mejor nuestro espacio:

—Si vas a seguir con tu deporte de los garage sale, vale más que te dejes de coleccionar fantasmas y me consigas algo útil. Hace tiempo que te pedí que me busques unos frascos para conservas, o una aspiradora que funcione, ya que no quieres comprar una nueva.

En el tiempo que llevamos fuera de Chile habíamos tenido que cambiar de país dos veces (porque en unos para conseguir visa de residencia hay que tener primero contrato de trabajo, en otros para conseguir trabajo hay que tener primero permiso de residencia, sin contar con que hay otros donde no nos aceptan ni de turistas) y estando en Estados Unidos veníamos recorriendo más de cinco estados, hasta encontrar un trabajo más o menos estable en Eugene. Oregón nos atrajo de inmediato, como un imán secreto, por su extraordinario parecido con el Sur de Chile. Nuestros desplazamientos nos obligaban a hacer y deshacer maletas, vender o regalar los pocos muebles que juntábamos, embalar y desembalar los libros de Darío, porque eso sí, una debe despedirse de la aspiradora, las ollas, y hasta el juego de loza, pero al perla los libros hay que instalárselos en la mejor parte del camión, allá vamos a comprar todo nuevo, mijita, no se preocupe. También había que enviarles la nueva dirección a algunos familiares y a los amigos que aún nos reconocen en el mapa, presentar en otra escuela los certificados de colegio y vacunas de Marisol, quién ya no sabía qué poner en la sección país de orígen, optando finalmente por escribir con sus mayúsculas MARISOL (lo que al menos le garantizaba un puesto seguro en las clases de Geografía), y hasta diseñar una huerta improvisada en el patio de la casa para plantar un poco de cilantro y albahaca. Porque eso sí, estos exiliados tan orgullosos siempre están dispuestos a viajar, a "buscar nuevos horizontes," pero donde van siguen suspirando por las empanadas y humitas que les solía preparar la abuela. Cuando le dio por los garage sales no me preocupé mucho, porque me parecía una distracción inofensiva y hasta novedosa, pero cuando empezó a alabar ante los chilenos las ventajas de esos "mercados persas", como los llamaba, tuve que cortarle un poco la afición, pues los amigos, como me confidenció Hilda, ya nos estaban llamando "Los Persas."

En la escuela no saben dónde queda Chile, y por eso me llaman a veces *hispanic* o *latin*. Una vez que le dije a la *English teacher* que era un país muy bonito, con muchas montañas y frutas, me sonrió y me dijo que era una gran verdad, que ella tenía muy buenas memorias de un viaje que hizo a Acapulco. Quizás no lo ubican porque en el mapa se ve tan chico, como un fideo, y por eso han tenido que salir tantos chilenos a vivir en otros países. Pero lo que no entiendo entonces es por qué si es tan chico, todo lo que hay allá es tan grande. Cada vez que se juntan los chilenos en la casa, porque en cada ciudad donde hemos vivido siempre hay un grupo de chilenos que se llaman por teléfono todos los días y se juntan a comer, se dedican a crear un país que no creo que entre en ningún mapa. A decir que las sandías de allá son mucho más grandes y dulces que las que venden en Safeway, que las uvas son del porte de las ciruelas de aquí, que el Mount Hood no le llega ni a los talones al Aconcagua, que no hay como un caldillo de congrio, que debe ser un pescado enorme como un tiburón pero que sabe muy sabroso, que el vino que se vende aquí parece tinta dulce o la cerveza tiene gusto a pichí, y que no hay comparación entre el pan amasado del Sur y las rebanadas de plástico que venden aquí. Un día se juntaron a discutir una cosa de pasaportes y a revisar una lista que traía el tío Romilio, inventándose sobrenombres que empezaban con la letra L (como Loco, Lampiño, Lolosaurio, Lucifer, Latoso, Libertador de Lanco, y así). Nosotros los niños nos pusimos a hacer dibujos. Yo dibujé una Cordillera y se la fui a mostrar a mi papi. El miró mi dibujo un largo rato, se puso serio, y luego me corrigió con un lápiz la Cordillera diciendo que era mucho más alta y difícil de cruzar. No se dio cuenta que también había dibujado un avión. Esa tarde se dedicó a criticar todo lo que decían los tíos, que así tenemos que llamar a los grandes pero no porque sean tíos, sino porque son chilenos que se visitan, a decir que las empanadas son originarias de China y que la cueca es un baile que llevaron a Chile desde Africa. Al final las visitas se enojaron y se fueron, y uno de los tíos le gritó desde la puerta a mi papi que lo único que le estaba quedando en claro era que nosotros ahora nos creíamos persas.

Marisol nos había puesto en aprietos una vez más con su lógica inocente, justo ese día de sol y kuchen de moras alemanas, cuando se me ocurrió hacer un comentario sobre la harina que venden en los supermercados y ella aprovechó para decir: si la abuelita sabe hacer mejores kuchenes, ¿por qué no vamos a Chile a visitarla? Darío se paró y caminó hacia la cocina, ¿alguien quiere más café?, dándome esa mirada de usted salió con el tema y lo resuelve. Pero como a estas alturas del exilio es difícil explicarle a una niña que creció en este país lo que significa tener una L en el pasaporte, traté de explicarle que los pasajes están últimamente por las nubes, que el papá ha estado haciendo esfuerzos por ahorrar dinero, pero apenas estamos en condiciones de comprar un pasaje, y no es justo que viaje a Chile sólo uno de nosotros, ¿verdad? No sé sí quedó muy convencida, pero se comió un pedazo extra de kuchen, estuvo haciendo figuritas con la servilleta y luego anunció que tenía la tele reservada hasta las doce.

Yo aproveché para ir a encerrarme a la oficina, pero al rato subió, levantó con curiosidad mis papeles como si estuviera muy interesada en ver lo que escribo, y luego, mirando por la ventana, me propuso: ¿por qué no invitamos a la abuela a que venga a pasar el verano con nosotros? Es sólo un pasaje, ¿verdad? Y a una niña a la que se le ha estado pintando por años un país hecho de sabores y olores definitivos, de memorias fijas y obsesivas, de rostros que parecen estar todavía a la vuelta de la esquina, y sobre todo de presencias familiares que van creciendo a medida que se alejan en el tiempo, que nos distanciamos, no se le puede decir de un día para otro que la abuela murió a los pocos meses de tener que abandonar nosotros Chile. Por eso sólo le sacudí un poco la chasquilla sabihonda, es buena idea señorita, vamos a ver qué podemos hacer, y salí.

Ese día recorrí varios garage sales, sin buscar nada en especial, y si me detuve frente a esa casa fue para examinar unas herramientas de labranza que tenían allí, con los precios cuidadosamente marcados en papelitos blancos, para ver si encontraba algún azadón para la huerta. Estaba por regresarme cuando descubrí a la anciana, instalada en una silla reclinable, con la vista perdida en un mundo anterior a todos los domingos de preguntas y garage sale. Al principio pensé que era otro maniquí, puesto artísticamente en la silla para realzar un vestido azul, con encajes de terciopelo, o la caja de diseños hindú que le habían puesto en el regazo. Pero al acercarme a revisar unas camisas y observarla de reojo, vi con sorpresa que la figura estiraba la mano, cogía un abanico de 25 centavos de la mesa, recuerdo de alguna excursión a Sevilla, y se empeñaba en abanicarse con movimientos enérgicos, pero con un dejo de coquetería.

El dueño de casa, viéndome estrujar el cuello de una camisa sport, se me acercó con una sonrisa de oreja a oreja y la típica pregunta de supermercado: *May I help you?* Acto seguido me aseguró que esas camisas estaban casi nuevas, y que habían decidido vender parte de sus pertenencias porque la hija acababa de casarse y ellos se mudaban a un departamento. Usted sabe, agregó, a medida que envejecemos necesitamos menos espacio.

Por una reacción impulsiva, que ponía en tensión los dilemas que me estaban fastidiando, le pregunté a mi vez, apuntando con el dedo:

—¿Y cuanto cobra por esta abuela?

El ciudadano me miró con la boca abierta, y luego se metió rápidamente en la casa.

Inicié rápidamente la retirada, anticipando una merecida colección de insultos que me darían una visión más académica del inglés, pero antes de doblar la esquina sentí que me llamaba, con un tono casi dulce. Una señora rubia estaba a su lado, secándose las manos en el delantal.

—¿*What about five hundred bucks?*—me dijo poniéndome una mano amistosa en el hombro, y bajando la voz en los números, como si fuera la proposición del año.

Tomando mi confusión por cálculo, la señora agregó:

—La verdad es que vale mucho más. Con decirle que ni siquiera habíamos pensado en venderla.

—Además—terció el marido—está completamente sana, y sólo recién ha comenzado a usar anteojos. Hace un mes le hicimos un chequeo completo, y el médico nos aseguró que vivirá muchos años más. Así como va, nos pronosticó el doctor—mi hipotético pariente iba a lanzar una carcajada aprobatoria, pero la señora se la cortó de un codazo—capaz que los entierre a ustedes.

—¿De verdad está para la venta?—les insistí, perplejo.

—Es que como el departamento es muy pequeño, la única solución que nos quedaba era mandarla a un centro de ancianos, y la verdad es que ella, tan acostumbrada a la vida familiar, no merece terminar allí. Nosotros no nos imaginábamos que existía esta otra solución: una familia joven, llena de proyectos, porque usted, por su acento, debe ser un inmigrante hispano ¿verdad? que le ofrezca una nueva oportunidad, y en ese ambiente latino donde se valoran tanto las tradiciones antiguas. . . .

—¿Cuánto puede ofrecer por ella?—agregó la señora—además se la entregamos con todos sus efectos personales, y no sabe usted todos los objetos valiosos que ha acumulado en su vida. Incluso le daremos varios artefactos de cocina, porque ha de saber usted que ella suele preparar unos pasteles de manzana de primera, con una receta secreta que heredó de su madre, y le gusta cocinar en sus propias fuentes.

Demoramos un par de horas en la transacción, y luego de convenir la forma de pago, decidimos que volvería a buscarla en dos semanas. Una decisión prudente, porque hay que tener en cuenta que estos cambios no se pueden hacer de un día para otro.

Esa noche, durante la cena, noté que Darío estaba más callado que de costumbre, y además se le ocurrió tomar mate, algo que casi nunca hace porque dice que le produce insomnio. Pero de pronto, mirando a Marisol que se entretenía en dibujar algo en una servilleta, empezó a proponer, con un entusiasmo de recién llegado, una serie de cambios en el orden de la casa, y a preguntar si todavía teníamos la cama plegable que compramos cuando vino a visitarnos el chilote Heriberto desde California.

Porque tenemos que preparar un dormitorio extra, les dejé caer, gozando por anticipado de la sorpresa: hoy le reservé un pasaje a la abuela, y viene a visitarnos en dos semanas más.

Luego salí al patio, porque todavía había luz afuera, y las colinas que rodeaban el Willamette Valley extremaban las gradaciones del verde hasta confundirlo con los destellos dorados del sol. Era como estar otra vez frente al Lago Llanquihue, respirando al ritmo secreto de las estaciones, pero sin estar allá.

Pero salí también porque quería cerciorarme que los porotos verdes estaban afirmando bien sus guías en las estacas, que había pasado ya el peligro de las heladas, y que el azadón que mis inesperados parientes gringos me habían dado de yapa era de buena calidad.

Garage Sale People

"I'm going for a spin," he said and, before I could ask him where he was heading, he had the car in reverse and was backing out over the daffodils he himself transplanted when we moved from Springfield. The daffodils suffer whenever he's angry or confused about one of the assignments they give him to write; he starts enthusiastically but then drops them saying he can't find the right tone.

My daddy's typewriter is like my mom's sewing machine that she bought at a garage sale; it works okay for a while and then breaks down. My mom says when he writes nonstop for an hour it's because he's answering a letter from one of his friends, those ten-page epistles they like to send each other. And when he writes for a few minutes and then there's a long silence in his room, it's because he's thinking over some problem . . . like those homeworks Miss Greenfield gives us? . . . and we know at any minute he'll come downstairs and cruise through the kitchen uncovering the pots on the stove or head straight out to the yard to water his tomatoes, saying it helps him concentrate.

"I bet your papa wanted to watch the news and you changed the channel on him," I said to Marisol who had settled in in front of the TV with a package of cookies and Def Leppard records scattered around her, glued to one of those music programs where the singers change scenes every verse.

"No, he told me he had to write some letters. Besides, the only program he likes is the news at 7. I went in to ask him why he didn't write Granny too and let's get her here finally, even if it's just for a visit. That's when he jumped up from his chair and pumm . . . was gone. You think he went to the Post Office?"

Since I don't understand anything about American football, much less baseball, and it's even harder for me to understand English in the movies (it's like speaking while you chew potatoes, Marta says, trying to imitate a phrase), the only way I can deal with Marisol's questions is to get out on the streets, to warm up my muscles. Even this metaphor doesn't fit, because every time I catch myself in a mirror it confirms that I'm gaining several pounds a year, and my first gray hairs have already arrived. It's the most interesting age for a man, Marta says, as she runs her finger along my incipient double chin. Besides, every time I decide to go running I find myself competing with hundreds of athletes all wearing their Nikes, and convinced that Eugene is the running capital of the world and every one of them—even the modest—truly believing they can win the NY marathon. So I finally opted for the classical wheel chair of this country, even if only to imagine that we are discovering new routes, gliding through these carefully laid-out streets with traffic lights and patrolmen regulating my exercise, swearing loyalty to this car which was so shiny at the beginning and now moves by jerks, like a Pinto with the flu.

When I was learning to drive and Chinaman (Chinaman was from Antofagasta and even he didn't know why he had the nickname) taught me a few basic maintenance tips like checking the pressure in the tires, changing the oil and putting antifreezing in the radiator, I thought it would be a good idea to get myself some of those tools he carries in the trunk of his convertible ("this is a real convertible, my friend," he exudes, flashing a sleeve over the canvas top . . . "from the good old days; you can even turn it into a bed should the occasion arise"), so I stopped once at one of those little signs that say "Garage Sale," looking for extra equipment for the car. Bit by bit my curiosity became an obsession, as I discovered that garage sales are small family markets *gringos* set up in their garages or on their lawns, where they put out second hand and even some new things, acquired on their tourist safaris, no doubt, or at those irresistible sales in the big department stores, stuff they accumulate until their boundless desire for new things forces them to offer it all up for a few bucks to make room for new purchases. My first few times out I got carried away by enthusiasm, enthusiasm for the variety of objects set out on little tables or casually placed on the picture-post-card lawns. I started bringing home unexpected trophies; Marta's reactions went from compassion to concern: a plow from before the era of the gas engine (the farm in the South we had to sell in a hurry to get out of the country in time), prints, fishing lures, picture frames, a new Mexican *guayabera* shirt which I wore even in mid-Winter, not so much to imagine how life would have been in that country had our visas arrived in time, but mainly to relive the goodbyes in the Bomba Bar, jot down addresses, go over the coded language we would use to communicate with one another, and *gringo* Hoefler looking warily at the chairs—every day one more was empty—his mind made up to remain till the last for some secret ancestral reason, and now a toast to the "Scourge of Puebla," a pair of imitation Colt 45s made out of tin, like those idealized in the westerns written by Marcial Lafuente Estefania who turned out to be a Spaniard who never left his own country, earning his living writing stories of the Far West which he diagrammed with the help of a map taken from the *National Geographic*, Frankie Avalon or Cinco Latinos records, and those best sellers so passé people have to throw

them into a box in hopes that someone will cart them off free, help yourself. I put a halt to my casual purchases one day when, coming home with a terrific mannikin worthy of space in my office, there was Marta in the midst of putting our own junk away in the garage, trying to make some room: "If you keep up this sport of yours, I'd appreciate it if you would bring home something a little more useful. I asked you a long time ago to get me some canning jars, or a vacuum cleaner that works since you don't want to buy a new one."

In our years away from Chile we had to change countries twice (in some countries to get a resident's visa you need to have a work contract first; in others you have to have the residency in order to get a job, and then there are other countries where they don't want us even as tourists) and being in the United States we had lived in more than five states when we finally got something more or less permanent in Eugene. Oregon drew us immediately, like a secret force, because it looks so amazingly like the South of Chile. Our moves had us packing and unpacking, selling or giving away what little furniture we acquired, crating and uncrating Dario's books, because there's one thing for sure—a woman can say goodbye to her vacuum, the pots, and even the china, but Mr. Big's books have to be put in the coziest part of the truck. We'll buy it all new there, dearie, don't worry. Then we had to send our new address to family and to the friends for whom we still exist, take Marisol's vaccination certificate and school records to yet another school, she didn't even know what to put anymore in the "country of origin" section, she ended up writing MARISOL (which guaranteed her a spot in the geography class), and even planning a little garden spot in the backyard to put in some cilantro and basil. For sure, these proud exiles are always ready to travel, "looking for New Horizons," but wherever they go they keep longing for the *empanadas* and *humitas* Granny used to fix for them. When he got into these garage sales it didn't bother me too much because it seemed harmless entertainment, but when he began to sing the praises of these "Persian markets," as he called them in front of other Chileans, I had to rein him in. Hilda told me confidentially that people were now calling us "the Persians."

In school nobody knows where Chile is, so they call me Hispanic or Latin sometimes. One time I told the English teacher that it was a beautiful country with a lot of mountains and fruit trees, and she smiled and said how true, she had wonderful memories of a trip to Acapulco. Maybe they don't know where it is because it's so small on the map, kind of like a string bean, and that's why so many Chileans have had to go abroad to live. What I don't get is if it's so small how come everything there is so big. Any time Chileans get together at my house—everywhere we've lived there's a group of Chileans who call each other every day and get together to eat—they create a country I don't think exists on any map. The watermelons there are bigger and sweeter than the ones at Safeway, grapes are the size of plums here, Mt. Hood doesn't come up to the ankle of Aconcagua, there's nothing like a stew of *congrio*, which must be an enormous fish like a shark but tasty, the wine they sell here tastes like sweet ink or the beer tastes like piss, and there is no comparison between bread baked in the South and that plastic stuff they sell here. One day they got together to discuss something about passports and to look at a list Uncle Romilio brought, inventing surnames that began with the letter "L" (like Lunatic, Limpid, Lolosaurus, Lucifer, Laborious, Lanco Liberator and so on). We kids began to draw. I drew a mountain range and went to show it to my papa. He looked at it a long time, then he became serious, and corrected my mountain range, saying it was much taller and more difficult to cross. He didn't see that I had also drawn an airplane. That afternoon he criticized everything my aunts and uncles were saying—we have to call all grownups from Chile aunt and uncle—saying that *empanadas* are originally from China and the *cueca* is a dance brought to Chile from Africa. Finally our visitors had had enough and left, and one of the uncles shouted at my papa that the only thing clear was that we considered ourselves Persians now.

Marisol had put us on the spot again with her innocent logic, just that sunny day with raspberry pie, when I said something about the flour they sell at the supermarkets and she spoke up to say that if Granny knows how to make better pies, why don't we go to Chile to see her? Dario stood up and walked to the kitchen, "Does anyone want more coffee?", giving me that "You brought it up, you answer her" look. But at this point in exile it's hard to explain to a girl who grew up in this country what it means to have an L on your passport—I mean, we don't even know what the "L" stands for—so I tried to explain that airfares were out of sight these days, that Papa had been trying to save money but we barely have enough for one ticket and it's not fair for just one of us to go back to Chile, right? I don't know if I convinced her, but she ate an extra piece of pie, played with her napkin a bit, then announced that she was reserving the television until 12.

I closed myself up in my office, but in a while she came up, lifting my papers as if interested in what I write and then looking out the window, she proposed: "Why don't we invite Granny to spend the summer with us? It's just one ticket, right?" And this girl for whom we have spent years painting a country filled with specific tastes and odors, fixed and obsessive memories, faces which still seem just around the corner, and above all family presences which grow even as they fade in time, how can we just up and tell her her grandmother died a few months after we left Chile? I gently mussed her hair and said, "Good idea, Miss, let's see what we can do," and I left.

That day I hit a couple of garage sales not seeking anything in particular, and I stopped at one house to take a look at some gardening tools they had, with prices precisely marked on those little white papers, in the hopes of finding a hoe. I was about to go back to the car when I found the old woman, installed on a reclining chair, staring off into a world prior to all Sundays filled with questions and garage sales. At first I thought she was another mannikin, artfully arranged on the chair to show off a blue velvet dress with lace or the box of Hindu prints placed on her lap. But when I drew closer to inspect some shirts and look at her, I was surprised to see her reach out her hand for the 25-cent souvenir-of-Seville fan, and begin to fan herself energetically with perhaps a bit of coyness.

Seeing me stretch the collar of a shirt, the owner of the house came up with an ear-to-ear smile and the typical supermarket question: "May I help you?" The shirts were practically new, their daughter had gotten married and they had decided to sell off some of their belongings because they were moving to an apartment, he offered. "You know," he added, "as you get older you need less space."

Impulsively responding to all my dilemmas, I pointed with my finger and asked him: "How much are you charging for that granny over there?"

The man stared at me, then quickly disappeared into his house.

I started retreating fast, fearing well-deserved insults which might improve my grasp of the English vernacular, but before I got around the corner I heard him call me, almost sweetly. A blond lady was standing beside him, wiping her hands on an apron.

Putting a friendly hand on my shoulder and dropping his voice at the numbers, he said, "What about five hundred bucks?" like he was making me the deal of the year.

Taking my confusion as a bargaining ploy, the woman added, "She's really worth much more. To tell you the truth we weren't even thinking of selling her."

"And besides, she's completely healthy," her husband interjected. "She's just started to use glasses. A month ago we got her a complete checkup and the doctor said she'd live for many more years. In her condition, the doctor predicted . . ."—my possible relative was about to let out an approving guffaw, but his wife cut him off with her elbow—"she might outlive us all."

"You really want to sell her?" I asked in perplexity.

"The thing is, the apartment is so small, and the only way was to send her to a retirement center, and really, she's so used to family life she just doesn't deserve to end up there. We hadn't imagined that there might be another solution: a young family, full of plans, because—judging by your accent—you must be a Hispanic immigrant, right? You can give her a new opportunity, and in a Latin environment where you value the old ways. . . ."

"How much can you offer for her?"—the woman went on, —"Besides, we'll give you all her personal effects and you can't imagine how much of value she's accumulated over her lifetime. And we'll throw in some kitchen items because you wouldn't believe what great apple pies she makes, from a secret recipe she inherited from her mother, and she likes to cook with her own pans."

We spent a couple of hours on the deal, and after working out a way to pay, we agreed that I would come back for her in a couple of weeks. A wise decision, because you can't just up and make these changes from one day to the next.

That night during dinner, I noticed that Dario was quieter than usual, and he even drank *mate*, which he practically never does because he says it gives him insomnia. Looking at Marisol who was drawing something on her napkin, he suddenly started proposing a series of changes in the house routine, asking if we still had that cot we bought when Heriberto El Chilote came from California to visit.

Anticipating the surprised reactions, I casually allowed, "Because we've got to get another bedroom ready. I booked a reservation for Granny today, and she'll be coming to visit us in two weeks."

Then I went outside into the backyard because it was still light, and the hills surrounding the Willamette Valley intensified the degrees of green, stretching towards the last golden sparks of the sun. It was like being on Lake Llanquihue once more, smelling the secret rhythms of the seasons, but without being there.

But I also went outside because I wanted to make sure that the beans were climbing up their stakes, that the danger of frost had passed, and that the hoe was really of good quality—that hoe my new North American relatives threw into the deal as an extra.

Translated by R. M. Jackson

Suggested Further Reading

WORKS BY EPPLE

Juan Armando Epple, ed. *Cruzado la Cordillera. El cuento chileno 1973-1983.* Mexico: Secretaría de Educación Pública—Casa de Chile, 1986.

Juan Armando Epple, ed. *Brevísma relación del cuento breve de Chile.* Concepción: Editorial LAR, 1989.

Barry Lopez

Barry Lopez, born in 1945 in New York state, has lived on the McKenzie River above Eugene since 1970. After a long period of apprenticeship, Lopez achieved renown with *Of Wolves and Men*, for which he received the John Burroughs Medal for Nature Writing in 1979. With *Arctic Dreams* in 1986, he won the National Book Award. Revealing a sensitivity to language and to the human imagination along with a keen scientific intelligence, these works have established Barry Lopez as one of the two or three most distinguished writers of natural history at work today. As an Oregonian, living in a forested and beautiful river valley, it is fitting that he continues to present us with the dreams and the realities which link us to our natural environment. Barry Lopez is also an accomplished writer of fiction, as *Winter Count* and *Crow and Weasel* reveal. The story which follows is a recent one, set in eastern Oregon.

Jordan Valley, 1977

The land began to lose its edges in the light of early evening, and it passed him like dross. The car shimmied in winds that came in fits across the high desert. He passed below Scott's Bluff and across Crooked Creek and stopped for supper in Rome. He considered going on ahead, but was afraid nothing would be open in Jordan Valley.

As he got out of the car, Esterver momentarily lost his grip on the door in the wind. Beyond the café a chained Weimaraner barked from a line of white-washed bungalows with red roofs. The branchlets of a weeping willow ticked wildly at the metal roof of a pickup beside him and the dog's barking hammered monotonously.

When he entered the café, Esterver entered an empty, electric silence of neon and fluorescent light, the radiation of an upright gas heater. He forgot the wind, the bored dog.

He hoped the waitress would be young, pretty. They would talk, he thought. As he slid into the booth, he realized this was repeatedly his hope. A small woman in her fifties came quietly across the linoleum floor with a clipped stride, an irritated look, as though she'd been about to close up. He glanced furtively at her when he took the menu. Her skin was pallid, her arms flaccid with age. He was embarrassed by his longing. He ordered. She turned away without writing anything down, without speaking to him.

Out past the window, across the valley, foothills of the Owyhee River rose against the evening sky. In what was left of dusk he could make out sheep grazing beneath the hills in their nervous way, unprepared for calamity. To the north, beyond a fence, a dozen stolid Herefords. He remembered reading that at the beginning of the 19th century two men had disappeared in the mountains to the east, where the river heads, Hawaiian beaver trappers killed by Shoshoni Indians. *O-w-y-h-e-e* was the best their companions could manage for Hawaii, and that was how the country got named.

Esterver thought suddenly of his father. He would be leaving Dubois now, if he hadn't already. Overnight in Pocatello maybe, changing buses in Boise. He took a notebook from his jacket: 7:22 was what he had written down, the time the bus would arrive the following evening in Jordan Valley.

He had not seen his father since the wedding, five years ago.

Esterver watched dusk fall away from the hills and ate the listless food slowly from the Melmac plate. Outside, stars burned incandescently in a moonless sky. In childhood, he reflected, he had known the names of most of the constellations. He held his hand up to the glass now to block the reflection in the room. He searched his memory for the names.

The waitress, washing dishes alone, studied Esterver with aimless suspicion through a kitchen portal. He turned suddenly to look at her and she smiled an ingratiating, impersonal smile. Esterver read insincerity in it and it brought his disaffection to the surface. Anger flared in him, focused not on her but at what was before him—the heavily salted gravy glutinous on the leathery meat, the decrepit beans, the spoiling lettuce and tomato. The food, he thought, lay humiliated before him. He ate dozens of meals like this now. He recalled still mornings in California when he had ridden with his father in a truck full of fresh produce, his arm braced in the open window on the passenger side, in imitation of his father. They would drive into Farmers Market in Hollywood through Coldwater Canyon from Calabasas, or sometimes down Topanga Canyon so they could see the ocean first. And then they would set out the flats and crates of vegetables and fruit, all of it firm and ripe.

The food is handled differently now, he thought.

It was nine when Esterver got into Jordan Valley. He got a room at Sevier's Motel and debated going out for a beer. No, he would stay in and read. By ten o'clock he had finished the Boise *Statesman* and all the pamphlets in the room and turned the TV on and off twice. He changed his mind.

The main highway, U.S. 95, came in from the west and then turned north abruptly toward the cemetery, as though fleeing the town. He walked up past Jim's Texaco and crossed the street to where *Esther's* hummed audibly in the still air, in rose neon script. In the country beyond these sheltering hills, he knew, the wind gusted wildly. Here the night was quiet, full of late winter.

A small Oriental woman sat smoking in isolated reverie at the bar. In a corner booth a middle-aged couple leaned toward each other, an attitude of failed conspiracy. Two cowboys, lank, their faces drawn by worry, weather, or emphysema, talked desultorily before the bar, one paddling the air with stiff, outsize hands. He felt conspicuous in wool slacks and a corduroy jacket, and ill at ease, though he had grown up with people like this. He had also, he cautioned himself, walked away from such a community. He ordered a draft beer. He tried to finish it slowly, and then went back across the street to his room.

He couldn't sleep. He stared at the dinette set under the window, at the gray-blue light from a street lamp glowing on the Formica. He had selected a kitchenette in case his father wanted a meal before they left, but he had also reserved an extra room.

He rolled the thin pillow over to its cool side and remembered he'd forgotten to call his wife. There was no phone in the room but he had seen one in a companionway outside.

By now, he thought, as he walked, shivering, through the heavy night air, his father would be asleep in Pocatello.

"Hello?"

"Hey, it's me. I was tired from driving. Forgot to call. Just fell asleep when I got in."

"Oh it's all right, David, I'm glad you're O.K."

"I'm fine. . . . Listen, I've got a lot to do tomorrow, and I'm standing here, I'm out here in the cold—there's no phone in the room."

"What's the hotel?"

"Motel. Sevier's. It's a motel. Room eight."

"There's no phone?"

"I'm freezing, Vicki. I'll call you tomorrow, after Dad gets in. Maybe we'll leave right away."

"Can't you do it like it's planned, get here when I have dinner ready?"

"Yes, I will. I'll do that."

"Well. . . ."

"Vicki, I'm freezing. Call you tomorrow."

"I love you, you know."

"Me too."

"Good luck with your other stuff."

"Thanks. O.K. Bye."

"Bye-bye."

He hated these conversations with her. He hated feeling the estrangement.

The Oregon State Welfare office shared space with the county's social services division in a clapboard storefront on Main Street. The woman who ran both, tired and overweight, was sitting pensive in a straight caned chair when David Esterver entered. He wore a tie. The look of comprehension in her face, the earnest freshness of her clothing, put him at ease. He had never met Miss Peletier, but he was instantly empathetic. He saw in her a selflessness he admired intensely. Back in his office in Salem he had barely glanced at a duplicate of her case files. Now, he knew, he must dispel what bore down on him, and address each situation fairly, compassionately, insightfully. He realized that this had once been his gift.

He pulled a second chair over and took from his briefcase a set of folders. Together they stared down at the record of wounds looking up at them from the dismal sheets of paper. In malaligned typescript and cheap ballpoint pen they read: *No known relatives. Abused by step-uncle. Driver's license suspended. Behavior disorder.*

He showed her how to allot what funds she had more effectively. He told her he would look the other way if she ignored a new state law that required her to check on certain people at their houses unannounced. "It's an invasion of privacy," he said softly, indignant. She nodded. He asked her about specific families, the more intractable situations.

"What about—is it Crimmins?—the man who's trying to get insurance benefits for the boy. Did they find the policy?"

"No. It's Christman, is the family. He's got a job working at a feedlot in Caldwell. He lives up there during the week in his truck, leaves the kids down here with his dad. But the insurance people, as far as that goes, I don't think he's going to get anything."

"The child—the child is deaf?"

"MS. The school won't take him. Mr. Christman, he was going to rent a room in Caldwell, care for him, but sleeping in his truck he saves the money for a room. But he's never going to make a dent in them hospital bills without the insurance."

It went on through the morning like that, dozens of lives marred by violence, by cruelty of one sort or another. They ate small, dry hamburgers in a café for lunch. In the afternoon he tried to explain that, barring some last-minute trade-off, the legislature would approve a budget with an 8% reduction in social services.

He knew she knew about it, but he watched rage cross her face as though she were hearing it for the first time. "Those damned people," she said.

He tried to soften the blow, but she waved him off. "Oh I know, I know all about it," she said.

"None of them ever had needs like these to speak of," she offered. "They look down on this kind of charity. They don't see the point of it."

He felt more sympathy than this for the legislators, but he was not sure, either, what they actually thought, or meant. To speculate about a politician's reasons for generosity was to wade into a swamp. Miss Peletier and her clients had one instinct for survival, the legislators another.

By five in the afternoon they were finished. Miss Peletier poured him a cup of coffee and unplugged the machine. They sat in silence. The sparsely furnished storefront had once been a hardware store, then an automobile parts store. He looked past Miss Peletier, out through the large windows. Across a dirt street, between two wooden buildings, were fields. Polled Herefords grazed. He saw a man moving irrigation pipe in a hay meadow. There were jobs out there, in the Idaho mines, the De Lamar and the others, but the wages went too fast, spent in wild generosity, in reckless anger, in self-pity. Never enough saved. He imagined the faces that passed through this room, mute and meek before Miss Peletier. People hounded by a sense of something gone enormously wrong, but too insensate with worry to act, accepting the implacable authority of whatever had been written down on interminable paper forms.

"Mr. Esterver?"

"Mmmm."

"Jordan Valley was built on a gold strike, did you know that?"

"It was?"

"Yes. May of 1863," she said. "Michael Matree Jordan was the man's name, and he found gold nuggets right up there on the creek."

He looked over at her and smiled and shook his head at the irony. "And, yea, verily I tell you . . . on the banks of the Jordan," he said. He began to laugh and she laughed with him.

He showered and shaved in his room. He read the afternoon paper and waited. At a little after seven, the sky still bright, he put on his jacket and went out. The bus would stop in front of Delmont's Café, but he didn't want to be standing right there when it did. He'd stand on the corner, watch it come in from the north and make the turn, then walk down. He didn't want to be right on top of his father, the first thing.

He walked with measured steps over rutted ground in the parking lot next to Esther's bar. He thought of his sisters, both married now, one gone off to Connecticut, the other to Iowa. The place in Calabasas, gone. His mother, dead of cancer. And of his father's equanimity. His kindness. He had denounced him years ago, in public, left for Stanford to study economics and then went to work for a congressman his father despised. He tended, even now, to believe his father spurned him because he'd had no children and lived a paperwork life. But even as he thought these things he knew it was fabrication, that he was indulging himself. His father had only wanted him to return to Calabasas, to the farm, for him to have that place.

He was chagrined by the bad faith in his thoughts.

One evening he'd sat in his father's room in the house in Calabasas, up on the second floor where you could look out over the orchards, his mother's beehives, and the vegetable and flower gardens. He'd come upstairs to strengthen their friendship. He'd begun to sense a gulf opening between them as he prepared to leave for college. His father, sensitive to his innocence and confusion, tried to allay his anxiety by describing his own fears, his own failings. One night, his father said, when he was working over his accounts, he had looked up to see in the chair opposite him the slumped body of a German soldier. Most of the head had been torn away. The blood-soaked tunic rose and fell with the whistle of his severed breaths. In his lap the soldier cradled the shattered remains of his left arm. The apparition, he told his son, was as vivid as the face of the full moon. He stared at it for a long time in disbelief, but it did not vanish. His terror, he said, gave way slowly to grief. He wondered if this was a soldier he had killed in a grenade attack at Argentan in 1944. He rose to his feet, his jaw quivering, he said, meaning to speak. And it vanished.

"You may believe in the essential goodness of men," he told his son, "but do not forget, either, the horror, the terrible meanness, the blood, the stupidity."

He had only a vague idea of what his father meant. Later he understood that war might bring human darkness to a nightmare focus. Most, however, found this darkness in pieces, in pockets, over a lifetime. It left them exhausted and made them angry or sad, but it fired in too few any resolve, any belief. Too many people, David Esterver believed, bleed to death in that darkness, between their own darkness and a darkness from without.

The bus's sudden appearance at the far end of the street startled him. Its bright headlights vibrated over the uneven road. How soundlessly buses could arrive, he thought. WINNEMUCCA, it declared. The bus swung into the turn, an impetuous, self-important movement, hissing, high-revving, double clutching, and winding down to a halt in front of Delmont's Café.

He recognized his father right away from the back, the unchanging khaki trousers, the dark blue Eisenhower jacket. He was shorter than he remembered. He walked toward him slowly. The strength of his father's embrace dissolved his apprehensions. He stepped back, clutching his father's lean forearms.

"You look great, Dad."

"You look good, like you've put on some weight."

"Well, I just don't exercise enough. I've been thinking about running."

"Oh, I meant you're filling out. You look healthy."

"Dad, when you're 34 you're not supposed to be filling out."

"Well—I had a fine trip. Slept last night in Pocatello."

"I made arrangements for us here tonight. Or if you want we can leave now, go part way."

"Let me take a walk. I need to stretch a bit."

He reached nervously for his father's small bag, which his father held away, but in a gesture without offense.

"The motel's over there. I was just going to run your bag over."

"Oh. Good. Fine."

He ran quickly across the street, feeling he'd made too much of taking the bag. And now, in his eagerness to accommodate, he'd left his father standing alone at the roadside.

They went east, out of town. David thanked his father for coming in from Dubois, so they'd have the extra day together, driving up to Salem. His father nodded. The older man walked with a deliberate placement of his feet, and moved his head often, looking around in the rising dusk. Beside him David felt inept. They walked past the edge of town, beyond a row of cottonwoods, out toward irrigated pastures.

He told his father about his job, what Vicki was doing, that they might have children soon. But his heart was in none of what he said and his father knew it.

"I wonder," said his father, "if these are Fremont Cottonwoods. Over there around Dubois you see a narrowleaf cottonwood, but there's also a Plains cottonwood and the two hybridize." He lifted a pear-shaped leaf from a cluster of roadside weeds. "I believe these are black cottonwoods."

His father tilted his head to examine the leaf more closely.

"You really know the trees, Dad."

"Oh, my, just a few. I like the willows. You find them no matter where you go, feel you haven't lost touch with home."

David heard insinuation in the remark, but didn't know whether his father meant it. Despite the poor light and the unfamiliarity of the road, his father walked on.

"Do you remember eucalyptus trees in California? Of all the trees, I was partial to those the most. You remember one called the manna gum? With thin leaves, long as your little arms when you were a boy?"

"Yes, I do, actually. They had a dusty smell. And I used to fill my pockets with eucalyptus buttons."

"People in Wyoming think of southern California as something that's, I don't know . . . televised." His father stopped to gaze at him. "They've no idea of the small farms still there, all the nurseries. They think it's just supermarkets, cars."

He resumed walking.

"Isn't the eucalyptus from Australia?"

"Yes," said his father. "Do you think it should be sent back?"

"No question. Send them all back—the tamarisk, the eucalyptus, the Lombardy poplar. Return the country," he said gravely, "to its native trees."

At the wedding five years before he had not been able to joke at all. His father had not taken to Vicki, a woman from suburban Portland who spoke in a vaguely pedantic manner about "the working class" and "the educated classes." He knew his father had regarded the marriage—his waiting that long to marry,

and marrying someone likeVicki—as a sign he had no intention of ever returning to live on land his father had lived on.

"I never asked if you ate, Dad."

"Ate in Boise, such as it was."

"You want to go back, get a cup of coffee?"

"What's up there?" He gestured with his chin, toward the darkness where
the road disappeared.

"It's farms. Cattle. Irrigated land along the creek. We can drive out that way
tomorrow."

He waited, to make his father turn around, so that they could start back. He
didn't like walking out of town in the evening like this, past farmhouses with
their lights on. It was a sort of trespassing only people like his father could
manage, people who had a certain authority, who could pick up another man's
tools without giving offense, and examine them closely without seeming to
judge. His father was free of schemes and disarming in this way with strangers.

"Do you like your work, David?"

"Oh, I think so. I'm good at it, which means a lot."

"You travel a good deal?"

"About 40,000 miles a year now. I'm away two or three nights a week. The way things have worked, I've been over here recently, east of the mountains, up around Pendleton, Baker. They grow a lot of wheat up there. Some of them are in rough shape. Bought equipment at the wrong time. Some done in by commodities speculation."

"It's the same in Wyoming."

"I like the work, trying to help people out, but there's a hopelessness about it that wears you down. You become a part of it yourself, get absorbed by it. It begins to affect everything in your life." He shook his hands out, as though to rid himself of tension. "And some of the people, some of what I deal with—I don't know what it is. Some people have no will to go on. If there was no unemployment, no food stamps, no help from outside, they'd go back to their trailer homes or to their cars and die. Quit. The despair, the cruelty—aaah."

"It would wear anyone down," consoled his father, "trying to understand the pain, deal with the embarrassment." His father paused. "Your compassion can turn to scorn, even though what's happening is past their control. You hate the ignorance that runs through it all.

"I'm sorry it's such a weight on you."

David pitied himself, an emotion he knew his father detested. Its cure, he knew, was learning to inhabit a world larger than one's own predicament. This is what always saved men like his father from a sense of failure. Already, he thought, his own friends had confided their resignation to him. They were indifferent to their failures. They were not moved by suffering. Their lives barely begun, they had retreated into their salaries.

"If I'm not careful," his father said, staring off into the distant fields, "I could begin to miss California." He reached out to pat his son on the shoulder. "I haven't had a *good*, a *perfect*, avocado, you know, in years."

"So how is your place, Dad?"

"It's grown." He glanced discreetly at his son. "I've got a hundred acres in hay, more next spring. Nothing affects those dude ranches, so I overwinter as many horses as I have room for, 400 last year. And I've gone full tilt into making honey."

"Bees?"

"Nine hundred and sixty pounds last year. I'm amazed at how well they do. In summer I move them up in stages in the Wind River Range, following the bloom of wildflowers, so they do all right. Lot of fireweed. We don't have any spraying around there. That's what's killing them off in California."

"All that acreage, and you're still a truck farmer."

"Yes," his father answered. "Yes. I've never understood why a person would want to risk everything in a single crop, put a place all in oranges, or all in wheat. You lose your feeling for the land and the weather. Only a corporation can farm like that."

They arrived beneath the rose light of Esther's bar.

"You want a beer, Dad?"

"No, thanks. Actually I was thinking about going to bed. The bus gave me a headache."

"I've got aspirin if—"

"I believe I just need to rest."

They crossed the street.

"I got you a room by yourself. I didn't know if—"

"Oh there's no need of that. I'll just stay with you. We won't use the other room, just tell them in the morning."

"Fine. Great."

While his father showered, David sat in an overstuffed chair by the window, looking out at the street.

When his father emerged he was wearing pajamas. In the black, unflattering light of the room's bare ceiling bulb his father's face looked lean. He was, David realized, still a handsome man, now looking more refreshed.

"What's that you're reading, Dad?"

"Well someone—" he put his glasses on, "—this man's name is Macaulay—has done a biography of Luther Burbank. I think it's pretty good." David sensed his father warming to a topic that held his deep interest. "Burbank was a kind of genius, you know, but he was also one of these people like Henry Ford, who wanted to revolutionize production. He wanted to breed fruits that would make people faint with pleasure at the first bite. He wanted to make a cactus with no spines that cattle could eat." His father paused and looked at the book where his finger held the place. "He was obsessed with hybridizing. There was something slightly mad about what he wanted to do."

"Maybe I'll read it when you're through."

His father got into bed. He couldn't remember when it had been so easy to talk to him.

"I'm really not tired, Dad. I'm going to go for a walk. I'll take a key so I won't wake you when I come in."

His father nodded, raising his eyeglasses to his forehead. "Well, that's fine. I'll see you in the morning."

"Dad—I'm awfully glad to see you."

"I'm glad to see you, too, son."

David walked back up the highway and east out of town. It was dark, but the sky was clear and after a while he could see well enough. Honey, he suddenly thought—his father was keeping honeybees.

He passed the cottonwoods, a windbreak planted 30 or 40 years ago. It was not his father who had caused the breach, he knew, but himself. He remembered the farmers he'd negotiated with, when he worked in the governor's office in Sacramento. Artichoke ranchers from Castroville, lettuce growers from the San Joaquin, men hell-bent on success. They wanted guarantees against every vagary in the market. Men like his father—who mixed crops, who changed, who adapted to the weather, to a buildup of salt in the soil—did not covet more land, did not expect such wealth.

He remembered with embarrassment the night in Calabasas when he'd screamed at his father that he didn't want the life his father had, that it fell short.

He remembered, too, with sharp pleasure, the days of his childhood—wonder at the interior of a pomegranate, tunneling through stacked bales of hay. And driving in early on Saturday mornings with the other farmers from Canoga Park and Sepulveda, over the Santa Monica Mountains into Hollywood. With eggplants and broccoli and beets, with carrots and casaba melons, cantaloupes and radishes and walnuts. Crates of olives. They would set the food out in wooden flats and half-barrels on sloping tables, and spray it all with water from green garden hoses. The people would feel the fruit and smile, touch him fondly on the head as they passed. The air under the canvas awnings was cool and damp with the precious water. There were demure Japanese families, whose farms were east of the city, out toward Pasadena. And kinds of plums for sale he never saw again.

The cold air penetrated his clothing and chilled him, but he walked on. Around a long curve the foothills finally opened into a valley. The air was utterly still, the wind that had blown the day before now gone. If it had been summer he would have expected to smell alfalfa, to hear the *chutch chutch chutch* of huge field sprinklers, the *chuh-chuh-chuh-chuh-chuh* of their recovery, to begin again the silver arc. Night watering.

Working in rural planning in California, he thought, had worn him out, had consumed his faltering idealism. He hated what had happened to farming in the San Joaquin. Calculating legislators in Sacramento, the farmers blaming everyone but themselves, the arrogance of the corporations. . . . He regretted mostly his own complicity. The soil he had grown up on, he reflected, had, over the years, become only a set of ideas in his head. That estrangement, he knew, was the real horror.

On the walk back he sensed how tenuous was his grasp of what he was thinking. His reasoning was uncertain, his thoughts vulnerable. But he recognized a shift within himself, away from reasoning and toward desire. His pure desire, he thought, was not to rectify, not to intercede. It was to affirm what he remembered, what his father still held to, to participate as well as he could in that.

He thought of Dubois, of Wyoming. He sensed the foolishness of it, the beckoning illusions of childhood, his presumption. He didn't know if there was actually any room for them there, or, if Vicki went, whether she would stay.

He walked as far as the telephone outside Esther's bar. He knew, from where he now stood, that his life was being devoured. He felt the cold night air falling. He knew that with hope he had also kindled doubt in his heart, and that it would not abate. He stood as still and composed as moonlight, waiting for the words with which to begin.

Suggested Further Reading

WORKS BY LOPEZ

Of Wolves and Men. New York: Charles Scribner's Sons, 1978.

River Notes: The Dances of Herons. Kansas City, Kansas: Andrew and McMeel, 1979.

Winter Count. New York: Charles Scribner's Sons, 1981.

Arctic Dreams. New York: Charles Scribner's Sons. 1986.

Crossing Open Ground. New York: Random House Vintage Books, 1989.

Crow and Weasel. San Francisco: North Point Press, 1990.

WORKS ABOUT LOPEZ

Aton, Jim. "An Interview with Barry Lopez." *Western American Literature,* 21 (May 1986), 3-17.

Wild, Peter. *Barry Lopez.* Boise State Western Writers Series, Number 64. Boise, Idaho: Boise State University, 1984.

Russell Working

Russell Working was born in 1959 in Long Beach, California. He attended Whitworth College and settled in Grants Pass, where he has lived for the last seven years. He works as a reporter at the *Daily Courier* in that city. His short story collection, *Resurrectionists*, was a winner of the 1987 H.L. Davis Award from the Oregon Institute for Literary Arts and the co-winner of the 1986 Iowa Short Fiction Award. Russell Working is now writing a novel set in southern Oregon. The story reprinted here, from the *Paris Review*, is based upon a Halloween festival in Ashland, a city famed for its Shakespeare theater. The festival has since been abandoned.

Halloween, Via Dolorosa

Though it was pitch dark on the road where the Foxes parked and you tried to keep from stepping in the black puddles of icy mud when you looked up at the stars, North Main Street was brightly lighted and decorated with lanterns and paper carved pumpkins in the windows, and the street was closed off with flashing barricades and crowded from one end to the other: from the tightly packed mob around the bandstand where a punk band was pounding out grating music and jumping sometimes with their guitars, to the end of the road near Gepetto's, where the crowd thinned out and everyone stopped and stood, puzzled and bemused, before turning back to walk again. They looked at each other, and now at this end of the street it seemed funny and innocent. Some of them were really good. A giant in a blue gown was lurching through the crowd, and small men held sticks attached to each arm. They made the giant wave. The pirate Jesse held his father's hand.

"Look!"

"Shakespeare," Fox said.

Fox was a monster. He had a Gila monster's head, with green fur on the pate and down the back of the neck, and he wore a coat and jeans and tennis shoes. He was smoking a cigar, stuck in a hole in the mask's gullet, and when he puffed smoke came out his eyes. People laughed and pointed at Fox. "Look at that guy," a witch said. "I love you." Fox was walking, and he bumped into her.

He said something, and she went on.

"You bumped her," said Jesse.

Fox said something.

"What?"

He bent over by Jesse's ear. "I can't see out of this thing. The eye slits are too small. Would you help steer your old man? I'll take it off in a minute."

"OK, Dad."

"Do you like this?"

"Yeah."

"Is it scary, kid?"

"No. A little bit."

"Good. A little scary is fun, isn't it?"

"Yeah."

"Let's head back down the street."

They went toward the noise.

Nuns were the most common and, after them, buxom women in shiny red low-cut dresses with fringe around the edges. Richard Nixon was popular, too. Some nuns wore real habits and rosaries and might have been nuns for all you could tell except that one of them was saying, "Son of a bitch," as she swished past. The Foxes were Lutheran, not Roman Catholic. There was no such thing as Lutheran nuns.

Fox was hot, and the mask full of smoke, making his eyes water. He blinked. His breath condensed on the plastic and ran in cold rivulets into his collar. He gritted the cigar in his teeth so it would not touch the plastic and melt it.

An eight-legged Chinese dragon danced past. It trotted in step, weaving its way through the crowd, and headed straight for Fox, until Jesse realized his father would be trampled and pulled him hard to the left and the dragon went on by. Its eyes were lit up.

"Boy, that startled me," Fox said. "Where did that come from? I ought to take this off so I can see. Maybe one more trip down the street to show off. I've got one more cigar. Then I need to see, too."

Fox pulled off his mask and lit another cigar. His hair was messy and damp, and he grinned and winked at Jesse. He put the mask back on. He could not find the mouth hole, and he nearly stuck the cigar in his eye.

"Everybody's staring at you, Dad."

"They envy my costume. K-mart special."

Fox managed to get the cigar in the hole of the mask, and he puffed away. His eyes smoked, and some girls came by and laughed and said, "Cool."

A cowboy came by with his horse attached around his midriff. He walked on his own feet, and the horse's legs dangled. He fired a cap gun in the air.

"Dad!"

"Yep."

Then a giant furry blond figure appeared, his head dark against a globe of light around a streetlamp, and Jesse stopped flat. The creature squatted beside the boy. He growled, "The Force be with you." Fox snarled at him and the creature rose and growled, hands on his hips. Then he strode on. He had tennis shoes instead of furry padded feet.

"He's a good guy, Dad."

"I know. Gorillas are always good guys."

"It wasn't a gorilla. It was Chewbacca from Star Wars."

"No kidding?" Fox looked back over his shoulder. "I couldn't tell."

"You growled at him."

"It was a friendly growl."

Jesse led his father along past a six-pack of beer trotting down the road. The cans were laughing. "We'd never make it through the door," a can hollered back at someone.

Nuns were everywhere. One nun knelt in the street, holding up a stick with a doll on the end. The doll was covered with ketchup, which dripped down the stick onto her hands. She cried out in a quavery voice, "Sinners! You're on the road to hell. Stop the slaughter of the innocents." A crowd stood in a circle around her, laughing. Ronald Reagan poured beer on her and made the sign of the cross.

"In the name of the Father and the Son and the Holy Ghost," President Reagan said.

The crowd howled.

"What are they doing, Dad?"

"What?" Fox looked around. He tilted his head back so he could see through the nostrils. He gripped Jesse's hand tight and said, "Let's walk on," and he shoved his way through the crowd, dragging his son by the hand. They bumped into a man in a dress, who said "Ooo!" Fox said, "We don't need to look at them."

"What were they doing?"

"Just being stupid."

"Were they taking the Lord's name in vain?"

"Yes."

Satan walked past wearing a red skintight suit. A pentacle was drawn on his forehead, and one of his arms was artificial, with a shiny metal hook on the end. Jesse was going to say something about the arm to his father when he realized it was real. He shivered. Fox was chewing the end of his cigar and looking the other way. Jesse squeezed his father's hand.

They were close to the band now, and the crowd made a noise, and through a gap Jesse saw Jesus. Jesus wore only a loincloth; he trudged along carrying a hollow plywood cross. A crown of thorns encircled his head, and stripes from a scourging were painted on his body. Jesse felt sick.

"Dad," he said. "Jesus."

Fox was puffing rapidly on the stub of his cigar; it was getting too short to be safe, and it might melt the plastic. He took a few final draws then dropped the cigar on the pavement and ground it out under his sole. He removed the mask and said, "Ah. Now I can breathe."

"Dad," said Jesse. "A man dressed as Jesus."

Fox looked, and his face hardened. The man Jesus was grinning, and he bellowed, "Eloi, Eloi, lama sabacthani." Some people laughed, but an old man standing near the Foxes told a woman dressed as Charlie Chaplin, "I can't believe it. I bloody cannot believe it." Fox clenched his fists.

"Let's get out of here," Fox said.

They walked up the street, and Jesse held his father's trembling hand. Fox wore his mask like a hat, and his face showed below the eyebrows. A couple of drunk college students staggered by, and one of them pointed at Fox and said, "Look at that one. He's fucking ugly."

Jesse started to cry. The other college boy said, "Now look what you've done," as they weaved away.

It was a long walk to the car, and Fox carried Jesse on his back. A small trailer was parked in a lot full of weeds up past the railroad tracks, and a light was on in the window, glowing through the yellow curtains and filmy broken window that was patched with duct tape. Jesse wiped his cheeks on his father's shoulders and thought, If only we make it that far. If we pass the window with the light on and the barking dog, we'll stay alive. If we make it to the car. Fox's pace was plodding, and Jesse thought, If he would run. If I stay awake that far.

The dog chained to an orange tree was barking, and it paced under the canopy of slick oily leaves and howled. The chain was long enough that the dog could reach Jesse if it tried, but a python was coiled around the dog's legs and torso. You should stay away from the dog, Jesse knew, but the snake was deadly. The snake left the dog and slithered across the grass at him. Jesse thought, A weapon, and there was a machete in his hand. He beheaded the snake. The head was snapping on the ground, and Jesse leaped out of the way of the fangs. Then the Devil said to him, "Pick it up."

Fox carried him away and brought him inside the trailer. Jesse said, "Why are we going in here?" "Shh," said Fox. "We're home." Jesse's mother was there. Fox said, "We've got one tired buccaneer here." They put him on the bed, and he began crying as they took off his jacket and pants and shoes and socks. "Ow!" Jesse said. His mother wiped his moustache off with a warm washcloth, and she said, "Stop it now. Here, blow your nose." He honked his nose in the washcloth. She tucked him in his pirate shirt and underwear.

"How did it go?" she said.

"I don't know if I want to go next year," said Fox.

"Why?"

"I'll tell you later."

"Did Jesse like it?"

"I think so, up until the end. I'll tell you about it."

Jesse started crying again.

"Shush," his mother said. But Jesse could not stop sobbing. "I dreamed I was in hell," he said.

Fox sat on the edge of the bed and stroked his son's messy hair. "It's OK," he said. "We're home now."

Suggested Further Reading

WORKS BY WORKING

Resurrectionists. Iowa City, University of Iowa Press, 1987.

Martha Gies

Born in Salem in 1944 and raised on a farm near Independence, Martha Gies is a fourth-generation Oregonian. During her 20s and 30s she attended a number of colleges, including Oregon College of Education where she received her B.A. in 1976, and worked at various jobs, including computer programmer, deputy sheriff, masseuse, stage manager, waitress, bookstore clerk, and taxi driver. She began publishing nonfiction in the mid-1970s. She later studied fiction writing with Raymond Carver and wrote *What We Talk about When We Talk about Love*, a screen adaptation of twelve Raymond Carver stories. "O'Keefe Sober," a winner of the 1990 PEN Syndicated Fiction Project, deals with the major contemporary problem of addiction in an urban Oregon setting. The story comes out of Martha Gies's concern for the homeless, her experience working in Skid Road sections of Portland and Seattle, and her ongoing contact with migrant farm workers.

O'Keefe Sober

Three days out of Hooper Detox, O'Keefe woke up scared. He lay in his assigned room at Bernadette House tasting blood in the back of his throat and heard the day start up with water whining through pipes and the food locker door creaking in the kitchen below. This time had been the time he was going to make it. But he was losing his nerve. With his eyes pressed closed, he patted the night table for an open pack of Parliaments. He figured it was the statuary in the dining room was doing it to him, that blue-robed madonna with her feet entwined in a plaster serpent, the black-robed friar toting a crucifix like a picket sign. This whole outfit reminded him of St. Vincent's Orphanage in North Platte, Neb., which he'd run away from at age 16. At least there were no nuns hanging around spying on him.

Thirty-four years old, with thinning hair, wiry in jeans and T-shirt, O'Keefe was a fighter. He was also a grinner, and people usually hit him first. These days his smile lines were the street map of a ghost town.

O'Keefe knew he'd have to fill every minute today. Bernadette House, which ran the 30-day program, required him to help serve breakfast and lunch to the homeless in exchange for his room and board. (This would eventually make him eligible for a job in the restaurant industry, he was told.) He worked the kitchen from 5 in the morning until 3 in the afternoon. At 3, he'd find the closest AA meeting, come directly back here for dinner with the other residents, and install himself safely in his room before 8:30 curfew.

The rhythm of the work pushed the day forward. The two meals were the strongest pulses, each bringing a surge of 200 people who lined up the length of the block. He patrolled the dining room, offering more scrambled eggs, more Cream of Wheat, more day-old pastry, more hot coffee. The room was painted green with a row of high windows from which streamed shafts of north light, fixing faces like photographs. O'Keefe found himself watching a gaunt old man with high-voltage black eyes, who wore a gray blanket over his shoulders and spoke to no one. O'Keefe didn't know how long he'd been staring.

After breakfast, O'Keefe helped swab down the long tables and benches, scalded plates in the huge dishwasher, and began chopping lettuce, cabbage, turnips for lunch. Then the room quickened and filled again, humming with footsteps, curses, cutlery, and laughter.

The hard part was evening. At 6 p.m., O'Keefe's fatigue suggested a drink, even though he'd just sat through the Marshall Street Community Center AA meeting. Something to pick him up, get him going again, lift the deadweight of routine.

The worst was dinner, where he had nothing to say. A dozen guys sat around chattering. About what, for godssakes? Just one drink, a quick jolt of whiskey eased down by a beer. O'Keefe was sure to utter something significant, maybe even shift the way everybody saw things. But he ate in mind-numb silence.

At the other end of the table, Tiny was waving a folded section of *The Oregonian*. "Here's just what I'm talking about: They got this kid with a messed-up heart. It's obvious he's never going to make it. But they spend thousands of dollars!" The bench creaked as Tiny shifted his massive weight to reach for the salt.

"They have hospital committees who decide that stuff," said Zack, who was sprinkling tobacco from a pouch onto a cigarette paper. He was considered a pretty bright kid because he'd worked on a salmon processor in Alaska and had learned to speak Tagalog. "That baby could have a life ahead of him." He lit one twisted end of the cigarette and inhaled.

"Could I see that over here?" O'Keefe asked with a grin.

"You're not getting the crossword puzzle," Tiny said, and he slipped off one page of news sheet and passed it down the table. O'Keefe finished his chili and lemonade and took the story upstairs to read slowly in his room.

The baby looked like a lively little tyke. He was photographed sitting up, wearing diapers, one hand buried in the fur of the sleeping cat. He had already had two open-heart surgeries. The young parents, who met in their freshman year of Bible College, had no other children.

O'Keefe kneeled down stiffly in front of the window. He hadn't prayed since the old orphanage days. After a moment he shut his eyes. "Dear Lord, please help this baby named Shawn Samuels. In Galesburg, Ill."

Then his mind froze, and he opened his eyes. A dead fly lay, legs up, in the dust of the sill, which was painted sky blue. He'd heard this used to be a brothel—spacious dining hall, 24 bedrooms, the river four blocks away. But wasn't the same thing said of every hotel, mission, and boarding house O'Keefe had stayed in from Nebraska to Oregon? It must be one of those things people said.

He knelt until his knees ached bone-white under his jeans. The next part of the prayer appeared in his mind: "Give this baby a perfect heart. In Jesus' name, Amen."

That's about as basic as it gets, he thought. He stood and shook out his thin legs. Then he lay on the flowered bedspread and smoked Parliaments and waited for the evening to be over so he could go to bed.

The next morning he thought about that baby as he mopped floors and watched the crowds shuffle through the dining room. He thought the part about the "perfect heart" was pretty well stated. It might do some good.

After work, he cut across the railroad yard on his way to a 4 p.m. AA meeting. Bottles and old clothing collected near the siding where people were sleeping in boxcars. Out of habit, O'Keefe eyed each bottle for a little Tokay or Mad Dog which might be left. When he caught himself doing it, he jammed his hands in his jeans pockets and picked up the pace. He remembered how little it took last time to fall off the wagon. He reviewed his prayer for that baby.

At AA, the subject was blackouts. O'Keefe sipped a cup of instant coffee and listened to a man with his arm in a sling tell a story about coming downstairs in the morning after his first alcoholic blackout. "I wasn't no more than 16," the man said. "I went right to the front window and looked out." The man lifted the sling and rubbed the back of his neck. He said he was sure glad to see his car parked safely at the curb, no ripped metal and no blood. "Then I realized my old man had come downstairs and was standing right there beside me, staring out the window at his car," he said. "We was worried about the very same thing."

O'Keefe said, "I'm Daniel, I'm an alcoholic." Then he passed. He didn't have any stories about his dad because he never knew him. This last blackout, he shuddered to recall, he was crawling across the Coliseum parking lot in the dark on his hands and knees. There was broken glass. A big motorcycle chopper wailed past.

Back at Bernadette House O'Keefe ate one helping of spaghetti and cole-slaw. Then he collected the leftover sections of *The Oregonian* and climbed the stairs to his room. He perused the paper, looking for someone who needed his prayers.

He studied the pictures of several brides, and one in particular, a pretty girl with seed pearls and a hyphenated name. But then he looked away. There were pictures of timber industry officials, a severe-looking black prime minister, a kidnapper in handcuffs and the power forward for Benson High School. There was nothing he could add to their lives.

He found the obituaries and read an entry about a school teacher named Alva Hauser who died of respiratory failure in a Portland nursing home. She had moved to Oregon from South Dakota, and taught for 41 years at Good Shepherd Elementary School. One paragraph. Was that a life?

"Dear Lord," he prayed, "please give Miss Hauser an easy death." He stopped and thought about that for a minute. He shifted his knees on the orange shag carpet, and he saw where a cigarette burn had welded the shiny strands together.

Was it too late to pray for that? How long does death take? Could his prayer still assist her? Between buildings a slice of the river glinted bronze in the evening sun. He had a bold thought: "Dear Lord, hear a prayer from Daniel O'Keefe in behalf of Alva Hauser. Forgive her sins, Amen." He got up and stretched his legs. He felt connected with events.

After that, he found himself coming in early to locate the obituary section of the newspaper. During dinner, he kept track of it as the newspaper made the rounds of the dining room.

The best were the dead. O'Keefe could not know what choices they had made, nor whether anyone was left behind to pray for them. Perhaps the dead needed him a little. He was impartial and maybe, because of that, his prayers just might carry some weight.

He began to think of his room upstairs as a factory of prayers for the dead, the place where his important work was done. He applied himself to it daily. And in this way, O'Keefe moved through his first 30 days without a drink.

Suggested Further Reading

WORK BY GIES
"Blue." *Zyzzva*, 3:2 (Summer 1987), 127-129.
"Blackbird." *Other Voices*, 8 (Spring 1988), 34-42.
"The Shoat." *Spindrift 88*, 26 (Spring 1988), 86-92.

Miles Wilson

Miles Wilson, born in South Dakota in 1943, lived in Oregon for sixteen years, in Eugene, Bend, McKenzie Bridge, and Port Orford. He taught at Central Oregon Community College, worked in fire management on the McKenzie and Blue River districts of the Willamette National Forest, and was a partner in a small logging company. He received his Master of Fine Arts degree from the University of Oregon, and now teaches at Southwest Texas State University in San Marcos. He has published his fiction in many leading journals. *Line of Fall*, his book of short fiction from which the following story is selected, was the 1989 winner of the University of Iowa's John Simmons Short Fiction Award. "The Lord of Misrule at Separation Creek" invites comparison with Nathaniel Hawthorne's classic tale, "The Maypole of Merrymount," and with Oregon's propensity for attracting cult religious leaders and followers such as the Bhagwan Shree Rajneesh and his devotees.

The Lord of Misrule at Separation Creek

On the west slope of the Oregon Cascade Mountains, deep inside the Three Sisters Wilderness, Separation Creek rises on the flank of the South Sister and flows west and north some twenty miles into Horse Creek. It is an ordinary stream, bright as ice and dropping steeply once it leaves the high meadow country. It had been called Whistling Jesus Creek by settlers after a circuit-riding preacher whose cabin stood near the stream's mouth. The name was changed with the coming of the U. S. Forest Service and the federal tidying up of bawdy or otherwise unsuitable place names.

Some few years ago, a party traveling north from Sphinx Butte broke out of heavy timber into Separation Meadow on the afternoon of the summer solstice. The group numbered perhaps a dozen, more women than men, and was led by a stocky man with a sprightly stride. They moved into the meadow, following the man toward a stand of pine, aspen, and spruce which covered a little rise in the grassy plain. The party was variously dressed, but the stocky man's cobalt shirt and lemon pants lit the meadow like a burning shrub. All carried heavy packs which they shrugged off clumsily when the buoyantly dressed man stopped at the verge of the rise.

They sank down beside the packs, but their leader, after scanning the meadow, walked on into the trees. Some time later he rejoined the group and spread his arms in wide embrace, facing east across the brilliant meadow towards the rising forest and the great snowy volcanoes of the Cascade summit.

A bright cheer rose from the group, and people began breaking out their gear. By late afternoon, tents bloomed at the edge of the rise, and the party was busy embellishing their campsite. Streamers, wind chimes, and globes of colored glass were hung from trees and from a network of lines run among the trees. Balloons were filled from a small tank and tied in clusters, and in the meadow ingenious miniature windmills were assembled, their vermillion and copper blades flashing as wind riffled the grassy flat. Bits of mirror and colored glass were tacked up on trees or wedged in the crotch of branches. One woman launched six kites, each resembling a different exotic beast. Through the afternoon, a storehouse of wood was gathered. The men dragged and rolled great logs to the pile and built a fire ring with stones carried from the creek.

The leader sat far out in the flat, facing away from the group, until the afternoon light thickened towards sunset. He swept up then and came across the meadow, gesturing like a mime, his face painted in an exaggerated mask of delight. Reaching the group, he bantered away questions, teasing the women and joking with the men. He sent the men away for more wood and settled around the cooking fire with the women, helping to prepare the evening meal, a richly spiced stew.

After supper the stained-glass lanterns were lit. Across the meadow the silver light drained away into the surface of Separation Creek. The man ignited the main fire, adding wood until it blazed up as high as his shoulders. He stepped back deliberately, thirty paces or so; then, with a yip of glee, he broke into a run towards the fire. Nearly there, he flung himself through three handsprings before vaulting in a double flip across the flames. Landing, the man spread his arms, palms up, and bowed to the applause. From a leather pouch on his belt, he drew out a bell and rang it crisply. At the sound each member of the group clasped his own hands, as if greeting himself.

"There is a place in the high desert, east of the Steens Mountains in the Alvord Basin. Gypsum flats, briny seeps, hot springs. Some alkaline lakes. Plants do not grow there; even the weather seems a stranger. But there are creatures here that are rare—rare and wonderful. A tusked fish that burrows into the sulfury mud. Blind, albino lizards far back in the basaltic caves. Carnivorous moths. I have seen these things." The man sprang into a back flip, and the people let go of their hands and rang bells like the one the man carried.

"My friends, are you less rare? The ordinary world has made you. So what? It has made you and made you and one day it must destroy you for being what it made. This is complicated and it is not fair and it fills us with fear." The man vaulted in front of the fire again, his face stretched like a tragic mask, and a moaning passed among the people.

"Therefore, everyone wants to save you. Everyone says: 'Change and you will be saved.' But I say to you, if you want to change go away from us." The man's arms flared out. "Here, I give you permission to be. I allow, I permit, I enable only one thing: that you be. Here you strip off all that encumbers, cast away old changes until you reach the pure vein, the pure joy that is your first self."

The bells pealed out across the meadow where nighthawks wheeled through the insect nations. The man dropped down, then pressed into a handstand, making one circuit of the fire before he resumed.

"Oh, the lords of law," the man said, his voice a husky whisper. "The masters of propriety, of discipline, of family. The grim captains of the church and the university and the marketplace. The magistrates of the superego and the Other. The lords of demand steal you away from your first self. You ask me who I am, and I tell you now, have brought you here to tell you." His voice rose out of him now like molten amber.

"I am the Lord of Misrule. I throw over the lords of rule and set you free."

The next morning the man led the band to the bank of a grassy oxbow of Separation Creek. He asked each one to call up some moment from his past, cup it in his hands, then sluice them through the flowing water.

"The lords of rule bind you with the past and the future. Only the present sets you free. Your past flushes out of your hands; your future sweeps away in the current and no man can know it. When your hands are no longer full of the past and the future, you may hold the present in them. You may hold a life which is your own."

Each morning at the oxbow the man repeated these words. At night before the fire, expansive and acrobatic, he amplified the doctrine. Sometimes he juggled as he spoke, weaving arcs with blue and lime and burgundy balls that glowed faintly in the dark.

"This is, all of it, about joy. If I ever grow too heavy you must remind me. Ring the small bells, the little tinklers.

"As you draw near to your first self you will shiver in delight, go blind with joy.

"You can see that I want nothing from you. Let us be candid. Not money, not sex, not power. It is my gift: I offer your lives to you."

As the summer deepened the man taught each of them a different acrobatic stunt. Whenever they performed the routine, he said, they were leaving their old bodies behind. Most had little talent for such feats but several women and one bantamweight man grew quite fluent.

The man set them other tasks as well. Some involved patterns of eating and defecation about which the man had a great store of riddles and puns. There was also a daily walkabout during which each member of the band went farther into the wilderness, leaving behind some small possession and returning with a piece of wood to be added to the effigy that was constructed during the week. At week's end, the man placed an article of his own on the effigy and it was burned. And in all of this the man insisted that they hold always before them their purpose: to strip away the overburden, turning over the layers of not-you until they struck the true ore of the self.

In late August two men slipped away with no explanation. Not long after, a woman, whose behavior had become increasingly erratic, stormed off after a dispute about the lyrics of a Cat Stevens song. The man was disconsolate, hunched in the meadow all one day until the group surrounded him at dusk ringing the tiny bells that sprung him into a goofy ragman dance which everyone joined. That night, he brought out the tank of nitrous oxide.

As the light tarnished towards autumn, the encampment took on the sadness of debris and things too long in the weather. Charred wood lay about the fire rings built near each tent. Tinfoil and shreds of plastic and scraps of parachute cord were scattered across the packed dirt of the cooking area, and bits of soiled tissue blew about. The kites had been torn away in a fierce and sudden wind that had left the streamers in tatters and uprooted the windmills. Bits of mirror and colored glass still glinted richly in the trees, but on the ground beneath, the tents were streaked and faded. The grassy soil of the oxbow had been beaten down into hardpan, and chunks of the bank had sloughed off where the group came down to flush their hands each morning. As the people came and went across the meadow, their trails deepened into ruts.

Their leader bore them above all of this, buoying the group with laughter and promise and forgetfulness.

"What we do here, remember, is peculiar. To take back your life from the hands of others is peculiar. To invent the present each day is peculiar. You must always surprise yourself; only in surprise and laughter are you free."

Two days before the equinox, the man directed that a feast be prepared from the remaining stores. The next morning in a great patchwork cloak he led the group in serpentine procession to the creek. Dressed in their brightest clothes, bells chiming in the crisp air, they wove through the meadow downstream from the oxbow where Separation Creek pooled behind a small logjam.

"You have scrubbed away the past and have forsaken the future. Still, there is one more thing. The last thing you must cast away is myself."

Distressed murmurs rose up from the people. The man waved them to silence.

"It is the right thing, you shall see. But first we must celebrate the self you have recovered. We must crystallize it in these waters; then travel over the crest and confirm it in the twin waters of the other side."

As he spoke, the man stepped apart from the group. His arms began to shovel air, and bruise-colored smoke rolled from his fingertips.

"The Lord of Misrule commands you: each of you now make a joyful run and extravagant leap into these waters." Each did, as the tang of smoke rode on the air and the man crinkled in laughter. When everyone was in the stream, the man snapped his fingers out and somersaulted into the pool, inciting a magnificent water fight.

Later, around the fire, the man explained what remained to be done. The next day, on the equinox, he would lead them across the pass between the Middle and South Sister. On the other side they would repeat their celebration in Blockhouse Creek. Then they must drive him away.

The next morning the band set out east across the meadow. Their leader carried a pack with provisions for an evening meal after the ceremony. Everything else was left behind. Pockets of ground fog hung in the meadow, and their pants were soaked with dew before they reached the timber.

By afternoon they were above timberline. Someone had wrenched an ankle crossing a patch of scree and had dropped behind with a companion. The rest went on up to a small cinder cone not far below the pass itself. By the time the stragglers had caught up, weather was rolling in from the southwest, already past Diamond Peak and careening along the crest.

The man urged them up, miming a frantic conductor making ready the departure of a train. Laughing, they rose and climbed on. Again, the same pair dropped back and were already out of sight of the rest when the rain struck. Within minutes snow was falling, driven in wild swarms by the wind.

The man gathered the group and told them they must keep moving. The pass, he said, was near, and the storm might beat itself out on this side of the summit. He approached each of them, rubbing their cheeks until the friction warmed them. Then he sprang ahead into the spreading snow.

Near dusk the man came through the pass and, dropping down a few hundred feet, left the storm above him. At timberline he built a great fire and waited.

Behind, blinded in the snow and oncoming dark, the band had separated into two groups with several lone stragglers. Some continued to climb; others felt their way downslope. Here and there bells rang out, the sound torn away in the roaring wind.

Two of the group made it down to the rain and the sheltering timber that night. One more came down the next morning. They rested a day at the encampment, eating a stash of licorice that one of them had left on a walkabout. The next day they hiked out to the Frog Camp trailhead.

It took the search party several days to find all the bodies. Two of them were frozen in grotesque acrobatic contortions. Another had a small bell clenched in her teeth.

Before the long snows reached Separation Meadow, a Forest Service packer and trail crew came in and cleaned out the encampment, burning what debris they could and packing out the rest on the mules.

On the tenth anniversary of the deaths, a staff writer for *Pacific Rim* magazine tracked down the leader of the group. His name was Jerry Corbet. He was director of recreation for a small chain of nursing homes in the mid-South. After the deaths, he had gone to the sheriff's office. They had taken his statement, but there was nothing to charge him with. The statement remained sealed, and Corbet left the state.

Corbet reluctantly agreed to an interview on the condition that his location not be divulged. He had little to tell the writer. Corbet refused to discuss his purposes in forming the group, except to say that recent medical research had confirmed the therapeutic effects of laughter. The writer prodded Corbet for an account of his actions during the storm and received an uninflected summary. When Corbet reached the pass, he waited. After no one came, he crossed over and built a signal fire. He stayed there through the night and into the next afternoon. By then it was apparent, he said, that everyone had chosen to return to the encampment, so he hiked out.

Corbet indicated that he was married, but would not say whether he had children. He said that the episode was not a part of his life that he dwelled on. At the end of the interview, he agreed to be photographed facing away from the camera in a handstand.

After a few summers, the meadow and grove were much as they had always been. Separation Creek carved a sharp, new bank in the oxbow, and saplings grew out of the mossy fire rings. Here and there, though, bits of colored glass remain, mostly now in the nests of Steller's Jays, those disorderly harlequins of the high country.

Suggested Further Reading

WORKS BY WILSON
Line of Fall. Iowa City: University of Iowa Press, 1989.

Lawson Fusao Inada

Born in Fresno, California, in 1938, Lawson Fusao Inada was a young boy during World War II. During that time, he and the members of his family, like other Japanese-Americans on the West Coast, were held in an internment camp. That experience marks much of his writing, including the story which follows.

Backin Fresno after the wat, he graduated from Fresno State College in 1959 and later, in 1966, he earned a Master of Fine Arts degree in creative writing at the University of Oregon. Since then, he has taught at Southern Oregon College in Ashland, where he is now Professor of English.He is known primarily as a poet and his first book of poems, *Before the War*, was the first poetry book by an Asian-American author published by a major press. This book joins Seattle writer John Okada's fine novel, *No-No Boy*, as a landmark of Asian-American writing in the Northwest.

The Flower Girls

For children everywhere

I. The Meeting

This is the story of Cherry and Rose, the two little girls who were almost sisters. They were almost twins, actually, because although they came from different families, they were both born on the very same day in the very same city of Portland, Oregon.

They met in the first grade on the very first day of school. They sat in the front row, right next to each other. They both had on pink dresses and white shoes. They even had their hair combed the same way—parted right down the middle. When the teacher saw them, she said, "Well, well, well—so you're Cherry, and you're Rose. Looks like we have a couple of real flower blossoms here. Why, I'll just call you my Flower Girls—and you can help me right now by passing out these pencils to the class. Come on, Flower Girls—let's go!"

Naturally, Cherry and Rose became best friends. From the very first day, they did everything together. They did very well in school, they ate lunch together, and during recess they jumped rope, played jacks, and played hopscotch together. They were good at things by themselves, but together they were even better.

II. After School

Now in those days, everyone walked home after school. The kids all lived close to school, but they went in different directions. Cherry went one way, and Rose went another. But one day, when school was over, Cherry said to Rose, "Rose, why don't you ask your mother if you could come over to my house to play tomorrow? I live just down over there and around the corner. We could have lots of fun, and I'll walk you home for dinner. Okay?"

"Okay!" said Rose.

So the next day, Rose went home with Cherry. As they got close, Cherry said, "I bet you can't guess where I live."

Rose said, "Over there?"

Cherry said, "No, silly—that's a newspaper office. Guess again."

Rose said, "Over there?"

Cherry said, "No, silly—that's the fish store. Guess again."

Rose said, "Over there?"

Cherry said, "No, silly—that's the manju-ya. You only get one more guess."

Then Rose said, "Well, how about that place?"

"Right," said Cherry.

"But what does that sign say?" said Rose.

"Don't be silly," said Cherry. "That sign says 'Sakura Tofu Company.'"

"But what does that mean?" said Rose.

"Don't be silly," said Cherry. "That means 'Cherry Blossom Tofu Company.'"

"But what is a tofu?" said Rose.

"Don't be silly," said Cherry. "A tofu is a tofu, don't you know?"

"But where do you live?" said Rose.

"Don't be silly," said Cherry. "We live in back of the store. Come on! My mom is waiting!"

Sure enough, Cherry's mom was waiting for them. A little bell tinkled when they went into the store. Cherry's mom said, "'My, oh my—don't you Flower Girls look pretty today! Cherry, here's ten cents for you and Rose to spend. Why don't you show your friend around?"

"Okay!" said Cherry. "Let's go!"

III. Snow Cones and Manju

The girls had a great time that afternoon. It was a nice, warm day, and they walked around the busy neighborhood, looking in stores and saying hello to people. After a while, Rose said, "Cherry, what are we going to do with the ten cents?"

Cherry said, "Come on—I'll show you!"

They went into the place called the manju-ya. There were many good things to eat on the shelves—everything looked so pretty and colorful, and everything smelled so good and tasty. Rose said, "Boy, oh boy—I've never seen anything like this! What are we going to get?"

Cherry said, "I'll show you."

When the man came out from the back, Cherry said, "We'll have two snow cones, please—with rainbow flavors."

The man went over to the snow-cone machine, put in a big, shiny piece of ice, and cranked the ice around and around. He made snow, scooped the snow into paper cones, and poured all the flavors of the rainbow on top of the snow. The girls watched with wide-open eyes, and licked their lips.

Cherry gave the man ten cents, and they got their cones. Then the man said, "Just a minute." He got a small paper bag and put in some of the prettiest manju for them to take home, for free.

Naturally, the girls said, "Thank you, very much!"

They had to eat the snow cones pretty fast because it was a hot day, but if they ate too fast, it hurt their heads. So they walked down the sidewalk very slowly, being careful to eat with good manners, to not slurp too much, and to not spill anything on their dresses. Rose bumped into an old lady coming out of the fish store, but since nothing was spilled, they all laughed.

At the street corner, though, as they were finishing their snow cones, tipping the cones upside-down, Rose looked at Cherry and started to laugh.

"What's the matter?" said Cherry.

"You should look at your mouth!" said Rose.

"You should look at *your* mouth!" said Cherry.

And both girls went and looked into a mirror in the window of the beauty shop. They laughed when they saw their colorful mouths. They laughed some more when they saw some old ladies inside with curlers on their heads. The old ladies were laughing at them.

On the way to Rose's house, they stopped in the park and sat on a bench. Rose said, "I hope that snow cone won't spoil my supper. Now why don't we try some of that stuff in the bag?"

Cherry said, "Sure." They shared bits of one that was very soft and white, with something sweet and red inside. Cherry said, "Why don't you take the rest home to your mother?"

"Okay!" said Rose.

IV. Shaving the Ice

Rose had a lot to tell her mother that night about her best friend's neighborhood, and, before long, Rose was visiting Cherry almost every day after school. They played in Rose's neighborhood, too, doing what they called the "regular things"—like going to the grocery store, going to the butcher shop, and walking by the noisy factory full of big machines and boxes—but they both agreed that Cherry's neighborhood was much more interesting, so they played there most of the time.

At school, their teacher said, "My, oh my—you Flower Girls are almost like a secret club, always talking about things like 'manju' and 'tofu.' Can you girls explain some of that to me and the class?"

Rose said, "Manju is manju and tofu is tofu, but eating a snow cone is like eating Mount Hood!" Everybody laughed. Then Rose said, "And after eating a snow cone, you look like a clown because your mouth is all orange and purple and red!" Everybody laughed. Everybody wanted to try eating a snow cone.

Then the teacher said, "Class, a snow cone is just shaved ice." That made the class laugh even more, because who ever heard of shaving the ice?

One boy put his hand up and said, "Teacher, my daddy shaves his face every morning, but I didn't know that the ice had to shave!" Everybody laughed again.

V. Learning Names

As the year went by, all the children learned to read and write and count at school. But the Flower Girls also learned how to count in Japanese, from Cherry's mother, and they could point to their fingers and say "ichi, ni, san, shi" just like that. Then Cherry's mother taught the Flower Girls how to write their names in Japanese. It took practice, over and over, because it was almost like drawing a picture, but when they learned how to do it right, their names looked very fancy, very beautiful, and the Flower Girls felt very special when they showed the kids at school. The other kids tried to write their names in Japanese, too, and made a lot of funny marks on paper. The teacher couldn't write her name, either.

Cherry's mother was like a teacher at home, but a fun teacher, and she would explain things to the girls as they went with her to make deliveries. They would walk down the sidewalks carrying packages of tofu, and when Cherry's mother got paid, the girls would also say, "Arigato." That always made the customers smile.

Sometimes, the girls would play with dolls in the kitchen in back of the tofu store, and Cherry's mother would teach them interesting things like how to make cinnamon toast without burning the toast or spilling the cinnamon, or how to blow soap bubbles without making too much of a mess, or how to make glue and clean up afterwards, or how to answer the phone even though your mouth is full of peanut butter, or how to fold and cut newspapers into snowflakes and birds.

One day, Cherry's mother told the girls that Japanese names had very interesting meanings in Japanese, like "Ricefield" and "Pine Forest" and "Mountain River" and "Rocky Seashore." She said that everybody's name means something, and that names like "Portland" and "Multnomah" and "Oregon" mean something, too. And the same for "Columbia" and "Willamette" and "Roosevelt" and "Studebaker" and "Chevrolet" and "Ford."

"How about 'Burnside'?" asked Rose.

"Yes," said Cherry's mother, "that must mean something, too."

"How about 'Atkinson School'?" said Cherry.

"Yes, that must mean something, too," said Cherry's mother. "And the same for 'Atlantic' and 'Pacific' and 'Blitz Weinhard' and 'Jantzen Beach' and 'Washington Park' and 'Meier and Frank.'"

"How about 'Nabisco'?" said Cherry.

"Yes," said Cherry's mother, "that just means National Biscuit Company. Na-Bis-Co—you get it?"

"Sure we do!" said the Flower Girls.

VI. More Places and Names

Actually, Cherry's neighborhood had so many people, places, and names that the girls couldn't remember everything. There were places upstairs, there were places downstairs; there were places in front, there were places out back. There were barbershops, beauty shops, bathhouses, laundries, fish markets, dry goods stores ("What's dry goods?" asked the girls), grocery stores, stores full of appliances, shoe repair shops, auto repair shops, many restaurants, very many hotels, one newspaper office called the *Oh Shu*, one newspaper office called the *Nippo*, another newspaper office called the *Ka Shu*, doctors' offices, dentists' offices, and pharmacies ("What's a pharmacy?" asked the girls).

Sometimes, the Flower Girls would just walk around, saying names like songs. "*Oh Shu* and *Nippo* and *Ka Shu*—step right up and get your latest news!" At other times, they would play a game to see if they remembered all the churches. Portland Buddhist Church—that was easy. It was also called Bu-kyo-kai. Then there was Japanese Methodist Church—that was easy. But how about Ken-jyo-ji, Kon-ko-kyu, Minori-nakai, Nichiren, and Sei-cho—those were not as easy. So the girls would have to count them all on their fingers, like a test, and they would always pass.

One time, Cherry's mother said, "Girls, listen to the names of these clubs: Fukuoka-kenjinkai, Hiroshima-kenjinkai, Okayama-kenjinkai, Wakayama-kenjinkai, and Nippon-kenjinkai. Do you think you can remember all that?"

And the girls said, "Sure! We'll try! Say those again! You can't trick us!"

And Cherry's mother said, "Well, go-men-na-sai, Flower Girls!"

VII. The Dog Named Cat

One day, when Rose got home, she told her mother, "Mother, did you know that Cherry has a new puppy? It's brown and very soft and furry, but guess what she named it?" Her mother couldn't guess, so Rose said, "Cherry wanted a kitten instead, but since she's allergic to cats, she named her puppy Nekko. And Nekko means 'cat.' Do you get it, huh? Do you get it? Isn't that funny? Don't you think that's funny? She has a dog and a cat at the same time!" And then, after a while, Rose said, "Mother, can I get a dog or a cat?"

Another day, Rose came home and said, "Mother, did you know that I was a hakujin? That's just what I am. And Cherry is a nihonjin. That's what she is. That's all. But we're both Americans. Isn't that interesting? And Cherry's mother says that we're *both* her Flower Girls."

Another time, Rose said, "Mother, did you know that where Cherry lives is called Shi-ta Machi? That means 'bottom town' or under or below. Isn't that interesting? Cherry's mother says that's because they live down by the river."

VIII. The Creature in the River

The teacher read a story to the class about the man in the moon. After it was over, Cherry raised her hand and told the class, "My mother says there is not a man in the moon but instead there are two rabbits with their hammers pounding rice." Some kids said that wasn't true, but Cherry said that when the moon was full they should go outside and *see* those rabbits that her mother showed her.

Cherry also said, "My mother says that the kappa is a creature who lives in the Willamette River. When you go down by the river, you can see his tracks. The kappa lives in the river, swimming under the boats and bridges, but he walks around on land at night. He likes to dump over garbage cans and play tricks on people."

One boy asked if the kappa likes to hurt people. Cherry said, "No, because he likes kids, but not even the police can catch him."

Another boy asked Cherry if she had seen the kappa.

Cherry said, "No, because I can't stay up at night. But one time I heard him. And in the morning, the garbage can was turned over."

One boy said that he had seen the kappa late at night, and that the kappa was big and hairy like a monster. Cherry said, "No, that's not the kappa, because the kappa is small, like a first-grader. Besides, he has a shell, like a turtle."

One girl asked if the kappa wore any clothes.

Cherry said, "No." Everybody laughed. Then Cherry said, "But you have to look out, because the kappa is very strong."

Then one boy said, "If the kappa ever came to my house, me and my dad would beat him up, just like that!"

Another boy said, "I would shoot him with a gun! Boom!"

And Cherry said, "Nobody could ever shoot or catch the kappa, because he's too fast. He could jump right into the river and swim right back to Japan. Or, if he wanted to, he could put on some clothes and walk around in a disguise, like a man."

One girl raised her hand and asked, "But why does he tip over garbage cans? Does he eat garbage?"

Cherry said, "No, he just does that, for fun."

One boy said, "But if he wears a disguise, how does he hide his face?"

Cherry said, "He wears a big, black hat. Besides, he could change his face to look like a man. And he wears a big overcoat to cover his shell."

Rose said, "One time, me and Cherry found a big overcoat in the alley. We didn't touch it. We ran home! The next day, it was gone!"

Everybody was quiet.

IX. The Celebrations

One day, after New Year's, Cherry told Rose that there was going to be a Girl's Day celebration in Shi-ta Machi, and that there would be many beautiful dolls on display, but not to play with. Then there was also going to be a Boy's Day when everybody would go on a picnic to a place called Montevilla, out in the country, to fly kites and play games, and that Rose could come with them. Then Cherry said that they could both dance in the Cherry Blossom Festival, too, but they would have to practice dancing after school.

"Oh, that will be fun," said Rose.

"Yes," said Cherry, "and we also get to wear special clothes."

Rose couldn't wait to get home to tell her mother. On the way home, she sang her own cherry blossom song. "Sakura, sakura," she sang, as she skipped along. "Sakura, sakura. . . ."

The Flower Girls had a lot of fun at those special celebrations, and everybody said, "My, you Flower Girls are so beautiful!"

And one day, in the summer, Rose came home and told her mother, "Mother—guess what! Our teacher says we get to be in the Rose Parade! Isn't that great? We get to ride on a float! And Cherry says she's going to ride on the Shi-ta Machi float! Her float is going to have roses, too, but it is also going to have lots of fruits and vegetables on it, like strawberries and radishes and onions! Oh, I can't wait! Won't that be neat?"

X. In the Second Grade

So the Flower Girls rode in the Rose Parade, and they had a lot of fun playing together all that summer. Then, when school started again, they were both in the same class in the second grade, and they even sat in the same front seats, right next to each other. On the first day, the new teacher said, "Well, well, well—looks like we have the Flower Girls together again. Now, Flower Girls, will you help me pass out these brand-new books?"

School was so much fun, as usual, but one day, after Thanksgiving, when the class was going to start practicing on a Christmas play about Santa Claus and all the good little children, the teacher said, "Class, as you all know, America is having a war against Japan. But let's be good boys and girls and put on the best Christmas play we can. Okay?"

And all the kids said, "Okay!"

But that day, at recess, there were fights among the older kids in the playground, and a lot of kids got called "Jap!" Then a sixth-grade girl came up to Rose and Cherry and said, "You guys aren't supposed to play together because *she's a Jap* and *you're enemies*!"

And Rose said, "No we're not! *We're friends!*"

And the older girl said, "No you're not! You're enemies! You're having a war! Ha, ha, ha—you're having a war-ar! You're having a war-ar! Boo hoo hoo! Enemies, enemies, enemies! Ha, ha, ha—you're having a war-ar!"

XI. Just Because

The Christmas play was canceled, and it was not a very happy Christmas for anybody. The Flower Girls did not visit each other anymore, and one day, after New Year's, Cherry said to Rose, "We're not going to have a Girl's Day or a Boy's Day or a Cherry Blossom Festival this year."

And Rose said, "Why not? How come?"

And Cherry said, "Just because. Because we're having a war."

Then, on a fine, spring morning, the teacher said, "Class, as you know, some of you kids are going to be moving away soon, so this week let's all have a real nice good-bye party, okay?"

Nobody knew what to say.

At recess, Rose said, "Cherry, where are you going?"

Cherry said, "I don't know."

Rose said, "What do you mean you don't know? How come you don't know?"

"Because I don't know, stupid!" said Cherry. "All I know is that we're going down the river."

"But how come you're going down the river?" said Rose.

"Because we're going down the river, stupid!" said Cherry. "Because we're going to war."

"But how come you're going to war?" said Rose.

"Because we're Japs, stupid!" said Cherry.

"But how are you going?" said Rose. "I know—maybe you get to float on a boat! Maybe you get to float on a float!"

"Don't be stupid, stupid!" said Cherry. "I bet you wouldn't want to go."

"Yes, I would!" said Rose.

"That's because you're stupid, stupid!" said Cherry.

"I'm not stupid!" said Rose.

"Yes, you are!" said Cherry. "You're stupid, stupid, stupid!"

The next day, Cherry said to Rose, "Rose, my mother wants to know if you could take care of Nekko for us."

"Why?" said Rose.

"Because we can't take her with us, stupid!" said Cherry.

"Why not? How come?" said Rose.

"Just because!" said Cherry. "Just because!"

XII. The Letters

On a warm, beautiful summer day, the mailman brought a letter to Rose. The letter said:

Dear Rose,

How are you? I am fine. How is Nekko? This place stinks. P U GARBAGE. Are you my friend? I can see Portland.

Your friend,
Cherry

With the help of her mother, Rose wrote a letter back to Cherry. The letter said:

Dear Cherry,

How are you? I am fine. Nekko got ran over. She went to heaven. I am your friend. You are in the map of Portland.

Your friend,
Rose

XIII. More Letters

On a lovely fall day, with a warm wind blowing, Cherry sat up in a bed and wrote a letter. The letter said:

Dear Rose,

How are you? I am fine. I am in the third grade. Who is your teacher? My teacher is American. We live in Idaho. I went to the hospital. This is my picture of you and Nekko. She is eating a manju. You are eating a snow cone. This is my picture of you in the Rose Parade. The float is beautiful. You are my friend.

Your friend,
Cherry

The letter was never answered.

XIV. No One Knows

No one knows what happened to Cherry. No one knows what happened to Rose. Shi-ta Machi is no more. The buildings are still there, with different stores and businesses in them, but the Shi-ta Machi people did not return to Shi-ta Machi. Shi-ta Machi is no more.

There are still Shi-ta Machi people, though, living in all parts of the city, and if you want to see Shi-ta, you have to look deep into the eyes of the Shi-ta Machi people. You have to look deep into the eyes, under the surface; you have to look deep below the surface of the shining eyes. You have to look deep down to the bottom of the eyes of the Shi-ta Machi people, and you will see Shi-ta Machi shining in their eyes. You will see the shining streets, the sidewalks full of people. You will see children like Cherry and Rose, playing after school.

You will see the tofu store, you will see the manju-ya (you can even smell the sweet manju, you can even hear the manju-man shaving the ice, you can even taste the snow cone, oh, so cold, with all the flavors of the rainbow). You can walk down the sidewalks past all the stores and offices, and when you stop at the corner, you can look into the window of the beauty shop and see your face in the mirror.

Then, in the blink of an eye, Shi-ta Machi will be gone. Shi-ta Machi is no more.

XV. The Song of Cherry and Rose

There is a beautiful park in the hills of Portland. It is full of trees and lawns, with many places to sit and play and walk and run. In one part of the park is a Japanese garden, full of beautiful plants and rocks, with a beautiful pond. In the Japanese garden, a very special cherry tree grows.

In the same part of the park, there is a beautiful rose garden. There are roses with all the colors of the rainbow, and in that garden grows a very special rose.

When the park is quiet, you can walk through the Japanese garden, and you can hear the wind blow. When the park is quiet, you can walk through the rose garden, and you can hear the wind blow.

The song you hear is the song of Cherry and Rose.

It is a beautiful song of friendship, of being best friends together, of going to school together, of playing together, of growing up together. It is a beautiful song of being the Flower Girls, of being sisters. It is a beautiful song of becoming women together, of always being sisters.

The song you hear is the song of Cherry and Rose.

XVI. The Continuing Story

On a fine summer day, a family was on a picnic in the park. After lunch, the little girl said, "Mother, I'm going for a little walk through the rose garden. Okay?"

The little girl went walking through all the beautiful roses. Everything smelled like roses, felt like roses, everything was colored like roses. When the little girl was right in the middle of the rose garden, right when she was sniffing a big, red rose, she looked up and saw another little girl doing the same thing.

Both girls said "Hi!" at the same time. One girl said, "My name is Cherry. What's your name?"

The other girl said, "My name is Rose."

And Cherry said, "Do you want to walk over to the Japanese garden?"

And Rose said, "Okay. I'll ask my mother."

And Cherry said, "Okay. I'll ask my mother."

And Rose said, "Okay. I'll meet you back here. Okay?"

And Cherry said, "Okay. I'll meet you back here."

And off they went.

Acknowledgments

This story was made possible by a grant from the Metropolitan Arts Commission, Portland, Oregon.

Special thanks to: Terry Akwai, Keiko Archer, George Azumano, Kay Capron, Phin Capron, Chisao Hata, Corky Kawasaki, Kaz Kinoshita, Dr. and Mrs. Matt Masuoka, Peggy Nagae, Joan and Vern Rutsala, Lury Sato, Chiyo Shiogi, Woodrow Shiogi, Chiyoko Tateishi, Dr. James Tsujimura, Dr. and Mrs. Homer Yasui.

Suggested Further Reading

WORKS BY INADA
Before the War. New York: William Morrow, 1971.
AIIIEEEEE! (ed.) New York: Penguin, 1991.
The Big AIIIEEEEE! (ed.) New York: New American Library, 1991.
Legends from Camp. Minneapolis Coffee House, 1992.

A Selected Bibliography of Oregon Fiction

Editor's note: Because the Oregon Literature Series includes only short fiction, the following bibliography lists selected examples of Oregon novels, as well as short fiction, for the interested reader.

Athanas, Verne. *Rogue Valley.* New York: Simon and Schuster, 1953.

Bailey, Margaret Jewett. *The Grains, or Passages in the Life of Ruth Rover.* 1854; rpt. Corvallis: Oregon State University Press, 1986.

Balch, Frederick H. *The Bridge of the Gods.* Chicago: A. C. McClurg, 1890.

Berry, Don. *Moontrap.* New York: Viking 1962; rpt. Sausalito: Comstock Editions, 1971.

——. *Trask.* New York: Viking, 1960; rpt. Sausalito: Comstock Editions, 1969.

Brautigan, Richard. *Revenge of the Lawn.* New York: Pocket Books, 1971.

Carpenter, Don. *The Murder of the Frogs.* New York: Harcourt, Brace, 1968.

Carr, Mary Jane, *Young Mac of Fort Vancouver,* New York: Thomas Y. Crowell, 1940.

Carver, Raymond. *Will You Please Be Quiet, Please?* New York: McGraw Hill, 1976.

Cleary, Beverly. *Ramona the Brave.* New York: William Morrow, 1975.

Davis, H. L. *Collected Essays and Short Stories.* Moscow, Idaho: University of Idaho Press, 1986.

——. *Honey in the Horn.* New York: Harper, 1935.

Domini, John. *Bedlam.* San Diego: San Diego State University Press, Fiction International, 1981.

Drake, Albert. *Beyond the Pavement.* Adelphi, MD: White Ewe Press, 1981.

Duncan, David James. *The River Why.* San Francisco: Sierra Club Books. 1983.

Everett, Percival. *The Weather and Women Treat Me Fair.* Little Rock: August House, 1987.

Gloss, Molly. *The Jump-Off Creek.* Boston: Houghton Mifflin, 1989.

Grey, Zane. *Rogue River Feud.* New York: Harper, 1948.

Haycox, Ernest. *The Earthbreakers.* Boston: Little, Brown, 1952.

——. *Pioneer Loves.* Boston: Little, Brown, 1952.

Hedrick, Helen. *The Blood Remembers.* New York: Alfred A. Knopf, 1941.

Heynen, Jim. *You Know What Is Right.* San Francisco: North Point Press, 1985.

Higginson, Ella. *From the Land of the Snow Pearls.* New York: Macmillan, 1897.

Hoyt, Richard. *The Siskiyou Two-Step.* New York: William A. Morrow, 1983.

Hyde, Dayton. *The Major, the Poacher, and the Wonderful One-Trout River.* New York: Atheneum, 1985.

Jacobs, Elizabeth D. *Nehalem Tillamook Tales,* ed. Melville Jacobs. Eugene: University of Oregon Books, 1959; rpt. Corvallis: Oregon State University Press, 1989.

Jones, Nard. *Oregon Detour.* New York: Payson and Clarke, 1930; rpt. Corvallis: Oregon State University Press, 1990.

——. *Swift Flows the River.* New York: Dodd, Mead, 1940.

Kesey, Ken. *One Flew Over the Cuckoo's Nest.* New York: Viking, 1962.

——. *Sometimes A Great Notion.* New York: Viking, 1964.

Kittredge, William. *We Are Not in This Together.* Port Townsend: Graywolf Press, 1984.

Lampman, Ben Hur. *At the End of the Car Line.* Portland: Binford and Mort, 1942.

Lampman, Evelyn Sibley. *Rock Hound.* Garden City, NY: Doubleday, 1958.

Le Guin, Ursula. *The Lathe of Heaven.* New York: Charles Scribner's Sons, 1971.

——. *The Wind's Twelve Quarters.* New York: Harper and Row, 1975.

Lerner, Andrea, ed. *Dancing on the Rim of the World: Contemporary Northwest Native American Writing.* Tucson: University of Arizona Press, 1989.

Lesley, Craig. *Winterkill.* Boston: Houghton Mifflin, 1984.

Lesley, Craig, ed. *Talking Leaves: Contemporary Native American Short Stories.* New York: Dell, 1991.

Lopez, Barry. *Winter Count.* New York: Charles Scribner's Sons, 1981.

Lucia, Ellis, ed. *This Land Around Us: A Treasury of Pacific Northwest Writing.* Garden City, N. Y.: Doubleday, 1969.

Lyons, Richard. *A Wilderness of Faith and Love.* Daleville, Indiana: Barnwood Press, 1988.

Malamud, Bernard. *A New Life.* New York: Farrar, Straus, Giroux, 1961.

Miller, Joaquin. *Selected Writings,* ed. Alan Rosenus. Eugene: Urion Press, 1977.

Monroe, Anne Shannon. *Happy Valley.* Chicago: A. C. McClure, 1916; rpt. Corvallis: Oregon State University Press, 1991.

Moore, Lucia. *The Wheel and the Hearth.* New York: Ballantine, 1953.

Morey, Walt. *Year of the Black Pony.* New York: Dutton, 1976.

Overholzer, Wayne. *Hearn's Valley.* New York: Macmillan, 1958.

Powers, Alfred A. *History of Oregon Literature.* Portland: Metropolitan Press, 1935.

——. *Marooned in Crater Lake: Stories of the Skyline Trail, the Umpqua Trail, and the Old Oregon Trail.* Portland: Metropolitan Press, 1930.

Ramsey, Jarold, ed. *Coyote Was Going There: Indian Literature of the Oregon Country.* Seattle: University of Washington Press, 1977.

Reyes, Karen S. "Finding a New Voice: The Oregon Writing Community between the Two World Wars." Unpublished Master's Dissertation, Portland State University, Department of History, 1986.

Shetzline, David. *Heckletooth 3.* New York: Random House, 1969.

Stevens, James. *Big Jim Turner.* Garden City, NY: Doubleday, 1948.

——. *Homer in the Sagebrush.* New York: Alfred A. Knopf, 1928.

Venn, George. *Marking the Magic Circle.* Corvallis: Oregon State University Press, 1987.

Victor, Frances Fuller. *The New Penelope and Other Stories and Poems.* San Francisco: A. L. Bancroft, 1877.

Wetjen, Albert Richard. *Way for a Sailor.* New York: Grosset and Dunlap, 1928.

Wilhelm, Kate. *The Hamlet Trap.* New York: St. Martin's Press, 1987.

Wilson, Miles. *Line of Fall.* Iowa City: University of Iowa Press, 1989.

Winther, Sophus K. *Beyond the Garden Gate.* New York: Macmillan, 1946; rpt. Corvallis: Oregon State University Press, 1991.

Working, Russell. *Resurrections.* Iowa City: University of Iowa Press, 1987.

Wren, M. K. *Nothing's Certain but Death.* Garden City, NY: Doubleday, 1978.

Copyright Acknowledgments

Every effort has been made to find the legal copyright holders of the material reproduced herein. If for some reason we have inadvertently overlooked a copyright holder who should be acknowledged, we have done so inadvertently or because our best efforts to do so failed. Thus all of these works are reprinted in good faith. If anyone can bring to our attention copyrighted material the holders of which we have not acknowledged, we will be happy to do so in a subsequent edition.

TEXTS

Berry, Don. "A Trap for the Moon" from *Moontrap* by Don Berry. New York: Viking, 1962. Copyright © 1962 by Don Berry. Used by permission of Viking Penguin, a division of Penguin Books, U.S.A., Inc.

Carver, Raymond. "Why, Honey?" from *Will You Please Be Quiet, Please?* New York: McGraw-Hill, 1976. Copyright © by Tess Gallagher. Reprinted by permission of Tess Gallagher.

Cleary, Beverly. "Owl Trouble," pp. 44-58 from *Ramona the Brave*. New York: William Morrow, 1975. Copyright © 1975 by Beverly Cleary. By permission of Morrow Junior Books, a division of William Morrow & Co., Inc.

Davis, H.L. "Old Man Isbell's Wife" from *Team Bells Woke Me and Other Stories*, Morrow, 1953. Copyright credit to University of Idaho Press and Curtis Publishing Co., Philadelphia.

Epple, Juan Armando. "Los Persas." Reprinted by permission of the author. Translation, "Garage Sale People." First printed in *The Americas Review* 5 (1991). Reproduced by permission of *The Americas Review*, Arte Publico Press, University of Houston, Houston, Texas.

Everett, Percival. "Cry About a Nickel" from *The Weather and Women Treat Me Fair*. Little Rock: August House, 1987. Reprinted by permission of August House Publishers, Inc.

Gies, Martha. "O'Keefe Sober." First printed in *The Oregonian*, Northwest Magazine (Sunday, April 21, 1991), pp. 36-37. Published by permission of the PEN Syndicated Fiction Project.

Gloss, Molly. "The Doe." First printed in *CALYX: A Journal of Art and Literature by Women*, June 1981. Copyright © 1981 by Molly Gloss. Reprinted by permission of *CALYX* and the author.

Haycox, Ernest. "Cry Deep, Cry Still" from *Pioneer Loves*. Boston: Little, Brown, 1952.

Heynen, Jim. "Who Kept One Hand in Her Pocket" from *You Know What Is Right: Stories by Jim Heynen*. San Francisco: North Point Press, 1985. Reprinted with permission from the author.

Higginson, Ella. "Zarelda" from *From the Land of the Snow Pearls*. New York: Macmillan, 1897.

Howard, Ellen. "The Blood of the Lamb." First printed in *CALYX: A Journal of Art and Literature by Women*, Issue 7:1, Summer 1982, pp. 21-26. Reprinted by permission of the author.

ART